"*Surprisingly Supernatural*" is a practical, yet inspirational way for a believer to exercise the power of the kingdom of God within them. Neil Gilligan is a prophetic evangelist that teaches the power of the Word and Spirit with his personal life examples. As his readers put into practice Neil's guidance in the ministry of the gifts of the Spirit, they too, will find that they are surprisingly supernatural believers.

With Open Heart

Mary Oliver

Pastor and President of Open Heart Ministry

Newcastle, WA

www.openheartministry.org

"*Surprisingly Supernatural*" is just that! Practical, Thought provoking, Biblically based, timely and Powerful. First of all, every new believer should have this book right away as a foundation to begin to operate and walk in the fullness of the Gifts of The Spirit.

Then to those who have known The Lord for a while it will challenge you out of the "status quo" and get you functioning and walking in The Supernatural where God has called us all to walk in. You will be Blessed by this book and encouraged to demonstrate the power of The Kingdom of God everywhere you go.

Elvin Gladney

Senior Pastor

Real Life International Church and Ministry Center, Seattle WA.

Director of 'C.A.A.P.P' "Cascadia Alliance Awakening People to their Purpose"

"I highly recommend Neil's book entitled, "*Surprisingly Supernatural*" to any Christian who desires to walk in the fullness of the spiritual gifts that Jesus Christ died and rose again to release to us. Be sure to get the most out of the book by answering the chapter questions, visiting his book website, and sharing the gospel with people that you meet every day. Also, pray about having Neil come to minister in your church or for your ministry. He brings a strong revelatory teaching gift which will enable the saints that you walk with to be trained and equipped to become mature sons and daughters of the Living God"

"*Surprisingly Supernatural*" is inspiring and an easy read. It will provide a deeper understanding of the continual infilling of Holy Spirit and the gifts that are available to us to do the works of the Father! You will find yourself excited about drawing closer to the Lord and thus being able to release the gifts to those you meet when led by the Holy Spirit.

Rev. Ann Ott
In His Presence Ministries
Houston, Texas

Ryan Ellis
Abbotsford, BC, Canada

"Surprisingly Supernatural" is a life changing book. Neil explains how to live a life in the supernatural for it to be normal. It is practical, relational and full of God stories that will build your faith into action. Read it and then watch for Mark 16:17-18 that says these signs will accompany those who believe… as they will become the normal part of your Christian life.

Mervin Strome
PACE (adult) Program Coordinator
Alberta Bible College

I read Neil's book *"Surprisingly Supernatural"* after I had a chronic back problem that was consistently relieved by Neil's prayers. His intuitive response to exactly where and how to heal me inspired me to learn more about his methods in his book *"Surprisingly Supernatural."* Thanks to Neil, I can do Ballroom Dancing without any pain. I recommend *"Surprisingly Supernatural"* as I found it assists people not only to learn historical religious anecdotes, but also how to appropriate relevant applications to their own lives through Christ. Written clearly and concisely and presented in a straightforward way, this book is for anyone who wishes to become a believer or for anyone who already is a believer, as Neil will help you learn the steps to be more proactive in your Christian life through aiding others.

Alyson Loney
Vancouver, BC

Endorsement for *"Surprisingly Supernatural"*

This practical guide will help you go deeper in understanding and experiencing the Holy Spirit and the gifts of God. As we draw close to Him and His Spirit we cultivate a love relationship with Him, we understand our identity in Christ, and walk in His presence. As we carry His presence and power with us into our everyday life and use our authority as sons and daughters of the living God, we are able to demonstrate His Kingdom here in the earth through signs, wonders, and miracles changing history as we go.

Elaine Perkins
Associate Director, Healing Rooms Ministries
Spokane, Washington

Love your third book!!! Here's my endorsement for *"Surprisingly Supernatural"*!

"It's time to ACT!!!" Just like in the Book of the Acts of the Apostles, it is time to "act upon" what we have been learning through Neil Gilligan's wonderful books. Now is the time to demonstrate the Gifts of Holy Spirit! Don't be afraid of who God says you are and what He will do through you. Decide today to be a *believing believer*. Receive the continual flow of Holy Spirit, step out, and be overjoyed operating with Him in the surprisingly supernatural. A vessel that is full always has something to pour out!

Pastor Carol Kindt
Sequim, WA

"*Surprisingly Supernatural* is a book the Holy Spirit will use to help prepare His bride to clothe herself in these last days. Neil has crafted a practical guide to enable His church to walk in the power and authority the Lord has granted her. You will find it helpful, practical and needed. I recommend it to you as a work that will help you walk in all the fullness God desires for his disciples."

Pastor Paul Taylor
County Line Christian Fellowship

"If you are troubling over the working of the Gifts of the Spirit and the practicality of their use in your daily life, you will find '*Surprisingly Supernatural*' an encouragement and a blessing in your Christian walk with some One greater and higher. '*Surprisingly Supernatural*' will lead and guide you from defeat to victory in every aspect of your Spiritual walk. I would encourage to seek the Lord thru this book and to be continually filled with the Holy Spirits' influence that will cause you to be '*Surprisingly Supernatural*' in your daily walk. Be filled with the knowledge and all wisdom and spiritual understanding for your walk with Him. (Col 1:9)".

Richard O. Tedeschi
President / Gen. Manager/ Radiant Light Broadcasting TV

Surprisingly Supernatural

A Practical Guide to Releasing
the Gifts of the Spirit

Neil Gilligan

Copyright © 2012 by Neil Gilligan.

All rights reserved. No part of this book may be used or reproduced by any means, graphic, electronic, or mechanical, including photocopying, recording, taping or by any information storage retrieval system without the written permission of the publisher except in the case of brief quotations embodied in critical articles and reviews.

Unless otherwise identified, Scripture quotations are taken from the HOLY BIBLE, NEW INTERNATIONAL VERSION ®, Copyright © 1973, 1978, 1980 International Bible Society. Used by permission of Zondervan. All rights reserved.

Scripture quotations marked KJV are taken from the King James Version. All emphasis within Scripture is the author's own, as is the use of capitalized certain pronouns in Scripture that refer to the Father, Son, and Holy Spirit, that may differ from the Bible version quoted.

The author has attempted to diligently research from both a biblical basis and historical records to justify his conclusions; however, the author is aware that the conclusions reached in this book may be changed in the future when further information is researched and analyzed. The reader needs to pray about the revelation in this work and proceed in faith from what you perceive is true.

WestBow Press books may be ordered through booksellers or by contacting:

WestBow Press
A Division of Thomas Nelson
1663 Liberty Drive
Bloomington, IN 47403
www.westbowpress.com
1-(866) 928-1240

Because of the dynamic nature of the Internet, any web addresses or links contained in this book may have changed since publication and may no longer be valid. The views expressed in this work are solely those of the author and do not necessarily reflect the views of the publisher, and the publisher hereby disclaims any responsibility for them.

Any people depicted in stock imagery provided by Thinkstock are models, and such images are being used for illustrative purposes only.

Certain stock imagery © Thinkstock.

ISBN: 978-1-4497-7242-0 (hc)
ISBN: 978-1-4497-7243-7 (sc)
ISBN: 978-1-4497-7244-4 (e)

Library of Congress Control Number: 2012920344

Printed in the United States of America

WestBow Press rev. date: 11/9/2012

TABLE OF CONTENTS

Foreword ix
Preface xi
Introduction xix

Chapter 1: Definitions and Hindrances to Releasing the Gifts 1
Chapter 2: Surprisingly Supernatural Step #1 Be Filled with the Holy Spirit 12
Chapter 3: Surprisingly Supernatural Step #2 How to Receive the Gift of Prophecy 41
Chapter 4: Surprisingly Supernatural Step #3 How to Ask for the Gifts of Healings and Miracles 70
Chapter 5: Surprisingly Supernatural Step #4A Asking for The Gift of Discernment 104
Chapter 6: Surprisingly Supernatural Step #4B How to Ask for the Authority to Bind Evil Spirits and Drive Out Demons 115
Chapter 7: Practicing the Release of the Gifts of the Spirit 149
Chapter 8: Becoming the Bride of Christ 166

Bibliography 183
About the Author 199

FOREWORD

Neil Gilligan has written a book, *Surprisingly Supernatural*, about the Holy Spirit's relationship with us. The book is filled with scriptures and the author's many experiences of the Holy Spirit working with him and through him. I would rather be taught by someone who is writing from personal experience rather than reforming other people's ideas as the only basis they have written. The author's personal experiences help shed light on the scriptures and other books he has quoted.

I also enjoyed the exercises Neil has put in the book to help us grow spiritually and to help us move in the gifts of the Spirit. The teaching on healing, discernment, deliverance, words of knowledge and wisdom and the other gifts are extremely practical. Neil has a desire to see us surprised by the Spirits' work in our life to develop a lifestyle of evangelism that touches others with God's love. Authentic spiritual gifts open people's hearts to the love of God.

I encourage you to read and enjoy the book. And I encourage you to not be surprised when you are surprised with what the Holy Spirit might speak to you.

Dan Hammer
Senior Pastor
Sonrise Chapel, Everett, WA

PREFACE

If you have followed my writings you would know that the Lord Jesus wooed me. First, He appeared to me in a vision where He was in the clouds and His light flowed out from Him in waves. Then He wooed me to be filled by His Holy Spirit and led me to ask the Heavenly Father to clothe me in power. All of that is described in the book: *"Transformed by the Power of God: Learning to be Clothed in Jesus Christ."*[1]

I was transformed and became a miracle worker only because Jesus was with me. During that time I went to Benny Hinn's healing crusade in Billings, Montana and the Lord told me,

> You are going to be part of a new movement that will be different from Hinn's style of ministry. This movement is not going to involve orchestras, teams of singers, staging and lighting. It is going to involve individual believers who will release the gifts of the Spirit right where they live, work, and play.

I began to see that God was leading me to lay my hands on people and I witnessed healings and miracles performed right before my eyes. I was in shock that God was working through me! I started to understand that this new movement was for the ordinary saints like me. It was for all believers who wanted to believe for more of God in their lives.

I ministered in the church and I also witnessed to people in the marketplace. When I ministered in the marketplace, I began to discern evil spirits on a great number of people's backs. I began to cast them off of them and then those people were healed. This alerted me to the fact that evil ungodly spirits were attacking people and trying to steal, kill and destroy their health and their birthrights.

Then I was led to write "*Wake Up! Preparing for the End-Times Outpouring.*" In this book I shared how the Lord showed me the character traits and practices that Daniel and his friends had and the first disciples had, and then I recognized that many Christians do not practice those same practices. *Wake Up!* implores the body of Christ to begin to embrace those lost practices.

The most significant practice that was lost was the the first disciples' practice of being *continually filled by the Spirit of God*. I shared that they were continually filled because they had the Spirit of the Lord upon them like Jesus had (see Luke 4:18). Then whenever they would slow down and wait, the Holy Spirit would begin to start filling them again. I testified that this is what I had experienced, because I had been clothed in Jesus Christ (see Rom. 13:14). This practice of believers being clothed in Christ has been stifled by the evil one, the little horn, who plans to defeat the saints unless we wake up to his plan (see Dan. 7:21).

I showed in *Wake Up!* how the little horn had influenced the Western culture and demonstrated how the saints were being defeated over the past three centuries and cited that the vast majority of believers failed to demonstrate the gifts of the Spirit, because there were few *believing believers* around.

A believing believer is someone who has woken up in the end of the end-times and wants to respond to Jesus' question about the end of the end-times when He asked, will there be faith on the earth when He comes back? (see Luke 18:8). Consequently, the believing believer will exhibit great faith as he walks out his spiritual journey of faith during the end of the end-times. Therefore, the believing believer believes the Scriptures and obeys them, and is continually filled by the Holy Spirit; as a result, the believing believer can release the gifts of the Spirit around him in his relational networks. Daniel 7:22 revealed that the Ancient of Days was going to release the kingdom to the saints with successive outpourings of His Spirit. And that is still happening, so the saints are called to wake up and receive these outpourings and become believing believers.

In *Wake Up!* I also showed how the Ancient of Days had released the kingdom, the Holy Spirit, to the saints shortly after the Enlightenment started, and He continued to release the kingdom to the saints in consecutive outpourings. I derived statistical data from Edwin J Orr and Phil D Oxion's book: *The Outpouring of the Spirit in Revival and Awakening and its Issues in Church Growth.*[2] From their records they show the historical outpourings:

The Great Awakening 1727—	**65 Years**
The Second Great Awakening 1792—	**42 Years**
Tonga/Hawaii 1830—	**28 Years**
The Third Great Awakening 1858—	**22 Years**
The Welsh Revival to Azuza 1905—	**17 Years**
North Ireland 1921—	**14 Years**
Norway 1935—	**15 Years**
South America 1952—	**12 Years**
The Charismatic Movement—1961—	**11 Years**

The outpourings that have run completely according to Edwin and Oxion are graphed as follows:

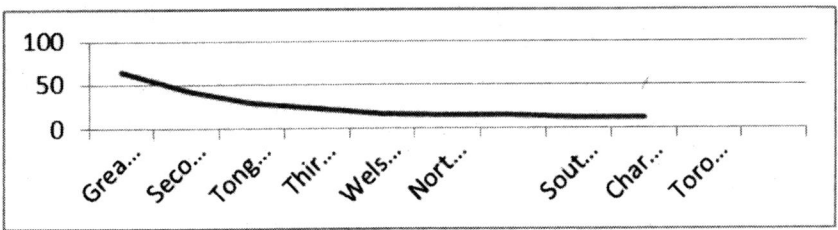

As you can see the line appears to be getting flatter. This apparently indicates that the time between notable outpourings is getting closer and closer together. Every 12 to 15 years is the interval of the most recent outpourings. The Father's Blessing was released in Toronto, Ontario and it began January 20, 1994, and that outpouring has lasted for 18 years. Consequently, it appears as if the next outpouring is now overdue. If it is following the same pattern, then it will arrive very soon. Unless this next outpouring is another Great Awakening, then it may tarry a little longer for the preparations to come into place.

The primary preparation that must take place is for the saints to wake up and receive the current release of the Holy Spirit, so they will be transformed and become miracle workers themselves. When enough of the saints learn how to release the gifts of the Spirit into the world around them, then the Ancient of Days can release this next Great Awakening upon the saints. Then the saints will be able to release the gifts of the Spirit to nonbelievers. And they will also teach other believers how they can learn to receive the Holy Spirit and learn to release the gifts of the Spirit as well. This is the time for the body of Christ to prepare for the Great End-Times Harvest that will sweep a great number of people into a relationship with Jesus Christ and His body on the earth.[3] But the body of Christ needs to wake up.

In *Wake Up!* I determined from the prophetic words from Daniel and the historical evidence, how the little horn has already been defeating the saints. Daniel 7:21 gives us the clue as it says,

> As I watched this horn was waging his war against the saints
> and defeating them…(Dan. 7:21).

I showed that the acceleration of the defeat of the saints had occurred during the Enlightenment. But the Ancient of Days did not want the saints completely defeated, so He released the kingdom to the saints shortly after the Enlightenment had begun. The outpouring was first poured out on the Moravian believers who lived on Count Zinzendorf's estate, called "*Herrnhut,*" which was located in Germany. These Moravians had cried out for the release of the Holy Spirit, and the Ancient of Days released it and as a result the *First Great Awakening* began on August 13, 1727.[4]

What is significant is that from Daniel 7, we read how the horn waged his war and was defeating the saints, but the response of the Ancient of Days was to release the kingdom to the saints, so they could counteract against their defeat. August 13, 1727 was the beginning of the response from the Ancient of Days, which coincides with Daniel 7:22.

The Ancient of Days has continued to respond by repeatedly releasing the kingdom of God to the saints ever since then. This corresponds to the phrase "the time came" which is the Hebrew word "*zawman*" from Daniel 7:22, which means "a season, a time, an appointed season or occasion."[5]

The Ancient of Days has been releasing the kingdom of God over the past three centuries for the saints to wake up and receive it, and then to learn to counteract against the evil ungodly powers that are aligned with the little horn. The saints need to wake up and counteract against the little horn, as this ungodly power's influence is accelerating in the world today through the plans of the elite bankers that are linked with the Illuminati who control a majority of the world's resources, military powers, judicial powers, and political powers.[6] And they want to form the New World Order, and the One World Religion and they want to eliminate Christianity completely. That's why the saints must awaken today.

Christian believers who are alive today are living in the "in-between period of time." They are living in the post-defeat of the saint's era, but they are not to remain defeated. Christians are called to rise up and counteract against their defeat by being continually filled by the Holy Spirit, learn how to receive the gifts of the Spirit, and then learn how to release the gifts of the Spirit. The eventual goal of these Christian believers is to work with God to bring about the prophetic word in Revelation 11 that says,

> The kingdom of the world has become the kingdom of our Lord and of His Christ… (Rev. 11:15).

I call these Christian believers, who live at the end of the end-times, "*believing believers.*" They act just like the first disciples acted, which shows they are just ordinary Christian believers who can release the kingdom of God and see miracles, deliverance, and prophetic words regularly happen as they go about their daily business.

These influences on my life and my previous writing have led me to write this book: *Surprisingly Supernatural: A Practical Guide to Releasing the Gifts of the Spirit*. This book is intended to help the contemporary believers to receive the Holy Spirit, to receive the gifts of the Spirit, and then to learn how to practice the gifts until they can release the gifts of the Spirit everywhere they go.

At first believing believers may appear to be surprisingly supernatural, but that is due to the little horn that successfully inhibited Christians from releasing the spiritual gifts. But all Christians are supposed to operate in the supernatural gifts of the Spirit; however, they have been impeded by the little horn's influence over the past few centuries. Consequently, many Christians have never realized that they were actually called to heal the sick and cast out demons (see Mark 16:17-18; Matt. 10:7-8). But in order for the kingdom of the world to become the kingdom of our Lord and His Christ, believing believers need to arise at this time.

This book: *Surprisingly Supernatural: A Practical Guide to Releasing the Gifts of the Spirit* is a training manual for believers so they can learn to become surprisingly supernatural, which means they will eventually become believing believers.[7]

ACKNOWLEDGEMENTS

I want to thank all my friends who helped me bring this book to maturity and in all the various, different and wonderful ways you helped me. I want to thank you from the bottom of my heart: Vicki Duffy, Ryan Ellis, Wanda Gladney, Linda Hackett, Carol Kindt, Veronica Lecheler, Leslie Preskitt, and Jeremy Smith. Thank you for all your help.

I also want to thank my teachers who have shared their knowledge about the gifts of the Spirit with me. I want to thank Randy Clark and Global Awakening, and the "Healing Schools" and the "Short-term Mission Trips" that you offer. I want to thank Dr. Paul Cox and Aslan's Place with your "Discernment and Generational Deliverance Schools" that you offer. I want to thank Dr. Bill Hamon and all your staff at Christian International for the "Apostolic Prophetic Training" courses that you offer. I want to thank Mary Oliver for your "PrayerCare Training Course" and the other supernatural training classes that you offer at Open Heart Ministries. I want to thank Cal Pierce and all your staff at the "Healing Rooms International" for the training on healing that you offer. And I want to thank Mark Sandford and all the Elijah House staff for the "Inner Healing courses" and the "Prophetic Schools" that you offer. And to all the other teachers I have not mentioned, but who were significant in allowing me to grow in the gifts of the Spirit. I thank you.

I also want to thank my God: the Heavenly Father, the Lord Jesus Christ, and the Holy Spirit for choosing me to be a vessel of your power and love so I can bring in the harvest and bring glory to your name. Thank you for your mercy on my life and for not leaving me the way I was, but for waking me up and transforming me so I can go from glory to glory. Lord this is such an amazing journey of faith. What an adventure. Thank you so much for a life that is exciting and thank you for giving my life significance. I pray you will bless this writing and prosper the message among your saints, so we can all represent you on the earth by releasing the gifts of the Spirit. Thank you so much for giving me this message to live and to share with others. I love you Lord.

INTRODUCTION

Becoming Surprisingly Supernatural

Becoming surprisingly supernatural does not happen like you might have expected. The change is not all that apparent. You don't wake up one morning and have a red S emblazoned on your T-shirt. And you don't burst out of your clothes and turn extremely muscular and green. No, it's not like that. It kind of creeps up on you, and one day you notice someone with a physical ailment and you feel compassion for her. So you work up your courage to ask her about it, "How do you feel? Is there anything I can do for you?" Then you ask, "May I pray for you?" And then when you pray, you realize that you are surprisingly supernatural, because she gets healed.

The change is not all that apparent. It just kind of slowly began to grow inside of you ever since you asked God to use you, and you asked Him to allow your life to be lived out significantly for His purposes. And oh yeah, you also started to ask for the Holy Spirit to come and fill you regularly. But that was it. Nothing else had really changed. Except now, every so often, you suddenly have become surprisingly supernatural. You are finding it wonderfully enjoyable to be operating in the supernatural realms, and joy bursts forth from your heart as you exclaim: "This is what I was made to do! I have waited all my life for this!" You are surprised at being supernatural, yet deep down inside you knew that someday it would be revealed that you really are surprisingly supernatural.

This book, *Surprisingly Supernatural: A Practical Guide to Releasing the Gifts of the Spirit* is to help you, the believer, who has faith in Jesus Christ, to take those few steps that lead into the supernatural realms of the kingdom of God where miracles, healing, power, and love flow from. This book defines the term "believing" and it is describing the practices of a believer who has faith in Jesus Christ and faith in the Scriptures and obeys them. When the adjective "believing" is linked to "believer," and if it is a "true believer," then fireworks go off, and an explosion occurs. Faith is a currency of heaven. When you have real faith in Jesus Christ you will have access to all of the resources in heaven. With real faith you will have access to all the spiritual blessings in Jesus Christ and you can draw on those resources, and then you will be changed into a surprisingly supernatural believing believer (see Eph. 1:3).

I share this writing with you because that was what the Holy Spirit has been doing with me since the summer of 2007. He would give me words of knowledge for my waiter, let me minister physical healing to the guy who sat next to me on an airplane, and allow me to drive out a demon from a client where I work. These occurred quite regularly, and I started teaching a series based on these experiences. Then in late 2008, a few more chapters came to me and I realized I must have been given the basis for this book: *Surprisingly Supernatural.*

I was amazed at what the Lord had opened up to me and I was reflecting on some of my spiritual experiences when I remembered that as a child I went to church and I learned the "Lord's Prayer," which is also called the "Our Father." I would recite it saying,

> Our Father in heaven, hallowed be your name,
> Your kingdom come, your will be done on earth as it is in heaven (Matt. 6:10).

I prayed it dutifully for years. I repeatedly would ask for the kingdom to come, but I failed to understand it.

All that has changed now since I learned to be continually filled with the Holy Spirit. Since I was continually filled with the Holy Spirit the kingdom of God came with its supernatural world of healings, miracles, driving out demons, prophecy, and angels. All of that opened up to me only after I was continually filled by the Holy Spirit and as a result, I was catapulted into the kingdom itself. I had become surprisingly supernatural, as I had learned to release the gifts of the Spirit and demonstrate that Jesus Christ was the King of kings wherever I went.

Lisa is one example that shows how I am now surprisingly supernatural because the gifts of the Spirit are released through me. I was proof reading a draft of this book, when I sensed I was being led by the Holy Spirit to go to the Denny's restaurant in Bellevue, Washington. I was at my table drinking coffee and a woman came by and poured coffee into my cup. Then my waiter came by and I asked him, "Does she work here?" He replied, "Yes, she works the morning shift." I had seen her rub her back so I asked him, "Would you please ask her if her back is sore? If it is, I would like to pray for her healing." He said he would, and he went over and told her. She began to look around to see who had said that.

I walked over to her and I introduced myself and found out her name was Lisa. Then I told her, "Sometimes when I pray for people they get healed. And I noticed you rubbing your back, as if it was sore, so may I pray for you?" She said, "Okay." I had her put her hands on her back and I put mine on top of hers. And I commanded the pain and soreness to go, in Jesus' name. In about three minutes she was healed. I told her that I had prayed in Jesus' name and He was the one who healed her. I asked her "Do you know anything about Jesus?" She replied, "I have been to church a few times."

I tested Lisa's hand with the anointing of the Holy Spirit and she felt it, but the Holy Spirit left when I pulled my hand away. I explained that when people are born again and become children of God, the Holy Spirit would stay with them. I asked her, "Would you like to ask Jesus to be your Lord and Savior now?" She turned away and thought about it for a minute and then she said "Yes." She prayed with me and afterwards I imparted to her some of the gifts of the Spirit. I had a word of knowledge that the Spirit was moving up to her shoulders and she confirmed that she felt it up to her shoulders. Afterwards I asked Lisa, "Do you have any Christian friends?" She told me she did. I suggested she tell them about her decision today.

Two days later, I went and spoke with her and tested her again with the anointing, and it still remained. So I told her, "You are now born again." I gave her the booklet, *Congratulations on Your New Life in Jesus Christ* and also a New Testament. And I confirmed with her that she would speak with her Christian friends soon and tell them about her new found faith in Jesus Christ. I also gave her phone number to a Christian lady in the city where she lives who will phone her and help her to grow in her faith. Lisa's story is a good example of being surprisingly supernatural, as I was able to release the gifts of the Spirit, a healing occurred, and Lisa was born again.

Video Illustrations

I have uploaded a number of videos onto the book's website, www.suprisinglysupernatural.com, to help illustrate some of the points I share in this book. The first video I would like you to look at is called: *Surprisingly Supernatural from Being Healed to Being Born Again.* To access this video you will need to log onto the web and go to www.suprisinglysupernatural.com. When you get to the webpage, click on the video tab, and then find the video you want to view, click on it, and it will begin to play. The videos are organized by chapter. Go to the Introduction and then click on the picture and the video will upload and begin to play.

I hope you enjoy watching a testimony about a believing believer who released healing, so that Lisa could be born again. Also on the website is a free download under Chapter 7 for the booklet: *Congratulations on Your New Life in Jesus Christ.* This booklet is an invitation to new converts to help them to step into the supernatural blessings that all believers can have in Jesus Christ. You can give it to new converts or to other believers who are not walking in the supernatural gifts themselves.

I find releasing the gifts of the Spirit is fun and exciting, because I get to operate in the supernatural realms of my Father's kingdom, and I also get to do my Father's will. It has taken me a very long time to understand what the prayer called "The Our Father" meant when it said, "Your kingdom come, your will be done." But now I understand it, for I am seeing His kingdom operating through me and around me almost every day, as I go out to do the will of my Father in heaven.

The ministry of releasing the gifts of the Spirit is for the believing believer, it is not just for special believers. But many believers have tried to share their faith, but have found it difficult to bring nonbelievers to the level of faith where they would accept Jesus Christ as their Lord and Savior. Others have tried prophetic evangelism, but those believers did not find how they could fit that prophetic practice into their lives, so it was primarily forgotten. And some have tended to refrain from witnessing and have said, "I don't think I am called to be an evangelist." I am aware that many believers have shied away from sharing their faith. But what I believe the problem has been is that believers were not doing it naturally.

Many believers have never learned how to live so that the sharing of your faith literally flows out from you. Instead, believers have been taught habits that they had to memorize and do, but that is not a lifestyle of sharing. I believe that is called "works." But if believers learn to have the lifestyle of releasing the gifts of the Spirit, then all the gifts will flow out of them for God's glory.

The ministry of releasing the gifts of the Spirit is to glorify the Lord Jesus Christ on the earth. The greatest thing about this lifestyle is that it's not about doing. It's about being. Being in a relationship with the Lord Jesus Christ through His Spirit and walking with the Lord in partnership with you, so you just release the supernatural realms of heaven and bring glory to the Lord.[8] It's not about works. It's about a lifestyle of walking in the Lord's presence and simply expressing that relationship around you as you go about your daily routine.

I want to reassure all believers who read this book and follow its teachings that you will learn how to become surprisingly supernatural, as you will begin to learn to release the gifts of the Spirit. This book is practical, so if you practice the exercises in this book, then over a period of time you will begin to flow in the gifts of the Spirit. Then you will have fun just being yourself, just being a believing believer who is playing in your Father's kingdom. When you see someone in front of you during your day, and if the Lord directs you, you can lay your hands on him and when he gets healed, then he will be thankful and blessed because you laid your hands on him. If he was a nonbeliever, he may be interested in learning more about the Jesus you spoke about, when you prayed for his healing.

I think you will be delighted if you will learn to release the gifts of the Spirit, as it will bring a supernatural dimension into your life, and you will recognize that you were made to be a believing believer who can bring

God's supernatural love and power to other people to demonstrate that Jesus Christ is the Lord. It will not be a pressure on you, as you will just bring the kingdom of God with you wherever you go, and it will be natural for you to release it. You will not have to argue or debate someone about theological issues for you will just demonstrate the gifts of the Spirit, and when the miracle happens, the miracle will speak for itself.

I believe that we are now in a time where the Father in heaven is going to equip believers, so they will find themselves surprisingly supernatural, and they will be enabled to release the gifts of the Spirit everywhere they go. For I believe that believers will be equipped with the power and love of the Holy Spirit. Jesus told His disciples that you must testify about Him (see John 15:26-27). Jesus was addressing the believer who is a disciple of Jesus Christ. If the believer wants to obey that command, you need to see that your testimony is tied to Jesus sending you out with the Holy Spirit. Therefore, the believer needs to learn to be continually filled by the Holy Spirit and then you are enabled to testify. And you must testify. Jesus sends the Holy Spirit so we can testify; our testimony comes out of the partnership with the Holy Spirit. You need to awaken to the reality that,

…The kingdom of God is at hand (Matthew 3:2 KJV).

When the kingdom is at hand, then you can easily testify to people about Jesus. Jesus does not want to make it onerous for you, so He gives you the Holy Spirit. When you receive the Holy Spirit then you just have to have faith and trust that He is with you, and that He wants to release His kingdom through you. Then He will direct you to where you are to release it. The Lord began to show me that my role was to help other people do what the Holy Spirit had taught me to do. I have written this book in hopes of getting the message out that the kingdom of God really is at hand! Not too long ago that statement was only a figure of speech for me, but now it is literal as the Holy Spirit's power flows out of my hands. I shake my head at all the obvious things that the Scripture revealed, but that I had failed to understand, because I had not understood the ways of the Spirit.

If you believe in the Lord Jesus Christ, then all you have to do is to access His Holy Spirit and then you can release His power and the miracles will happen. Sometimes it feels like I am dancing with the Holy Spirit. I was a professional dance competitor, teacher, and judge, so I know a little bit about dancing. When you dance, one partner is the leader, but a good leader does not make his partner follow; instead the leader gives an indication about what he wants his partner to do and then waits to see if the partner will respond. The person who follows has to pay attention. The best dancers in the world hardly touch one another when they dance together, and they respond to the slightest indication of the lead or the movement from their partner.

This is like the dynamic that occurs when I am led by the Holy Spirit. From my experiences when I hear the Lord's voice or when His Spirit nudges me, or if I am being led by the Spirit, I have learned that I must be sensitive to His lead. I must pay attention and follow. The Spirit's cues appear to be very subtle. If I am not paying attention, I might miss it. Sometimes, I do not realize I am dancing with the Spirit until I see God doing something through me that is impossible for me to do without Him. It is only then that I become aware that: *Oh, now I am being led.* Believers are told that we are sheep, and now I understand why. Sheep are not stubborn and sheep do not go their own way; sheep inherently follow the Good Shepherd (see John 10:3, 11, 14). I have finally learned to enjoy the process of knowing that I am not in control of my life all the time, but that I just have to yield to the Holy Spirit's lead and then I get to participate in releasing the gifts of the Holy Spirit.

Bishop and Prophet Bill Hamon, founder of "Christian International," gave the "2009 Word of the Lord" which states that we are now in the third reformation period for the church, and it began in 2008. This period is where the believers are to activate the restored truths of Scripture in our lives, so we can demonstrate the kingdom of God in the entire world (see Matt. 24:14). Hamon says, "The church has now been commissioned to infiltrate and dominate every kingdom and nation until Revelation 11:15 is fulfilled." Hamon says that "the five-fold ministers must expand their vision to go beyond maturing the church to activating and equipping every saint to be a kingdom demonstrator in their sphere of influence."[9]

I believe *Surprisingly Supernatural: A Practical Guide to Releasing the Gifts of the Spirit* is in the same spirit that Dr. Hamon speaks about, as it was birthed by the Holy Spirit at the right time, in the spring of 2008. It is calling out to each and every saint who can read or hear this message to be continually filled with the Holy Spirit, and filled with His gifts and His fruit. Then they can demonstrate the kingdom of God everywhere they find themselves in the world. This is a glorious time for believing believers. I encourage you to step into the river of God, and join me in the fun of being swept away in His power and His love, as we share the release of the gifts of the Spirit with all the people in our relational networks.

The wonderful part of releasing the gifts of the Spirit is that the Lord Jesus Christ has placed you exactly where you need to be to do it (see Acts 17:26-27). So when you release the gifts you do it in your sphere of influence, in your relational networks where you live, work, and play. Some people you touch will be your family members. Some people you touch will be your friends. Some people you touch will be acquaintances. And some people you touch will be strangers. Some of the people you touch will be believers, and some will be nonbelievers.

The reason the Lord has you release the gifts of the Spirit is to help other people to know the Lord better. Knowing the Lord Jesus Christ and the Only True God is what eternal life is all about (see John 17:3). Some believers that you touch, you will help to know the Lord better, as you will show them how they can receive the Holy Spirit and show them they can release the gifts of the Spirit themselves, as well. Some nonbelievers you touch, you will help them to know the Lord better too, especially if you give them a word of knowledge or if they get healed. The nonbelievers will either find out that the Lord knows about them or the Lord has the love and the power to heal them. The gifts are to bless other people and to help them to know Jesus' love and power.

I have some recurring themes in this book which essentially come from being filled with the Holy Spirit, for when you are continually filled with the Holy Spirit, His fruit and the gifts come along with it. Then you can just go out and follow the leading of the Spirit in the dance. He will teach you all things for Scripture tells us,

> As for you, the anointing you received from Him remains in you, and you do not need anyone to teach you. But as

> His anointing teaches you about all things, and as that anointing is real, not counterfeit—just as it has taught you, remain in Him (1 John 2:27).

So that's the secret. That's what happened to me. The Holy Spirit taught me to be surprisingly supernatural once I was clothed in Jesus Christ and I learned to remain in Him. Then I learned to release the gifts of the Spirit wherever I went. You can read this book to encourage yourself or you also can receive some new insights yourself. But if you already have the Holy Spirit filling you continually, then the Holy Spirit can teach you what I want to share with you in this book. If you hear the Spirit speak, we should be in unity, for I believe He will encourage you to freely receive and to freely give the kingdom of God away to the other people in your relational networks.

As I mentioned earlier, the focus of this book is for the reader to learn to release the gifts of the Spirit in your relational networks, and the consequence of that is that some evangelism will occur. But evangelism is a fruit of releasing the gifts of the Spirit; therefore, I do not address conventional evangelistic practices in this book. Conventional evangelistic resources cover many other points, which are important, but I do not cover them in this book. I believe those principles serve to support the presentation of the gospel and help in discipleship. However, this book focuses on the main points of accessing the gifts of the Spirit, so true believers will become sons and daughters of the Father in heaven, and then they will release the gifts of the Spirit.

When a believer truly becomes a son, like the Father in heaven had wanted all along, then the believer will begin to act like a son of the Father is supposed to act, which happens to be the way Jesus Christ acted. Now I am not advocating for you to wear one of those WWJD bracelets (What Would Jesus Do?).

This is not about memorizing principles to live by. No! This is because Jesus is literally with you via His Spirit. You will no longer think: *I wonder what Jesus would do?* Instead, you will just ask Jesus, because He is right there with you, so you ask Him: "Jesus, what would you like me to do here?" And then He will respond and tell you what you are to do. When

Jesus is there with you, you will be assured that you have become a son or daughter of the Father in heaven.

Believers who are sons of the Father are empowered to release the power of God into their relational networks. Jesus did not heal everyone or cast out all the demons. He just did what the Father told Him to do (see John 5:19). That's what the believing believers who read this book will begin to do, they will act like sons of the Father in heaven, and then they will do what the Father tells them to do. Because the believing believer is a son of the Father in heaven, it is natural that some evangelism will happen. Probably much more than you have ever experienced before, but that is not the goal, that's the fruit of obeying the commands you hear from the Father.

When all the followers of Jesus Christ understand that you are to continually receive the Holy Spirit and then copy Jesus' model by releasing the gifts of the Spirit into your relational networks, then you will operate in a surprisingly supernatural manner. There will be no stress or fear, for you will know that the Lord is near. When you know that, you will know you are endowed with God's supernatural power that you can release everywhere you go. Then you will behave the way the sons of God are supposed to; in this book I call them "*believing believers*" for they will copy how the Son of God, Jesus Christ, operated.

The term "Christian" has been watered down so much that it has lost its meaning. A Christian is supposed to be a son of God and should be identified by the Spirit of God testifying on his behalf (see Rom. 8:16). But that proof of the faith has been lost over the centuries and the church has accepted a lower standard of faith for Christians. Therefore, in this book I use the term *believing believer*, which captures the essence of being the child of God that the Heavenly Father wanted. The believing believer will act just like the elder brother Jesus acted when He walked upon the earth and released the gifts of the Spirit.

I am inviting you to lean on Jesus Christ, and I am asking you to implore Him to move through you with His Spirit, so you can demonstrate His kingdom, His power, His gifts, and His love in this next season so that millions and millions will come to receive Him as their Lord and Savior.

Yet this will not occur because you are a zealous believer. No! It will only occur because each one of you will have become a believing believer who receives the Holy Spirit, and then you will reach out and touch a few nonbelievers every month who are in your relational networks, and you will invite them to receive Jesus' mercy and save them. This is the body of Christ coming alive and demonstrating Jesus Christ's love and power.

Each one of you is called to be continually filled by the Holy Spirit, and then you can touch the people in your relational networks that the Father in heaven directs for you to touch for His glory. When you become a believing believer, then you can release the gifts of the Spirit, and then millions and millions of people will receive Jesus Christ as their Lord and Savior. When this happens it will be the Day of the Saints.[10]

After each chapter, I have some discussion questions that are intended to further help the reader's study on the topic and to help the reader absorb the material. These questions can be done individually or as group projects. The questions should help the reader to grasp what I am sharing in this book as many of the ideas may require the reader to change her ways of doing things. Romans 12 tells us,

> Do not be conformed to the pattern of this world, but be transformed by the renewing of your mind (Rom. 12:2).

The experiences I share with you in this book, and the perspectives on Scripture I share with you may challenge you. I hope you see that in my heart I want to see Jesus Christ glorified on the earth by inspiring all "believers" to become *"believing believers"* who will demonstrate the gifts of the Spirit in their relational networks. I hope you will reflect on the Scriptures I present, the testimonies I share, and the video clips that I direct you to watch on the website. I hope you will allow the ideas that you previously held to shift, so your mind will be transformed. Consequently, you will overcome the lies of the enemy, and you will become a believing believer who will be continually filled by the Holy Spirit; and then you will release the gifts of the Spirit into your relational networks.

The questions after each chapter are to help you to engage with the Scriptures around this topic, to wrestle with the new ideas proposed, and to wrestle with your own courage and your faith, so that you can step into the presence of God's Holy Spirit with me and other believers, and become transformed into Jesus Christ's likeness (see 2 Cor. 3:18).

This book is not just a book for you to read and put down. It is a training manual and I suggest that you will want to read and reread it, and use it to help you practice acquiring and releasing the gifts of the Spirit. It will probably take several months, before you are able to release the gifts of the Spirit regularly as you go about your daily routine. So apply yourself and become an overcomer who understands we are in a war and the evil spiritual powers want to extinguish your flame. But don't let them. Learn to be continually filled by the Spirit of God and to have the Spirit of God upon you. That way your flame will never grow dim, but instead you will be made holy and be transformed by the Spirit that is in you and surrounds you. Be patient, passionate and persevere in receiving the gifts of the Spirit and releasing them in your relational networks.

CHAPTER 1

DEFINITIONS AND HINDRANCES TO RELEASING THE GIFTS

This book is intended to empower the saints to become overcomers and demonstrate the gifts of the Spirit in their relational networks. However, I need to start by defining some of the terms and understandings that I have put into my writing.

Relational Networks

Your relational networks would include family members, neighbors, schoolmates, workmates, friends, acquaintances, and anyone you meet along the way like a grocery clerk, or someone in a line at a coffee shop, or a stranger you run into during your day. Because believing believers are continually filled by the Holy Spirit they will release the gifts of the Spirit in their relational networks with a wide variety of people as they go about their daily lives.

Believing Believer

When I use the term: "*believing believer*" it refers to a Christian who is a true believer. The believing part of the believer responds with great faith to Jesus' question when He asked: If He will find faith on the earth when He comes back? (see Luke 18:8b). Jesus was speaking about the very end of the end-times when He spoke about coming back again.

The believing believer will respond with great faith at the end of the end-times and will ask for the Holy Spirit to fill her until she is continually filled by the Holy Spirit.[11] Because of that practice, the believing believer is distinguished from her culture because the Holy Spirit regularly testifies that the believing believer is a child of God with healings, miracles, deliverance and prophetic words being given out. The believing believer is the kind of follower that Jesus envisioned that He would have (see John 20:21-22).

The believing believer loves the Lord, loves the Word of God, and obeys all of the Lord's instructions, which includes being continually filled by the Holy Spirit, so she is overshadowed by the Holy Spirit. Consequently, she has become a home for the Lord Jesus and the Heavenly Father (see John 14:23). The believing believer is the protagonist in this book.

Misunderstood Teachings on Spiritual Gifts

Some people in the church have what I believe is a misunderstanding. They think the gifts of the Spirit are distributed in a limited fashion. This thinking comes from their reading of the passage in 1 Corinthians 12,

> All these are the work of one and the same Spirit, and He gives them to each one, just as He determines (1 Cor. 12:11).

Some people have viewed the phrase "He gives them to each one" in a limited fashion. They believe that the Holy Spirit limits the believer to a maximum of one gift. These same people also look at the preceding Scripture and note that it repeats the phrase "to another" (see 1 Cor. 12:8-10). And they believe this phrase supports their understanding that each person will get only one gift, but not more than one.

However, Jesus tells you that the Holy Spirit will not speak on His own. The Holy Spirit will only speak what He hears from the Father (see John 16:13). Jesus also tells you that the Father wants to give good gifts to His children *who will ask* the Father for them (see Matt. 7:11; Luke 11:9-13). The Scripture also tells us that the believing believer should desire the greater gifts, and they also should come to the waters and drink (see 1 Cor. 12:31; Isa. 55:1).

The Father in heaven, that I know, wants to give good gifts freely to His children who will use them. He is not stingy with His Holy Spirit, if you want to walk out as one of His obedient children and demonstrate the kingdom in your relational networks. Those who want to use the gifts to demonstrate the kingdom will be recognized by the Father in heaven. And He will be pleased to give the gifts of the Spirit to all of His obedient children who want to go out and demonstrate the kingdom.

Paul writes,

> Now you are the body of Christ, and each of you is a part of it...Are all apostles? Are all prophets? Are all teachers? Do all work miracles? Do all have gifts of healing? Do all speak in tongues? But eagerly desire the greater gifts (see 1 Cor. 12:27, 29-31).

You are all part of the body of Christ and each of you has your own part to play, but Paul also says "...eagerly desire the greater gifts" (1 Cor. 12:27). You may start with one gift, but if you express your desire for more than one of the gifts to the Father in heaven, He is pleased to expand the selection of the gifts that will operate through you. All the gifts are available to the children of God once they have desired them, and have asked for the spiritual gifts. Then they will receive many of those different spiritual gifts from the Father in heaven that you desired and asked for.

When I asked the Father in heaven to give me the gift of prophecy, I felt that the Holy Spirit had encouraged me to ask for it. But after that no one in my church informed me that I could ask for different gifts or told me that I was to desire them. So I didn't ask for them. However, fifteen years passed and I sensed that the Holy Spirit wanted to encourage me to abide in Him.

Then I learned to be continually filled by the Holy Spirit. After having soaked in God's Spirit for several hours a day over a four month period, I began to see healing gifts start to operate in my life. Then deliverance and discernment came. It took me fifteen years to realize that if I desired another spiritual gift, I could ask for it, and the Father would respond and give me more than one spiritual gift. My Father in heaven is not stingy with His spiritual gifts. Instead, He is pleased when His children understand they are to desire them and ask for them.

I also discovered that when I asked for the Holy Spirit to fill me, and I asked to be used by God for His purposes, other gifts started to appear as well. Jesus did tell you,

> You did not choose me, but I chose you and appointed you to go and bear fruit—fruit that will last. Then the Father will give you whatever you *ask in my name* (John 15:16).

Jesus chose you to bear fruit. Bearing fruit means you are being used by God for His purposes. With that motive in mind, wanting to bear fruit for Jesus, the doorway will open up to all believing believers to receive all of the gifts of the Spirit they desire and ask for, so they can release them in their relational networks. I had asked God to use me and to allow my life to be fruitful, and then I received additional gifts of the Spirit. But I first had to desire them, and then I had to ask for the gifts of the Spirit (see Matt. 7:7; 7:11; 18:19; 21:22; Luke 11:9-13; John 11:22; 14:13-14; 15:7; 15:16; 16:23-26).

The most significant key was that I responded to the Holy Spirit when He encouraged me to be continually filled by Him.[12] Then the other gifts seemed to come to me without having to ask for them, once I had the Holy Spirit continually filling me. However, there were other times when I expressed my desire and I specifically asked for more spiritual gifts. I also asked for an increased level in the gifting that operated through me. Then often the gifting level would increase. The gifting and the increase in gifting was attributed to my learning to align my will with the Father's will and ask Him to use me for His purposes. Then it appears as if He responded to my faith and my requests.

The Father wants to give good gifts to His children. *All believing believers who want to be used by God, and are continually filled with the Holy Spirit will receive more than one of the gifts from the Holy Spirit.* But they have to express their desire for the Holy Spirit and for the gifts of the Spirit, and then ask for them.

Besides asking for the gifts of the Spirit, I also activated the Spiritual gifts by using the gifts whenever I could. The result was I grew in many of the spiritual gifts. And I also believed what Paul wrote "...eagerly desire the greater gifts" (1 Cor. 12:27). So that's what I did. I desired the greater gifts and I asked the Father for them. But I also tried to demonstrate the gifts whenever I could. Then my Father in heaven sometimes would bring out a spiritual gift whenever He wanted that gift to operate through me. But I also found that I could press into the gifts in faith.

Pressing into the Gifts of the Spirit in Faith

Paul writes in Romans 12,

> If a man's gift is prophesying, let him use it in proportion to his faith (Rom. 12:6b).

I found that by faith I could prophesy, so I pressed into it and practiced prophesying. Then by faith I found I could pray for the sick, so I pressed into it and practiced praying for healing, and then I saw the sick start to be healed. Then by faith I pressed into and practiced the gifts of discernment and I discerned angels, demons, and demonic structures and then I drove out the demons. The result was that I saw the spiritual gifts that I had access to begin to grow. And they began to become even more accessible because I exercised my faith. Jesus did say,

> 'Consider carefully what you hear,' He continued. 'With the measure you use, it will be measured to you, and even more. Whoever has will be given more, whoever does not have, even what he has will be taken from him' (Mark 4:24-25).

The Lord said that more will be given to those who have. I believe He was referring to the gifts of the Spirit. The increase is based on how the believing believer uses the spiritual gifts. If you are intent on demonstrating the kingdom of God in your relational networks, you will develop greater access to the gifts that you have been given.

You will also be given more spiritual gifts to add to your repertoire. All believing believers will be given an assortment of spiritual gifts, because they will desire the greater gifts. And they will be continually filled by the

Holy Spirit, as that is where the gifts of the Spirit come from. And they will ask the Father for those gifts, and they will practice using the gifts by releasing them to the people who live around them.

Now it is good that even if you have all the gifts of the Spirit, you need to know that you are still dependent on other believing believers, as you need other believing believers to confirm the spiritual insights that you will receive. It is good for the believing believer to work with other believing believers, so you can learn to complement one another with your gifts during your ministry time together.

Even though it is good for you to work with one another, I still believe it is incorrect to think the Spirit limits the gifts of the Spirit to one per person. The Spirit does what the Father says. And the Father responds to the faith and obedience of His children. I believe that everyone who asks in faith for the gifts from the Father in heaven, and intends to use them to glorify the Lord Jesus Christ, will receive all the spiritual gifts that they ask for.

Paul also writes,

> There are different kinds of working, but the same God works all of them *in all men* (1 Cor. 12:6; emphasis added).

Paul meant that God's power is at work in the gifts of the Spirit regardless of who has them. And with the phrase "*God works all of them* in all men," Paul could have been implying that the key to having access to all the gifts of the Spirit is for the believers to have God with us. Whoever wants the spiritual gifts will get all the gifts that they ask for, when they are continually filled by the Spirit of God, because that's when God is with us (see John 4:24). All believing believers will have God with them working all of the spiritual gifts.

Paul did write in 1 Corinthians 12 for believing believers to desire the spiritual gifts. All believing believers will desire the gifts and will ask for them. The phrase "all of them in all men" could imply that all believing believers can have all the spiritual gifts. And if not all the gifts, then they will certainly have at least a variety of the spiritual gifts, as long as they desire them and ask for them, and they are intent on releasing them in their relational networks to demonstrate that Jesus Christ is God. This appears to correspond with what Moses had said,

> I wish that *all the Lord's people* were prophets and that the Lord would put His Spirit on them! (Num. 11:29b; emphasis added).

"All" in this verse indicates that Moses was expressing God's heart the same way Paul did in 1 Corinthians 12:6. They both implied that the Lord wants *"all"* of the believing believers to possess a variety of the spiritual gifts. Especially since the gifts listed in 1 Corinthians 12 will help the believing believers to avoid being ignorant of idols, demons, and demonic structures. And they will help them to destroy the devil's works. I believe that if you hunger and thirst for more of God, and if you become a son, daughter, servant, or sheep like all believing believers are, then the gifts of the Spirit will be freely given to you.

The Father in heaven wants to give the good gifts to those who ask Him, especially if the one who asks is a believing believer who wants to love and obey the Lord Jesus and the Father in heaven, and become a home for them. The natural response of the Father then is to give the believing believer a variety of spiritual gifts, so he can access them whenever they are needed (see Isa. 55:1-5; Matt. 10:6-8; Luke 11:9-13). Consequently, I believe the Father in heaven wants His sons, daughters, servants, and sheep, who are believing believers to desire the gifts, and then ask Him for the gifts of the Spirit. Then they will surely receive all of the gifts that they ask for.

With this understanding the next five chapters will teach you how the reader can continually receive the Holy Spirit and receive the gifts of the Spirit. Then the reader can practice those gifts, so eventually you can take them out into your relational network to bring glory to the Lord Jesus Christ.

Warning about the Gifts of the Spirit Becoming an Idol

One cautionary note that is clear from the Scriptures, as it tells us the manifestation of the gifts of the Spirit can become idolatry, if they are sought outside of a relationship with the Lord. Matthew 7 tells us,

> Not everyone who says to Me, 'Lord, Lord,' will enter the kingdom of heaven, but only he who does the will of My Father who is in heaven. Many will say to Me on that day, 'Lord, Lord, did we not prophesy in Your name, and in Your name drive out demons and perform many miracles?' Then I will tell them plainly, 'I never knew you. Away from Me, you evil-doers' (Matt. 7: 21-23).

The pursuit of the gifts of the Spirit outside of a relationship with Jesus Christ and the Holy Father is inadvisable, as you might end up in hell if you pursue the gifts outside of those relationships. Many New Age practitioners pray and do Healing Touch or *Reiki* healing, and then they invoke the name of Jesus, but they are not in a relationship with the Lord Jesus Christ. They are some of the people who might be represented by Matthew 7:21-23.

Consequently, I suggest for the reader to note how the subsequent chapters show various Scriptures that indicate your need to be in a relationship with the Lord as a son, daughter, servant, or sheep. And the Scriptures also encourage you to listen and obey whatever the Lord directs you to do. I believe we are now in a special time where the Lord wants intimate relationships with all His children. I also believe He wants to see us transformed, so our lives can obtain a greater likeness to the Lord Jesus Christ. This will result in greater manifestations of the gifts and the fruit of the Spirit.

The Phrase "*Surprisingly Supernatural*"

I use the phrase "*surprisingly supernatural*" in the title of this book to address the believer who does not really believe Jesus' promise when He said He would be with us,

> And surely I am with you always to the very end of the age (Matt. 28:20b; John 14:18).

If you renewed your mind so you really believed Jesus' promise, then you would not be surprised that you operate in the supernatural realm. But Jesus told you, He would be with you when the Holy Spirit comes. Not when you have mental assent to biblical principles, or when you have mentally accepted Jesus as your Lord and Savior. With the believer's un-renewed mind, he fails to understand that he is a true believer when he becomes a son of God, and that only occurs when he has asked Jesus to forgive his sins and save him, and then asks for the Holy Spirit to fill him, and to testify through him demonstrating that he is a son of God (see John 3:6 Rom. 8:16).

A renewed believer's mind in this book means that the believing believer has developed the practice of being continually filled by the Holy Spirit; consequently, he will be assured that Jesus is with him always. Therefore, he will not be surprised that he operates in the supernatural realms of God's kingdom, because the Holy Spirit is with him and so is Jesus, who happens to be the Creator of the universe (see John 1:3).

You may not have believed the promise that Jesus would always be with you, because you were not continually filled with His Spirit, and because you did not see the Spirit testify that you are a son of God. The believer's un-renewed mind is partially attributed to the devil leading the whole world astray (see Rev. 12:9). But I want to encourage you to resist the devil's lies. This book addresses your unbelief and it encourages you to explore the gifts of the Spirit, so you will surprise yourself when you see that you can release the supernatural gifts of the Spirit within your relational networks.

Use the Surprisingly Supernatural Cards to Practice Releasing the Gifts

If you practice using the Surprisingly Supernatural Cards that are associated with this book, which are found on the book's website, then you will declare to the Father that you want the gifts of the Spirit and your life will never be the same again. You will become a believing believer who will carry the Spirit of God with you all the time. And when you are directed to release it, then you will participate in healings, miracles, and demons being cast out.

You will be walking in the birthright that God the Father had planned for your life since before the foundations of the world. You will become a member of the end-times army of God, and you will walk out as an overcomer during the final hours on the earth. You will be an active participant during the Days of the Saints, as you will become the Bride of Christ! I bless you as you pursue intimacy with the Lord, and as you make your body, soul, and spirit a home for both the Lord Jesus Christ and the Heavenly Father.

Surprisingly Supernatural Cards Are Free Downloads

On the book's website www.surprisinglysupernatural.com, I have made available to the reader all of the Surprisingly Supernatural Cards for you to download for free. You have my permission to print them and give them out to as many believers as you can, so you can to encourage them to become believing believers as well.

This book is not intended for you to just pick it up, read it, and then put it down. No, this book is a practical book with exercises in it, and with Surprisingly Supernatural Cards that you can download so you can practice asking for the gifts of the Spirit and practice releasing the gifts of the Spirit in your relational network. This book and the associated Surprisingly Supernatural Cards will probably stay with you for a number of weeks, and maybe even for a few months until you can acquire the skills associated with releasing the gifts of the Spirit.

This book is not just to give you more information. The intention is to transform you so you will become a believing believer who can regularly release the gifts of the Spirit in your relational networks. I hope you enjoy reading this book and declaring the Surprisingly Supernatural Cards, so you will be transformed into a supernatural believing believer who will glorify the Lord Jesus Christ by releasing the gifts of the Spirit into the world around you.

Receiving the Gifts of the Spirit

This book is practical and in each of the next five chapters you are invited to acquire one of the gifts of the Spirit. Each chapter has a Surprisingly Supernatural Card that is associated with it. The Surprisingly Supernatural Cards are to help the reader appropriate the Scriptures. The Surprisingly Supernatural Cards are in the form of prayers that you will decree and declare the Scriptural promises that are in the Bible back to the Father in heaven and ask Him for the specific spiritual gift.

I encourage the reader to use the reference material in this book over a number of weeks. During this time the reader will be asking for the gifts of the Spirit. Once the format in the Surprisingly Supernatural Card is memorized, the reader does not need to look at that card again, but can start on the next Surprisingly Supernatural Card, and begin to practice saying the decrees and declarations that are on that new Surprisingly Supernatural Card.

CHAPTER 2

SURPRISINGLY SUPERNATURAL STEP #1
BE FILLED WITH THE HOLY SPIRIT

The first step in becoming a supernatural believing believer is to learn to be continually filled by the Holy Spirit. This is absolutely the most important step for a believing believer to take, especially since it opens up your relationship with the Lord, and it will allow you to be taught and to obey what He wants you to do. This chapter will teach you about the importance of being continually filled with the Holy Spirit, and it also has a practical section for you to learn to practice asking for the Holy Spirit, which will enable you to be continually filled.

The Lord inspired Peter to read Joel's prophecy and He said,

> In the last days, God says, I will pour out my Spirit on all people. Your sons and your daughters will prophesy, your young men will see visions, your old men dream dreams. Even on my servants, both men and women, I will pour out my Sprit in those days, and they will prophesy. (Acts 2:17-18).

The Lord is still pouring out His Spirit today, and I believe that receiving the outpouring of the Spirit is just like receiving salvation in Jesus Christ. We must first *ask* Jesus to save us, and to forgive us for our sins. Jesus said,

> This is my blood of the covenant, which is poured out *for many* for the forgiveness of sins (Matt. 26:28; emphasis added).

We read in 1 John 4 that Jesus is the *savior of the world* (see 1 John 4:14; John 4:42b). If Jesus is the *savior of the world*, why do you think Jesus said *"for many"* in Matthew 26:28? I believe it is because not all people in the world know they *must ask* Jesus to be their Lord and Savior, and *ask* Him to forgive them for their sins, even though He has already died for their sins.

If people do not *ask* Jesus to forgive them for their sins, they are not automatically forgiven; even though His blood has been poured out to cover the sins of the whole world (see 1 John 2:2). Jesus' blood has been poured out, but only those *who ask* Him to be their Lord and Savior, and *ask* Him to forgive their sins will be forgiven and receive the blessing of salvation, and the invitation to spend eternity with the God of love.

If you understand that everyone needs to have their sins forgiven by Jesus, you will be compelled to try to share with other people the good news of the gospel, for if they do not receive salvation in Jesus Christ then they will spend eternity away from God in hell. They *must ask* Jesus to forgive them for their sins, and *ask* Jesus to come into their lives and become their Lord and Savior.

If you understand this and you are compelled by it to take some action and share your faith, then that is the innate evangelist responding within you. It is part of your spiritual DNA in Christ to want to save the world, but you will generally only do it one person at a time.

If you did not respond to this, I do not think you understand the gravity of your situation as a saint or understand your plight and your responsibility; for you must obey the Father and participate with Him to save all those in your relational networks that you can.

Our plight is that only those who do the will of the Father will enter the kingdom of heaven (see Matt. 7:21). *You do not become a sheep when you just receive Jesus Christ in a prayer, but you are a sheep when you follow the Father's commands. Clearly, one of the commands is to testify and make disciples.* You are told you *must testify* and that was the Lord's command to all of us (see John 15:26-27; Matt. 28:18-20). This command is to all disciples, to all sheep who want to obey the Father's will, not just to evangelists.

Your responsibility is to represent the Lord Jesus Christ as a vessel for His love and His power to be expressed through you, and to be experienced by other people. Jesus is still echoing these words in this hour "as the Father has sent me, I am sending you," so receive my Spirit and represent me to the entire world (see John 20:21-22; Matt. 9:38; Mark 16:15).

You have the responsibility to represent Jesus Christ in your relational networks, and you do that by going out like He was sent out, in the power of the Holy Spirit. Then you will release the gifts of the Spirit to reach those people who live and work around you. You also have a responsibility to tell them that *they must ask* for Jesus' blood to cover their sins, for their sins to be forgiven. They will not be forgiven unless they *ask* for the Lord's forgiveness.

To Benefit From God's Gifts Requires You to Ask for Them

Jesus' blood was poured out and the Holy Spirit is also poured out. To receive the benefit of these gifts from God, *you need to ask* for them. You do not receive the baptism of the Holy Spirit *unless you ask* for it, and wait for it. But when you do that, you then can go out like Jesus was sent out (see John 20:21-22).

When you are a believing believer, you operate out of simply being continually filled by the Holy Spirit, and then you can go out and demonstrate who Jesus Christ is to the world around you. If you demonstrate the gifts of the Spirit to a nonbeliever with healing, deliverance, and prophecy being released, then the nonbeliever may be motivated and willing to ask Jesus Christ to forgive her for her sins, and ask Him to be her Lord and Savior.

Being a believing believer is influenced by these two important points:

Point #1: Invite Them to Receive Jesus

People, who do not know they are sinners that need to be forgiven, must be told about Jesus' blood that atones for all sin. You also may need to define what sin is to them. Then if they are willing, you can invite them to receive Jesus Christ and His forgiveness for their sins. That is what we call evangelism, which is the good news that all sins are forgiven in Jesus' blood. But because the world now has a myriad of "truths" due to post-modernism, it is more difficult to talk someone into believing in Jesus Christ. Consequently, you need the second point.

Point #2: Believing Believers Need to Ask, Wait for, and Then Receive the Holy Spirit

Believers, who are believing believers, need to ask, wait for, and then receive the outpouring of the Holy Spirit, because Jesus tells you to ask for the good gift, which is the Holy Spirit (see Luke 11:9, 13). And then He later says in Luke 11 that when the Holy Spirit's power is demonstrated the kingdom of God comes to people (see Luke 11:20). When the kingdom comes to people through healing, deliverance, and prophecy, those people will discover that Jesus Christ truly is the King, because the kingdom of God touched them. I believe this is the type of testifying that God is calling the whole body of Christ to employ now. He wants believing believers to bring the kingdom of God, with all the spiritual gifts, to everyone they can.

Jesus frequently spoke about "the kingdom of God," so I have listed a few Scriptures here for you to see what Jesus meant when He used the phrase "the kingdom of God." You will see that it meant to demonstrate the gifts of the Spirit with prophecy, healing, and deliverance.

In Luke 8 it says,

> The knowledge of the secrets of the kingdom of God have been given to you, but to others I speak in parables, so that, 'though seeing, they may not see; though hearing, they may not understand' (Luke 8:10).

The kingdom secrets Jesus speaks about may be similar to what Paul tells us; that through the prophetic gift you can reveal the secrets of other people's hearts (see 1 Cor. 14:24-25; 1 Sam. 9:19-20). Once you have received the kingdom, you then can release it with prophetic insights like words of knowledge and prophecy.

In Luke 8:1 it says,

> …Jesus traveled about…proclaiming the good news of the kingdom (Luke 8:1).

Jesus proclaimed the good news of the kingdom both verbally and by demonstrating it with the Spirit's power, for in the next few verses it tells us some women who followed Jesus had received freedom from evil spirits, and their diseases were cured. Therefore, Jesus proclaimed the kingdom of God by releasing deliverance and healing (see Luke 8:2).

In Luke 9:1 it says,

> When Jesus called the twelve together, He gave them power and authority to drive out all demons and to cure diseases, and He sent them out to preach the kingdom of God, and to heal the sick (Luke 9:1-2).

This previous verse shows the preaching of the kingdom of God is associated with driving out demons, curing diseases, and healing the sick.

In Luke 9:11 it says,

> He…spoke to them about the kingdom of God and healed those who needed healing (Luke 9:11).

Again, we see that the kingdom of God is linked to healing.

In Luke 11:20 Jesus says,

> But if I drive out demons by the finger of God, then the kingdom of God has come to you (Luke 11:20).

Here Jesus links the kingdom of God to the driving out of demons, which is also called deliverance.

In Matthew 10:7-8 Jesus says,

> As you go, preach this message: the kingdom of God is near. Heal the sick, raise the dead, cleanse those who have leprosy, drive out demons. Freely you have received, freely give (Matt. 10:7-8).

Here Jesus shows that when the kingdom of God is preached, three different types of healings may occur: 1) healing the sick, 2) raising the dead, and 3) cleansing the leper. And Jesus also said it involved driving out demons. The kingdom of God in this verse is expressed with healing and deliverance. When He said, "Freely receive, freely give," this seems to echo Isaiah 55 that implores believers to,

> Come all you who are thirsty, come to the waters; and you who have no money, come buy and eat (Isa. 55:1).

Since you freely receive the waters of the Holy Spirit, which is the kingdom of God, you are supposed to give it away freely. What is interesting is that it says come to the waters; even if you have no money, you can buy and eat (see Isa. 55:1). How do you buy and eat without having money? How do you buy without money?

I think the currency is your time. You need to spend your time to come and wait for the living waters to fill you. Every person in the world has 60 seconds to the minute. Everyone has the same opportunity to either spend their time to wait for and to receive the good gift of the Holy Spirit, which is the living waters, or not. But the Lord wants you to come and buy with your time, so you can wait and drink in deeply the living waters of God. Are you willing to spend your time to drink in the Holy Spirit of God?

In Luke 17:20-21 Jesus tells us,

> The kingdom of God does not come with your careful observation, nor will people say, 'Here it is' or 'There it is' because the kingdom of God is within you (Luke 17:20b-21).

Hidden inside of every true follower of Christ is the potential of the kingdom of God with its spiritual power for healings, miracles, words of knowledge, and the power to drive out demons. Once you have received it, this power of God is ready to be released everywhere the believing believer goes.

But like Isaiah 55 says, you must come to the waters and drink to receive the water, which is the Holy Spirit. It will require your time and your effort to come and drink. The *Surprisingly Supernatural Step #1: Be Filled with the Holy Spirit* card was written to help believers to learn to come to the waters and drink, and receive the Holy Spirit and His gifts within themselves (go to the website: www.surprisinglysupernatural.com to get the free download of this card). Receiving His Spirit is the key to receiving the kingdom of God. This card is to help believers to fill up with the fullness of the Spirit of God.

The significance for believers who are living at the end of the end-times is to respond to what Jesus tells us He wants us to do, which He told us in Matthew 24,

> ...this gospel of the kingdom will be preached in the whole world as a testimony to all nations, and then the end will come (Matt. 24:14).

The Scriptures we have examined above have shown that an important key to preaching the gospel of the kingdom of God would certainly include demonstrations of healings, miracles, deliverance and prophecy. The body of Christ needs to wake up to this reality and learn to demonstrate these gifts of the Spirit, as "then the end will come" (Matt. 24:14b). All believing believers will awaken to the urgency of this call and learn to be continually filled by the Holy Spirit, and then learn how to demonstrate the gifts of the Spirit into the whole world in this hour.

Guard Your Heart by Keeping the Kingdom Message

Remember that 1 John 3:8 says that Jesus came to destroy the works of the devil. The devil does not want you to read this book to learn about the kingdom of God and to learn how to release the gifts of the Spirit, because you will be learning to destroy the works of the devil.

In Matthew 13 Jesus tells us an important fact,

> When anyone hears the message about the kingdom and does not understand it, the evil one comes and snatches away what was sown in the heart (Matthew 13:19).

Beware! The evil one wants to snatch this message of the kingdom of God from you. The evil one wants to prevent the kingdom of God and its gifts from getting inside of your heart. Make every effort to understand it. Guard your heart! Keep the kingdom message that you will learn from reading this book intact.

When Jesus said the kingdom of God is within you, He was referring to the Holy Spirit. Therefore, the first step in becoming surprisingly supernatural is to use the *Surprisingly Supernatural Step #1: Be Filled with the Holy Spirit* card, which was written to help believers to learn to come, drink, and receive the Holy Spirit and His gifts within themselves, like all believing believers will do. After this first step, the other steps follow naturally, as the gifts of the Spirit will flow out of you once you have received an abundance of the Holy Spirit.

The Scripture Shows the Disciples Received Multiple Fillings of the Holy Spirit

When I was learning to be filled by the Holy Spirit, He led me through the Scriptures and I saw that the first disciples were filled a number of times in succession. It began after Jesus' resurrection in John 20 when Jesus told the disciples,

> … 'Peace be with you, as the Father sent me, I am sending you,' and with that, He breathed on them and said, 'Receive the Holy Spirit' (John 20:21-22).

Then the second time the disciples were filled by the Holy Spirit was when the disciples were in the upper room on the day of Pentecost, which we read about in Acts 2 where it says,

> Suddenly a sound like the blowing of a violent wind came from heaven and filled the whole house where they were

> sitting. They saw what seemed to be tongues of fire that separated and came to rest on each of them. All of them were filled with the Holy Spirit and began to speak in other tongues as the Spirit enabled them (Acts 2:2-4).

Then the third time being filled by the Holy Spirit is mentioned in the Scripture is in Acts 4, that says,

> Then Peter, filled with the Holy Spirit... (Acts 4:8).

It appears that Peter had been continually filled by the Spirit. Then again we read that the disciples and possibly Peter were filled for either a third or a fourth time in Acts 4:31 where it says,

> After they prayed, the place where they were meeting was shaken. And they were all filled with the Holy Spirit and spoke the word of God boldly (Acts 4:31).

Once again we read that the disciples were empowered by the Holy Spirit and they were enabled to speak boldly. After multiple fillings of the Spirit of God, we then read about the fruit of those fillings. In Acts 3 a cripple was healed,

> Taking him by the right hand, he helped him up, and instantly the man's feet and ankles became strong (Acts 3:7).

Peter and John had released the power of the kingdom and the cripple was healed. Peter was so full of the Spirit that he also manifested a shadow of the Spirit, which we read in Acts 5,

> ...People brought the sick into the streets and laid them on beds and mats so that at least Peter's shadow might fall on some of them as he passed by (Acts 5:15).

Peter had been in the group of disciples who had received at least three, and probably more successive fillings of the Holy Spirit. The result was that Peter was filled to overflowing with the Holy Spirit. The overflow of the Holy Spirit made the spiritual shadow around Peter. And that resulted in the healing power and the deliverance power of the Holy Spirit being released in his relational networks.

When the cripple was healed, that cripple was just along the route Peter took regularly to go to the temple. The cripple was just someone in his relational network; someone who was a family member, a friend, a neighbor, an acquaintance or a stranger who came along Peter's path that day. Believing believers will release the gifts of the Spirit in your relational networks. Can you start to look for the people that God will bring along your path today?

Paul had a similar manifestation to Peter's, for in Acts 19 it reads,

> God did extraordinary miracles through Paul, so that even handkerchiefs and aprons that had touched him were taken to the sick and their illnesses were cured and the evil spirits left them (Acts 19:11).

Paul had pieces of clothing around his body that carried the Holy Spirit's power for healing and deliverance; therefore, Paul must have been overflowing with the Holy Spirit's power as well. Paul had a spiritual shadow like Peter did. Peter and Paul were just following Jesus' example and following the instructions to ask and wait for the Holy Spirit, as Jesus had His own spiritual shadow (see Luke 11:9, 13; Luke 24:49).

In Mark 5, we read that the woman said, "If I just touch His clothes, I will be healed" (Mark 5:28). Then she touched the tassels on Jesus' garment and she was immediately healed, and "Jesus realized that power had gone out from Him" (Mark 5:30). By the woman touching the tassels on Jesus' garment, and then she received her healing, demonstrates that Jesus had a spiritual shadow as well.

Jesus had been baptized in the Spirit of God, was full of the Holy Spirit, and then He was full of the power of the Holy Spirit of God. Jesus did say, "The Spirit of the Lord is upon me" (see Luke 4:1; 3:22; 4: 14; 4:18). *Consequently, all of our New Testament role models Jesus, Peter, and Paul all demonstrated that they were full of the Holy Spirit and they had the Spirit of God upon them.* Jesus did tell us that,

> God is Spirit and His worshippers must worship in spirit and in truth (John 4:24).

The Father wants to continually fill all His children with His Spirit to make you as much like Jesus as He can. And that can only be accomplished by the Holy Spirit of God continually filling you. When you ask for the Spirit and then you wait for Him to fill you regularly, that's your spiritual act of worship.

Then when you wait for extended periods of time, and you practice continually asking the Holy Spirit to fill you, that's when the Spirit of God will begin to stay with you and will begin to overshadow you. When you express your desire for the Spirit to fill you, the Lord will eventually see your desire, and then He will place His Spirit upon you.

The Lord may even prompt you to ask Him to clothe you in power from on high (see Matt. 6:30; Luke 24:49). When the Spirit of God is upon you, then you will be able to be continually filled by the Spirit. Then you will walk out in the birthright that the Father in heaven had planned for your life, for you will be *in Christ*, and Christ will be in you, when the Spirit of God is upon you. Then your life will be fruitful! (see John 15:5; Eph. 2:10).

One Theme in Ephesians is to be Filled by the Spirit

Paul writes to the Ephesians and throughout the letter the theme of being filled by the Spirit is expressed, for he writes,

> "Praise be to the God and Father of our Lord Jesus Christ who has blessed us in the heavenly realms with every spiritual blessing *in Christ*" (Eph. 1:3; emphasis added) "… You were marked *in Him* with a seal, the promised Holy Spirit, who is a deposit guaranteeing our inheritance… of those who are God's possession" (Eph. 1:14; emphasis added) "… And God raised us up with Christ and seated us with Him in the heavenly realms *in Christ Jesus*" (Eph. 2:6; emphasis added) "…For we are God's workmanship, created *in Christ Jesus* to do good works, which God

prepared in advance for us to do" (Eph. 2:10; emphasis added) "...For *through Him* we both have access to the Father by one Spirit" (Eph. 2:18; emphasis added) "...I pray that out of His glorious riches He may strengthen you with power *through His Spirit* in your inner being so that *Christ may dwell in your hearts* through faith" (Eph. 3:16; emphasis added) "...that you may *be filled* to the measure of *all the fullness of God"* (Eph. 3:19; emphasis added) "...and become mature, attaining to the measure of *the fullness of Christ"* (Eph. 4:13; emphasis added) ... Instead, *be filled with the Spirit"* (Eph. 5:18; emphasis added) "...Finally, be strong in the Lord and *in His mighty power.* Put on the full armor of God so that you can take your stand against the devil's schemes..."(Eph. 6:10; emphasis added).

Paul writes that when you are *in Jesus Christ,* it is through Jesus Christ that you receive the heavenly blessings. He also writes that you are seated with Him. You receive the good works that God planned for you to do—but you will only receive those planned works and do them, when you are *in Jesus Christ.* Paul is repeatedly telling the Ephesians believers this theme: be continually filled with the fullness of God by His Spirit until you have the Spirit of God upon you, so you are *in Jesus Christ* (see John 15:5).

Being strong in the Lord and in His mighty power means you are filled with the Holy Spirit until He overshadows you like Jesus, Peter, and Paul experienced. Then you are literally *in the Lord.* Being overshadowed is being *clothed in Jesus Christ* (see Rom. 13:14). It may seem unbelievable, but we are literally to be *clothed in Jesus Christ.* That was one of the revelations I wrote about in my book, *Transformed by the Power of God: Learning to be Clothed in Jesus Christ.*[13]

The phrase in Ephesians 5:18 tells us to "be filled" and it means "to be continually filled with the fullness of Christ."[14] The early church was familiar with this teaching, but the contemporary church has missed this teaching that implores you to be completely and continually filled by the Spirit, until you are literally *clothed in Jesus Christ* and *in His power.*

The reason the contemporary church has missed this blessing of being clothed in Jesus Christ is due to the attack of the little horn, who has deceived the body of Christ and hindered them from understanding that all Christians were to be continually filled by the Spirit until you are literally clothed in Jesus Christ (see Dan. 7:21).[15] We are now in the post-defeat of the saints' era, and now it's time for the saints to wake up and get dressed![16]

Multiple Baptisms of the Spirit

The book of Hebrews mentions that one of the elementary teachings is about "baptisms." This is from the *plural* Greek word "*baptismoi*," relating to the Old Testament practice of absolutions, which was the ceremonial cleansing practice for the purification from sin by using water. This symbolized the cleansing of our sins by Jesus' blood (see Heb. 6:2; Num. 19:9).

What is significant is that in the New Testament, it is the living water of the Holy Spirit that sanctifies the believer (see John 7:37-39; Rom. 15:16). So with the plural form used for the word "baptisms" in Hebrews 6:2, and the associated sanctifying action of the Holy Spirit, we can see why the early church knew it was elementary to have plural baptisms of the Holy Spirit, because it was the Holy Spirit that cleansed them and made them holy.[17]

That's why it says you need to leave the elementary teachings about Christ, which is the anointing of the Holy Spirit, and go forward to maturity; because when you are repeatedly filled with the Spirit, you are becoming more like Christ. And the result is that you will become more mature (see Heb. 6:1). That's what you are encouraged to do today. *But you first have to learn the elementary teachings about Christ, which is learning about the multiple fillings of the Holy Spirit.*

The early church indicates, as do the first disciples, that there were multiple fillings of the Holy Spirit that they participated in. Learning about the multiple fillings of the Spirit was considered to be an elementary teaching according to Hebrews 6. Believing believers are strongly encouraged to renew their minds and practices and start receiving the multiple fillings of the Holy Spirit, so they will be able to release the gifts of the Spirit. You are told about the benefits of being full of the Holy Spirit in Acts 10,

> God anointed Jesus of Nazareth with the Holy Spirit and power, and how he went around doing good, and healing all who were under the power of the devil, because God was with him (Acts 10:38).

Jesus was anointed with the Holy Spirit and power, because God was with Him. The empowerment of the Holy Spirit allows believing believers to heal the sick and to overpower the devil's works. God's desire has always been to dwell with His people and to demonstrate that you are His child by empowering you. It appears that one of the battlegrounds with the devil has to do with real estate.

Whose Home Will You Become? The Lord Jesus Christ and the Heavenly Father Want to Have You as Their Home!

The previous Scripture notes that God was with Jesus (see Acts 10:38). That is one of God's prime desires; He wants to be with His children, which is described by the prophet Isaiah, in Isaiah 66,

> Heaven is My throne, and earth is My footstool. Where is the house you will build for Me? Where will My resting place be? (Isaiah 66:1).

This sounds as if the Lord was pining away, as He expressed His desire for a house where He could dwell.

What is shocking is that the temple of the New Testament church is to be within the believers themselves (see 1 Cor. 3:16-17). Jesus continued with this theme, and He expands on it when He spoke about the true believing believer who makes herself available to become a home for God, as Jesus tells us,

> If anyone loves Me, he will obey my teaching. My Father will love him, and We will come to him and make Our home with him (John 14:23).

If you love the Lord and obey His teaching, the Father and the Son will make your body, soul, and spirit their home. That is why I previously said it was "shocking," for I find it startling that our God is willing to make His home within the believing believer. What a privilege! You are permitted to host the Creator of the Universe, the Lord Jesus Christ and the Ancient of Days, who is your Heavenly Father within your being (see Heb. 1:2).

Paul said this was a "profound mystery" that Christ Jesus was one with the Church (see Eph. 5:32). It is shocking, startling, and a profound mystery, yet it is the reality that every single believing believer who loves the Lord and obeys His teachings and asks for the Holy Spirit to fill her continually will actually become a home for the Lord Jesus Christ and the Heavenly Father.

Lucifer, Satan, the Devil Wants to Make You His Home Too

Someone else is competing to make his home within your being. The enemy of your soul wants to make you his home too, because he is jealous. Lucifer is described in Ezekiel 28 which says,

> You were the model of perfection, full of wisdom and perfect in beauty…You were anointed as a guardian cherub, for so I ordained you. You were on the holy mountain of God; you walked among the fiery stones (Ezek. 28:12b, 14).

Lucifer was not only wise and beautiful, but he was ordained as a guardian cherub to guard God's throne. This may have meant that Lucifer also got to guard some of the things that were close to God's heart as well. Lucifer had a very special relationship with God. But Lucifer became jealous of the relationship that human beings were going to have with God.

George Otis Jr. writes, "What prompted Lucifer's fall?—centers on his jealousy over man's unique nature and the special attention Adam elicited from God. Jealousy led to prideful comparisons and exalted thoughts—and the rest, as they say, is history."[18] Lucifer was probably far more intelligent, wise, and beautiful than Adam. And Lucifer not only got to come near to

God's throne, but he may have been allowed to share in some of things that were close to God's heart.

But Adam, the first believing believer, had the Holy Spirit of God come upon him, and God's Spirit resided with Adam (see Gen. 1:27; 2:7; 2:25). God not only went for walks and talked with Adam, but God dwelt with Adam, as His glory resided with Adam and it covered Adam. That's why it said he was naked, but he felt no shame. God covered Adam's shame and his body with His glory, but sadly, the glory left Adam when he sinned (see Gen. 2:15-25; 3:6-13).[19]

Lucifer or Satan was jealous of God's relationship with Adam. And he remains jealous of human beings today. He wants to destroy as many human lives as he can by preventing people from worshiping the Lord, and preventing them from becoming close intimate believers. Lucifer is the Hebrew word *Haylele* which means "in the sense of brightness, the morning star" that was his name when he was a guardian cherub who walked among the fiery stones near God's throne.[20]

Lucifer's name was changed to Satan, which means "the accuser" when his role changed.[21] With his jealousy over human beings and with his rebellion, he shifted from being near to God's throne to being far from it. Satan's role changed from guarding God's throne—to accusing human beings day and night. And he tries to orchestrate temptations to entice humans to fall into sin. Satan also tries to incite human beings to rebel against God. But Jesus gave us the upper hand in this battle with Satan. Jesus demonstrated what believing believers are supposed to do, which is to act just like Jesus did.

The Son of God was manifested so that He might destroy the works of the devil (1 John 3:8). One of the main thrusts of the spiritual war between the kingdom of God and the kingdom of Satan is over whose home will you become? *The war is over who will get to have their home in you and around you?* (see Luke 11:24-26; Matt. 12:43-45).

That's why Jesus came to destroy the devil's works. The devil wants to prevent believers from getting the kingdom message into their hearts, because he is jealous that you actually get to have God within your hearts.

So the enemy tries to send evil spirits to dwell within your body, soul, and heart instead. One way to counteract the enemy's assault and destroy the devil's works is to give your body, soul, heart, and spirit to God and become His home by being filled with His Holy Spirit.

I was preaching in Sao Paulo, Brasil at a center that treated men with addiction problems and one guy who responded to my teaching from the previous night, asked: "How do I get more of God?" To answer him, I invited the whole group of men to lay down on the stage and taught them how to be filled by the Spirit. During the time we were being filled by the Spirit, I had a word of knowledge about a guy who had a stomach ache. At the end of the soaking time I asked, "Who has a stomach ache?" Two guys said they did, and that led into a time where I taught on deliverance. I demonstrated how to drive out demons by freeing those two guys from the evil spirits that had made their homes in those guys.

When the Holy Spirit was making His home in them, by filling them, He was simultaneously evicting the demonic spirits that had made their home in those guys. I just got to deliver the eviction notice: "All demonic spirits get out now, in Jesus' name!" That's the prime location of our battle in this war: it's a turf war, a real estate battle. So, whose home will you become? That's why Jesus modeled destroying the devil's works. Jesus wants you to be His home, and wants you to destroy any possibility that the devil can make his home in you.

A friend of mine was having problems praying for a girl whose stomach had been upset, so she brought her over to my house so I could minister to her. After a little while I had a word of knowledge about "rejection." This girl had been a Christian all her life and at first she did not think she was rejected, but when I asked, "Where have you not been accepted?" She rattled off a number of painful situations in her life.

I took that as a cue and said, "Let me point my fingers toward your stomach and see if an evil spirit was there." She agreed, but she was in shock that an evil spirit could be inside of her. I commanded it to come up and out on the breath, then I asked her, "Do you feel it coming up?" She responded with fear in her voice and said, "No, it's going down!"

She had lived a good life and was not conscious of any un-confessed sin. It broke her emotionally for her to learn she had an evil spirit who had taken up residence within her. Many Christians do not understand that the enemy wants to make his home in you, and if he can get in, he will. This girl had just felt rejected, and this *evil spirit of rejection* seized the opportunity when she felt rejected, and it came in through that open door of feeling rejected, and made his home in her.

The enemy does not want you to be continually filled by the Holy Spirit and make yourself to be a home for Jesus and the Heavenly Father. The enemy does not want you going out and act like Jesus did, by destroying the devil's works in the world around you, because if you do that, you will discern evil spirits and cast them out of the people that the evil spirits had made as their homes (see Luke 11:24-26). *Therefore, the enemy battles all he can to keep you from knowing about the kingdom message that you can be continually filled by the Holy Spirit, so he can prevent you from getting the kingdom within you, so he can live within you instead (see Matt. 13:19).*

Believing believers need to know the devil's schemes and counteract against his schemes (see Eph. 6:11). Jesus was with the Holy Spirit and power and went around doing good by healing people and breaking off the power of the devil that was over them. If Jesus is our model, then believing believers need to do the same thing.

When you have the Father and Jesus living in you, making their home in you, then they will give you the desire to destroy the works of the devil too. How badly do you want the Holy Spirit so you can do what Jesus did? How badly do you want to become a home for the Father in heaven and for the Lord Jesus Christ? How badly do you want the gifts of the Spirit? Today, many believers do not move in the gifts of the Spirit because they do not go after them, and that's partially the result of the devil having stolen the message of the kingdom from their hearts (see Matt. 13:19). But 1 Corinthians 12 tells you to,

>…eagerly desire the greater gifts (1 Cor. 12: 31).

Having an eager desire for the greater gifts reveals your pursuit for more of the Father, and it also displays your hunger and thirst for the Lord of Life,

Jesus Christ. This is one of the keys to learn how to receive the gifts of the Spirit is to have desire, hunger, and thirst for an intimate relationship with the Lord, because when you have that relationship, then the gifts of the Spirit will flow out from it.

Believing believers are called to seek a relationship with the Lord by seeking the Holy Spirit, the gifts of the Spirit, and the fruit of the Spirit earnestly and zealously. You also need to pursue the Holy Spirit's sanctification. The Father's goal is that you desire and pursue the Holy Spirit, so you will fall in love with the Father and with Jesus, and you will obey their commands. Then they will come and make their home within you (see John 14:23).

When you pursue the Holy Spirit and His power, then the gifts and the fruit will begin to manifest in your life the same way they did in Jesus' ministry, because Jesus will be with you. Then you can release the anointing and begin to destroy the devil's works. The first practical step for you to become surprisingly supernatural is to take *Step #1: Be Filled with the Holy Spirit*, so you get the kingdom within you, as it is only then that you will be able to release the kingdom by displaying the gifts of the Spirit.

Soaking or Being Filled with the Holy Spirit

Over the past decade people have been teaching believers how to be filled with the Spirit. One term that is used is "soaking." Soaking is simply asking the Holy Spirit to come, and then you lay in His presence like you would lie down in a bathtub of water. I believe soaking was coined at the Toronto Airport Christian Fellowship, where the outpouring of the Holy Spirit began in January 20, 1994 and has continued through to the time of this writing.[22]

Whether you call it "being filled by the Spirit," "soaking," or some other term, the basic process is to ask the Holy Spirit to come and fill you and overshadow you. The next section is a practical explanation on this soaking process. If you already soak regularly, you may want to skip this section or just glance at it, and then go to the next chapter. But if you have not learned how to be regularly and repeatedly filled by the Holy Spirit, then I encourage you to read this next section and practice it regularly.

One of the benefits I have had from reading and believing the Scriptures in which the disciples were filled and overshadowed by the Spirit, is that's what I now experience. After initially having spent four months soaking in the presence of God, I began to feel the presence over my face. Specifically, I felt the Spirit's presence over the bridge of my nose and over my forehead. Then a year later, I began to feel the presence of God around my body like a robe or a cloak.[23]

I have not walked by anyone and seen them healed yet, or seen demons flee when I walked by them, but I know I have Jesus with me. A couple of seer prophets have told me that Jesus was standing right next to me, or He was in front of me, when they were prophesying to me. The people I lay my hands on get healed more frequently than not. It seems that one kingdom rule is that the thing you focus on is the thing you get. I focused on and asked to be clothed by the Holy Spirit and clothed in power from on high, and the Father in heaven graciously answered. I never knew that this was possible before, but now I know this is what the Father in heaven wants for all His children. I hope you enjoy being continually filled by the Spirit and drawing near to your Father in heaven.

Guide to Soaking in the Holy Spirit

This section will cover many of the practical applications to soaking in the Holy Spirit.

Your Body Position When You Soak

Try to get in a comfortable position where you can be relaxed. I often soak when I am lying down on the floor with my face up, or I lay on my bed at night or in the morning. Sometimes, I just sit in a comfortable chair or I recline the front seat of my car. Just get into a comfortable position, so you can relax. I usually open my hands with the palms facing upward.

Emotional and Mental Position When You Soak

Try to calm your emotions and your mind. You want to focus your emotions and mind on Jesus. You do not want to be distracted by them. If you find you have random thoughts that are hitting your mind, place a pad of paper and pen next to you. Then you can write your thoughts down, and tell your mind and emotions: *I will take care of those problems later, I have made a note of them, but right now I am worshipping the Lord Jesus Christ, so be quiet.* Then go back and try to focus on the worship of Jesus. If your emotions are active, you may need to reflect and see if there is anything you need to confess to the Lord, or give over to Him for Him to take, so you can return your focus to the worship of Jesus Christ.

Sometimes, I use soft instrumental worship music to help draw my heart and mind into a place where I can be intimate with my Lord. The music helps me to position my mind and emotions to be in a relaxed state of peace. I raise the level of my faith, as I express my desire to spend time with my Heavenly Father, and with the Lord Jesus Christ, as I am filled with the Holy Spirit.

The Use of Scripture to Ask for the Holy Spirit

I invite the Father in heaven to fill me with His Spirit, based on what the Scriptures say about being filled. I say to Him:

- "Father, the Scripture in Isaiah 55:1 says, 'if we are thirsty we can come to the waters and drink,' so I ask you Father, let me drink your living water, please fill me with Your Holy Spirit."

- "Father, Your word says, 'It is not by might, nor by power, but by My Spirit' says the Lord God Almighty' (Zech. 4:6). I believe that it is only by Your Spirit, so please fill me with Your Spirit Lord."

- "Lord, I am dependent on the Holy Spirit to empower me, and to guide me into everything that You have for me. So I ask Holy Spirit, Counselor, Spirit of Truth, and the seven Spirits of God please fill me."

I also like to declare the Scriptures that are associated with the first disciples when they were being filled by the Holy Spirit, which are found in the gospels, and in Acts. In Luke, we read that Jesus tells us,

How much more will your Father in heaven give the Holy
Spirit to those who ask Him (Luke 11:13).

I personalize this Scripture and other Scriptures and say,

- "Heavenly Father, I read in Luke 11 that Jesus told us that You give good gifts to those who ask, and the good gift is Your Holy Spirit. So Heavenly Father, please give me the good gift of your Holy Spirit. Please fill me with your Holy Spirit" (Luke 11:13).[24]
- "Come Holy Spirit of God, please come and fill me, and teach me and guide me" (John 16:12-13).
- "Holy Spirit, please come and sanctify me" (Romans 15:16).
- "Holy Spirit, please come and transform me into Jesus' likeness" (2 Corinthians 3:17-18).
- "Holy Spirit, please come and take me from glory to glory" (Romans 8:30).
- "Holy Spirit, please come and quicken my body and heal me" (Romans 8:11).
- "Holy Spirit, please come and guide me into all truth" (John 16:13).
- "Holy Spirit, please come and show me what is yet to come" (John 16:13).
- "Holy Spirit, please come and remind me about everything that Jesus taught" (John 14:26).
- "Holy Spirit, please come and help me to testify about Jesus" (John 15:26-27).
- "Come Holy Spirit, please come and fill me and enable me to speak in tongues" (Acts 2:4).
- "Come Holy Spirit, please come and baptize me and empower me to speak boldly" (Acts 4:31).
- "Holy Spirit of God, I do believe it is 'Not by might nor by power, but by My Spirit says the Lord Almighty.'" "So please come and fill me with Your Spirit and baptize me" (Zechariah 4:6; Acts 4:31, 1:5).

Try holding the book in your dominate hand, for most people that is your right hand. With your free hand, hold the palm upwards and have your fingers open and rest it next to you. Then repeat the declarations on this page out loud and truly ask the Father in heaven for the Holy Spirit. Try to sense what happens. See if you can feel the Holy Spirit filling your fingers and the palm of your free hand. Also try to feel if your feet and legs are being filled by the Holy Spirit as well.

An alternative to using the personalized Scriptures above is to use the card, which is available on the website: www.surprisinglysupernatural.com. When you get to the website you can download the *Surprisingly Supernatural Step #1: How to Ask to be Filled by the Holy Spirit* card. The Surprisingly Supernatural Cards were made to help believing believers to practice asking for the spiritual gifts. This will help them to grow as believing believers. Then you can learn to release the gifts and fruit of the Holy Spirit. I want to encourage the believers to use the Surprisingly Supernatural Cards, and to continue to use them until you have incorporated the specific gifts and spiritual skills into your lives.

You do not have to follow the Surprisingly Supernatural Cards religiously, but it will benefit you to understand the principles and the skills that are behind the Surprisingly Supernatural Cards.

When you use them, you may read the entire Surprisingly Supernatural Card as it is written or just read part of it. You may also read it at a different pace each time. You may read it through in its entirety, or you may read only a portion of it. You may want to limit your use of the square bulleted points, and read only one or two of the bullet points. Some of the developmental points that are in the Surprisingly Supernatural Cards are listed below.

The Surprisingly Supernatural Card Skill Development

1. Awareness that God the Father wants you to ask Him for the gifts and fruit of the Spirit. This also helps you to remember that you are dependent on His Holy Spirit to do His will.

2. You personalize the Scriptures with the Surprisingly Supernatural Cards and this teaches that believers can appropriate the Scripture for themselves and can pray or declare them back to God. This skill helps to align the believer's life with God's will.

3. You will begin to memorize the Scripture, which will help you to transform your mind, will, and emotions, as you will get the Word of God into your heart.

4. The Surprisingly Supernatural Cards teach a model of prayer that includes praying the Scriptures, praying along a theme, and praying the Scriptures out loud as a declaration or as a decree.

5. The Surprisingly Supernatural Cards teach the believer to use specific themes connected to the first disciples when they were filled by the Spirit of God, so not only do you ask God for the Holy Spirit, but you will begin to do what the first disciples did.

Now practice being filled by the Holy Spirit. Put yourself in a comfortable position, which was mentioned earlier on page **42**, and open yourself up to God and ask for His Holy Spirit to fill you. Now turn to the *Surprisingly Supernatural Step #1: How to Ask to be Filled by the Holy Spirit* card, and read it out loud.

Try to spend at least ten minutes a day being filled by God's Holy Spirit; however, a longer period of time is better. It is also beneficial to regularly spend time throughout your day in God's presence too. The goal is for you to be continually filled until you are clothed in Jesus Christ. The Holy Spirit may even prompt you to ask the Father to clothe you in power from on high (see Matt. 6:30b; Luke 24:49).

When you feel the Spirit of God surrounding you that's when you will become continually filled by the Spirit of God. Then you will be able to release the gifts of the Spirit whenever you are asked to release them, and you will be transformed into a supernatural believing believer (see 1 John 2:5-6; 2:27).

Results of Being Filled by the Holy Spirit

Now that I have spent several years being continually filled by the Holy Spirit, I understand that it is not by my might, nor by my power, nor by my intelligence, nor by my education, but it is only by God's Spirit.

Apart from the Spirit of God I can do nothing worthwhile that has eternal consequences (see Zech. 4:6; John 15:5).

I am dependent on the Holy Spirit to empower me and guide me into everything that the Lord has for me. Everything else will be tested by fire. I want to receive my reward for building my Father's kingdom and giving Him the glory, not building my own kingdom (see John 15:6; 1 Cor. 3:12-14). I have finally understood that I am crucified in Jesus Christ; therefore, I have died, I no longer live, but Christ lives in me (see Gal. 2:20). So I now recognize my need for the Holy Spirit to guide me and lead me to do all that my Father wants me to do.

After I invite the Holy Spirit and the seven Spirits of the Lord to fill me, I wait expectantly for Him (see Isa. 11:1-2). I focus my mind and heart on Jesus and my attitude is to have more of Him. I want to know Him more. I spend as much time as I can in God's presence, so I can be transformed into the man of God He wants me to be. I regularly practice being filled in the morning when I wake-up, at a coffee break, during lunchtime, in the car when I am driving or when it is parked, at a quiet time at home, and at night before I go to sleep. I try to invite God's presence to fill me in just about every circumstance I am in, so I am continually filled by the Spirit of God.

I try to do it continually, which means each and every day. I have spent too much of my life trying to be equipped with human ways to do God's work, but now I understand that all those ways are bankrupt. So I just need more of Jesus, so I can release more of His kingdom around me.

One story I shared in my book, *Transformed by the Power of God* is that after months of soaking where I had felt the Holy Spirit filling me through my hands, then I went out to Starbucks and had coffee with a friend. When I sat down with my coffee, I just happened to rest my left hand on the arm of the chair and I turned my palm slightly upward. Suddenly, I felt the Holy Spirit land on my hand and He began to fill me. I was shocked! And I wondered: *Does the Holy Spirit like Starbucks too?*

Ever since those first few months, I have been aware that the Holy Spirit has been hanging around me and it has changed my life. Because of that everywhere I go I can release the kingdom of God. It's really fun! I realize I am walking out my birthright that God had birthed for me to live out. I am soaking all the time as the Holy Spirit is with me all the time. I just hold my hands open in any situation and the Holy Spirit falls on them and starts to fill me, because I am clothed in Jesus Christ. Jesus did tell us that He would be with us to the very end of the age (see Matt. 28:20). He verifies that He is with me every single day now, because I am continually being filled by the Spirit of God.

I encourage you to invite the Holy Spirit to come and fill you, and I hope you will wait for Him to fill you regularly. When you engage with the Holy Spirit, you are engaging with the Lord, for "God is Spirit and His worshippers must worship in spirit and in truth" (John 4:24). Practice waiting and being filled whenever you can, as that is one of the spiritual acts of worship that really pleases the Lord.

Filled Until the Flow Reverses and Goes Out for Impartation

One of the results of being filled continually by the Holy Spirit is that the flow now reverses out of my hands and goes the other way. Paul writes about the act of impartation in both 1 Timothy and 2 Timothy. In 1 Timothy we read,

> *Do not neglect your gift, which was given you through a prophetic message when the body of elders laid their hands on you* (1 Timothy 4:14; 2 Timothy 1:6; Duet. 34:9).

Acts 6 speaks about the act of impartation and says,

> They presented these men to the apostles, who prayed and laid their hands on them. So the word of God spread. The number of disciples increased rapidly, and a large number of priests became obedient to the faith (Acts 6:6-7).

The elders and the apostles both had the anointing of the Holy Spirit flowing out of their hands for impartation. That's because they practiced being continually filled by the Holy Spirit. The Lord has matured me and moved me into that role, because I am now able to impart the gifts of the spirit when I lay my hands on people. He only did that because I had spent extended periods of time in God's presence, so I could be continually filled by His Holy Spirit.

If you do that and you are continually filled by the Holy Spirit, then God will empower you too. He will bring you into a more intimate relationship with Himself. And He will give you more of His authority. He also may even bring you into higher levels of leadership within His church body.

If there is an opportunity to receive an impartation from the laying on of hands, I suggest that you go after it. You can never have enough of God, and you may be able to accelerate your birthright if you receive the impartation in faith. When you spend enough time being continually filled with the Holy Spirit, then you will become surprisingly supernatural, as the gifts of the Spirit will begin to manifest in your life. And you will never be the same after that occurs.

Chapter 2: Discussion Questions

1. Jesus breathed on the disciples and afterwards they continued to be baptized and filled by the Spirit so they could expand God's kingdom into the world around them.
    a. Can you imagine how the Lord is asking you to go out as He was sent out? What do you need to start doing to be repeatedly filled by the Holy Spirit?

2. When Jesus, Peter and Paul were filled with the Spirit, they had such an abundance of the Spirit that it surrounded them and they exuded the Spirit out from their bodies into the people and things around them.
    a. What do you need to do so you will have such an abundance of the flow of the Spirit that it will exude out from around your body?
    b. What do you need to do to decide to be willing to ask the Father in heaven for His Spirit and then wait for it?

3. The book of Ephesians has the theme of being filled with the Spirit, to the fullness of God, the fullness of Christ, and to be continually filled so much so that you have put on the armor of God through being filled by the Spirit of God.
    a. What had you noticed about Ephesians before? Was this theme of being filled by God's Spirit apparent to you before, and if not why?
    b. Now that you know about this theme, what do you plan to do with that knowledge?

4. When believers are filled with the Holy Spirit, they have access to all the gifts and fruit of the Spirit too.
    a. What do you need to do so that the Spirit of God will transform you and give you the gifts and fruits to operate with?
    b. What is hindering your faith to believe that you can receive an abundance of the Holy Spirit?

5. "Soaking in the Spirit" is another term meaning "Being Filled by the Spirit." I encourage you to practice being filled by the Holy Spirit repeatedly throughout your day.
    a. How can you make a time or times during your day to be filled by the Spirit of God?
    b. How can you make a goal or a vow to God that you will be repeatedly filled by His Spirit, if He gives you the grace to do that?
    c. What do you think about the people in your relational networks that could use a touch from the Holy Spirit, so they can come to the knowledge of the Lord Jesus Christ? Can you prepare yourself by being continually filled by the Holy Spirit or not?

CHAPTER 3

SURPRISINGLY SUPERNATURAL STEP #2 HOW TO RECEIVE THE GIFT OF PROPHECY

I believe being continually filled by the Holy Spirit is the most important thing a believing believer can do. When you are continually filled with the Holy Spirit, you will be assured that God is with you. And you will have begun to establish an intimate relationship with the Lord, out of which all the gifts and fruit of the Spirit will begin to flow through you, because the Holy Spirit is with you. Then you will begin to find that you are a surprisingly supernatural believing believer who will find that the gifts of the Spirit will start to bubble up as you go about your daily routine.

The next most important thing is to learn to hear God's voice for yourself and for other people. If you can hear God's voice, then you know how to respond to what He says, and that is crucial, for obedience is very important, as Samuel said,

> …Does the Lord delight in burnt offerings and sacrifices as much as in obeying the voice of the Lord? To obey is better than sacrifice… (1 Sam. 15:22).

All believing believers want to obey the Lord, but when circumstances are not covered by the biblical laws of God, how do we know what is obedience and what is not? Well, hearing the voice of the Lord is an important key to responding to those circumstances in obedience, and hearing the voice of the Lord is also called prophecy.

Various Ways to Receive Prophecy and Words of Knowledge

In this chapter, I will teach you some of the basic ideas about hearing the voice of God, which is also called the gift of prophecy, hearing a prophetic word, or hearing words of knowledge. When people speak about prophecy they frequently mean hearing from God. Hearing from God can happen from a number of experiences. The person could hear God's voice in her spirit or have a vision or a dream. She could get an impression, smell, feel, or taste something that is a revelation from God. She can hear an angel speak a message for herself or for another person. Or she can just know something that comes to her suddenly. God speaks to His followers in many different ways, as Job did say,

> For God does speak—now one way, now another—though man may not perceive it. In a dream or a vision of the night, when deep sleep falls on men as they slumber in their beds, he may speak in their ears and terrify them with warnings, to turn a man from wrongdoing and keep him from pride, to preserve his soul from the pit, his life from perishing by the sword (Job 33:14-18).

Prophecy may come to a person in many different ways. And prophecy is also categorized by time, as to whether it refers to the past, present, or future.

Time Categorizes of Prophecy and Words of Knowledge

Prophecy can be defined as a Word from God about the future. It occurs when a person gets a revelation from God for another person, or for his own personal guidance. The prophetic word is forward looking and it frequently speaks of a person's calling, birthright, or God's plans for that person's life. The prophetic word is always conditional and always requires the person who receives it to be obedient and to exercise his faith regarding it.[25]

When we speak of a word of knowledge, it can be defined as a Word from God about the past or the present. Words of knowledge occur when a person gets revelation from God for another person or for her own personal guidance. The word of knowledge is about something that has already occurred either in the past or is occurring in the present. When the word of knowledge is revealed, it helps the person who receives it to know that God knows about her life and is trying to get her attention.

Often times God will give a word of knowledge first to get the person's attention, to let him know that God knows him and is addressing him. Then frequently God will share a prophetic word about his future. This often happens when a believing believer hears God telling him to share something with another person and a word of knowledge will come first, and then a prophetic word will follow. Let's look in the Scriptures at an example that shows how words of knowledge and prophecy are linked together.

Words of Knowledge and Prophecy are Linked

In 1 Samuel Chapter 9, we can read how words of knowledge and prophecy are linked together. This section begins where the Scripture says,

> Now the donkeys belonging to Saul's father Kish were lost… (1 Sam. 9:3).

Saul was told to look for the lost donkeys. Then a few verses later the prophet Samuel meets Saul and tells him he is a seer, which is a type of prophet, and that he will prophesy to him in the morning. This is what he meant when he said he would tell him what is in his heart. Then Samuel gives Saul the word of knowledge about the donkeys that were lost. This word of knowledge was how God opened up Saul's heart to be able to hear the prophetic word that Samuel gave him afterwards. Samuel told Saul,

> 'I am a seer,' Samuel replied. 'Go up ahead of me to the high place, for today you are to eat with me, and in the morning I will let you go, and will tell you all that is in your heart. As for the donkeys you lost three days ago, do not worry about them; they have been found' (1 Sam. 9:19-20a).

Saul now knows Samuel is a seer who hears from God after this exchange. Saul had not told Samuel that the donkeys were lost. Consequently, Saul opened his ears and his heart because of the word of knowledge. Then Samuel gives him a prophetic word twice, but he uses a slightly different wording each time. First he said,

> And to whom is all the desire of Israel turned, if not to you and all your father's family? (1 Sam. 9:20b).

Then the second time Samuel spoke the prophetic word, he used different words, but implied the same meaning: Saul was to be Israel's king,

> …Has not the Lord anointed you leader over his inheritance? (1 Sam. 10:1b).

Samuel finishes this encounter by closing it out with another prophetic word, so that Saul can look back and realize that Samuel had really heard from God.

> When you leave me today, you will meet two men near Rachel's tomb, at Zelzah on the border of Benjamin. They will say to you, 'The donkeys you set out to look for have been found' (1 Sam. 10:2a).

Samuel prophesied about the rest of Saul's day, so when Saul meets these two men, and everything else happens the way Samuel had prophesied, Saul would realize that all that Samuel had said was true and was from God. This was particularly important for Saul to understand, as the Lord had wanted him to know that he was to become the king of Israel.

From this study in 1 Samuel 9, we can see that God linked words of knowledge with prophetic words to help open up Saul's heart, so he would know that the prophet Samuel had really heard from God. God frequently links a word of knowledge with a prophetic word, as the word of knowledge can build the faith in the person who hears it. When a person receives a word of knowledge, and he realizes that it is true, he is likely to conclude: *It must be from God!* That opens up the person's heart to be able to receive the prophetic word that follows after the word of knowledge.

In addition, this Scripture shows us that a prophecy that foretells about some short-term future event also serves to establish credibility and faith in the person that receives it. When the prophetic word that is given comes to pass, the person receiving it can reflect back and realize that all the prophetic words that he had received earlier from the prophet were probably true and were from God as well.

Now that I have defined words of knowledge and prophecy, I want to explain the Scriptural basis that supports my belief that all believers may prophesy today. It is very helpful for believing believers to have the gift of prophecy, as it is one of the ways you can demonstrate to nonbelievers that Jesus Christ is the Lord God Almighty.

A Word of Knowledge Opens Up the Door for Evangelism

On a ministry trip to Sao Paulo, Brasil, I went with my interpreter to a sightseeing venue. While we waited in line, my interpreter spoke with the man standing in front of her named "Wilson." As she spoke with him, I asked the Lord, "Do you want to show me something about this man?" Then a few seconds later, I saw an open vision of a small stringed instrument like a guitar that appeared in front of his torso. I told my interpreter that I had a vision, and I wanted her to ask him if he played a stringed instrument, like a guitar.

My interpreter asked Wilson if he played the guitar and he said, "Yes." But he then clarified that it was a smaller stringed instrument than a guitar. I was able to tell him I had seen a smaller instrument in the vision. I told Wilson, "I am a Christian and God showed me the small stringed instrument, because Jesus knows everything about you Wilson." He told us he was from Bolivia and he said that he did not have a religion, and was not spiritual.

We went up in the tower and enjoyed looking out at the sweeping panoramic view across the mega city of Sao Paulo. When we were coming down, I felt compelled to ask Wilson to coffee. Sometimes the Holy Spirit will move my emotions and then I feel enthusiasm for doing something, like inviting Wilson out for coffee. I trust these promptings as "enthusiasm" comes from a Greek word that means "inspiration by a god."[26] When

I become enthusiastic, I recognize that my God via the Holy Spirit is moving me to bring joy to my Father in heaven, as I know I will get to display His kingdom in some way.

My interpreter asked Wilson if he would come to coffee with us, but Wilson said he wanted to go to a meeting that would teach him about stock market investments. I told him that I was an investor, and I would like to share with him some of the things I had learned from investing in stocks. He became interested and agreed to come to coffee with us.

I spoke with him about the basics of investing: buy low, sell high, how to look for a good stock with fundamentals and technical indicators, but I mentioned to Wilson that timing was also a very important factor. I admitted that the quality of the information that he received was extremely important for investing in stocks. Then I reminded him that God had shown me that he played that stringed instrument, and I shared that "since I am with Jesus, He not only gives me words of knowledge about people, but He also does that with investments too." I shared how God helped me select investments and told me when I should buy and sell the investment, so I would have a profitable return. God's advice has turned out to be accurate and profitable. I told him since God knows everything, He is the best investment advisor to have, as you will have the best and the timeliest information for investments when you have Jesus Christ on your side.

I then did the impartation test with Wilson, and he felt the anointing of the Holy Spirit. I told him it was Jesus' Spirit. I shared with Wilson the gospel message and how Jesus knows him, and can save his soul because of His sacrifice on the cross. I shared that when he receives Jesus, He can also receive the Holy Spirit who will guide him throughout his life, and I could impart the gift of prophecy, if he wanted to hear Jesus' voice. I told Wilson that when he learns to hear Jesus' voice, he can ask Jesus to help him with all the decisions in his life, and he will get great advice.

Wilson prayed that day to receive Jesus. I imparted the Holy Spirit and the gifts of the Spirit to him. Then I discerned an angel was standing behind him. I got Wilson to feel the place where the angel was standing. Wilson felt the change in power where the angel was standing, and I was able to tell him that the angel was now assigned to him to help him and protect him in life, as he was now a child of God. My interpreter got his phone number and arranged to contact him so he could be discipled.

When people receive Jesus due to a demonstration of the gifts of the Spirit, it is not necessary to use wise and persuasive words. *Because I released the gifts of the Spirit with Wilson, I only had to speak briefly about Jesus, and that was sufficient for Wilson to be willing to invite both Jesus and the Holy Spirit into his life.* Believing believers are called to "snatch others from the fire and save them" (Jude 22a).

That's what happened with Wilson. He was snatched from the fire. I knew I might never see him again. However, discipleship is to be matched up with evangelism. Discipleship is part of the lifelong journey of getting to know the Lord. It is through discipleship that believers are made into disciples and then they learn the other details of following the Lord.

Releasing the supernatural gifts is a way to help nonbelievers to start to take a new road in life by accepting Jesus and His Spirit. Then when the nonbeliever becomes a new convert, he can continue on that new road by being discipled by other believers who are also taking that same road toward Christ.

Believing believers need to be able to release the kingdom gifts to bring people into a relationship with the Lord Jesus Christ. They also need to be able to disciple believers in their continued journey of faith. However, not every person who receives Jesus is discipled by the believing believer who brought them to Christ. Other believers may take over the role of discipleship. Believing believers need to discern what role the Lord is calling you to. With Wilson it was obvious. He lived in Sao Paulo, Brasil, so I asked my interpreter to follow up and contact Wilson to ensure that he will continue to walk with the Lord.

The gift of prophecy is one of the key tools believing believers use to help other people to learn about Jesus Christ. The gift of prophecy can help to bring a person around to the point where he will decide to invite Jesus into his life, like Wilson did that day. But the gift of prophecy does not always bring a person to the point where he decides to invite Jesus into his life. Sometimes it just provides one step toward the Lord, whether the person receiving the prophetic word is prepared to take that step or not.

I was in Chicago visiting my friend Jeremy, and we decided to go to a soccer game, so we boarded a bus. I sat in my seat and I began gazing at the back of the head of the guy who sat in front of me. Then the words *testicular cancer* came to my mind. I had never, to my knowledge, thought of those words before, and I had never spoken them out loud before either. I asked Jeremy if he knew anything about it. And he said, "A few of my friends have had it." I told Jeremy, "I heard, 'testicular cancer,' but it does not apply to you or me."

I tapped the shoulder of the guy in front of me and I asked him, "Are you working with this group?" He said, "No." Then I said, "I believe the Lord spoke these words to me, 'testicular cancer.' Is it relevant to you?" He responded with a sarcastic tone of voice "The Lord told you?" Then I replied, "Yes, and I think that you might want to check it out with your doctor." Then he said, "I don't want to talk about it, get out of here." I sat back in my seat respecting his request, but I wondered: *Was the word of knowledge was accurate?*

Although the word of knowledge could have been inaccurate, I had sensed that it probably was accurate. It was a strange word to surface in my mind from out of nowhere. And he did not deny it, but he only said he did not want to talk about it. It could have been a word of knowledge that this guy knew was correct, but since he had never seen me before, he was shocked.

Having acknowledged "The Lord" had spoken the word to me, this guy may have begun to ponder: *How could that stranger have known that I have testicular cancer?* Then he may have started to think about the Lord. That may have been all that was needed. I was just called to plant a seed in that guy, that the Lord knows him and knows about his medical condition.

However, I do not need to know the result of the prophetic words that I give. I just have to be obedient and release the prophetic word, when I am given one to release. What impact the release of the prophetic word has, is not my concern. The person's response is not my responsibility. My responsibility is to share the prophetic word, and anything else that the Lord gives me, but that's it.

The prophetic gifts can be used to plant seeds that show that the Lord knows them, or they can be used to help harvest new believers and bring them into a relationship with Jesus Christ. The gifts of the Spirit are not just for specially anointed believers. I believe they are for every believing believer who asks for them. At least that's what I understand from the Scripture, which I will now try to show you.

Scriptural Basis That All Believers Can Prophecy Today

The First Scripture: John 10

The first Scripture that supports all believers can prophesy today is found in John 10 where Jesus said,

> My sheep listen to my voice; I know them, and they follow Me (John 10:27).

The English phrase "listen to my voice" contains the verb "listen," which is the Greek word *akouo* that means "to hear, (in the) audience (of), come (to the ears), (shall) hear, be noised, be reported, understand."[27] In context, it does not mean only listening to Jesus' voice one time, like at the moment of your conversion. But it implies you are able to continually listen to Jesus' voice (see John 10:16). *It's as if you are continually in the audience of the Lord, and you are able to hear His voice and understand Him.*

The key aspect of this verse is that the believers who are Jesus' sheep are those who obediently follow the Lord Jesus. They are not just people who pray one time to receive Jesus, and then they make their own plans and merrily go on with their own lives. No, a sheep is a believer who is always willing to follow after the Good Shepherd. Jesus supports this idea about the believer who is in a close relationship with God is able to hear God speak, when He spoke in John 8 and said,

> He who belongs to God hears what God says (John 8:47a).

This verse implies that those people who belong to God, who are His possession, are the people who will hear His voice. Perhaps the questions you might like to ask yourself are: "Am I really a sheep?" And "Do I follow Jesus, the Good Shepherd?" If you are following Jesus and you belong to God, then these verses state you will be able to hear God's voice. That means you will also be able to prophesy.

Hearing God's voice is for the believing believers who live their lives with their hearts in line with God's will and ways. Hearing God's voice is not for a person who prays one time the prayer of faith to receive Jesus, but that's it. No, hearing God's voice is not for that kind of person. It is for the true follower, the believing believer, who tries to actively follow Jesus every day of her life.

John Wimber writes about God speaking to him, "He told me that I needed to listen to His voice rather than try to distill the Christian life down to a set of rules and principles."[28] The Lord desires a relationship with His disciples, who are His children. The believing believer's life is about being in a relationship with the Lord. And hearing the voice of the Lord is crucial for a successful and relational walk with the Lord. Wimber had learned to become a sheep, a disciple who belonged to God, for he chose to listen for the Lord's voice when he prayed. Wimber was a believing believer.

The Second Scripture: Acts 2

The second Scripture that supports all believers can prophesy today is found in Acts 2 when Peter read Joel's prophecy and declared,

> In the last days, God says, I will pour out my Spirit on all people. Your sons and daughters will prophesy, your young men will see visions, your old men will dream dreams. Even on my servants, both men and women, I will pour out my Spirit in those days, and they will prophesy (Acts 2:17-18).

Peter spoke that nearly 2000 years ago, so if it was the last days then, it certainly is even more so now.

One of the testimonies that validates the outpouring is still happening today is occurring in the Middle-East. One of the most prolific evangelistic methods in the Middle-East is God's use of dreams. God is giving dreams to Muslims and is identifying Himself as Jesus Christ. The result is that those Muslims become followers of Jesus Christ. God is pouring out His Spirit today on all people, and that includes nonbelievers who get prophetic revelation through visions and dreams.

We read in the Scriptures that pagan kings Abimelech and Nebuchadnezzar from the Old Testament both had prophetic dreams from God, and Pilate's wife also had a prophetic dream (see Gen. 20:3; Dan. 2:1-3; Matt. 27:19). It should not be difficult for us to understand that God is interested in communicating who He is to as many people as He can, and that includes nonbelievers.

The Heavenly Father is interested in sharing the knowledge of His Son Jesus Christ with others. Therefore, if God gives prophetic revelation to nonbelievers both yesterday and today, then surely He wants to speak to believing believers today as well. This is especially true if the believing believers want to partner with God by releasing the gifts of the Spirit in their relational networks to glorify the Lord Jesus Christ. Then surely the believing believers will receive prophetic insights like dreams and visions, and they will also hear God's voice as well.

On the book's website I have listed three videos that give testimonies of Muslims who have had Jesus appear to them in dreams and visions. These three videos are located under Chapter 3 on the book's website. The first video is titled: *Visions and Dreams of Jesus Christ Stir Muslims to Christ!* The second video is titled: *Egypt, More Muslims embrace Christ and Growing Persecution.* And the third video is titled: *Kamal Saleem: Arise, Body of Christ - CBN.com.*

Another fact that appears to support that Acts 2 is still happening is that Bishop Bill Hamon, who is also a prophet, wrote that he has taught over 250,000 people to prophesy.[29] This is an unprecedented number of people who have learned to prophesy. I believe this lines up with Acts 2, and confirms that God is still pouring out His Spirit to allow His sons and daughters to prophesy, if they believe that and they ask Him for the gift of prophecy.

The Third Scripture: 1 Corinthians 14:1

The third Scripture that supports the belief that all believers can prophesy today is found in 1 Corinthians 14 which says,

> Follow the way of love, and eagerly desire the spiritual gifts especially the gift of prophecy (1 Cor. 14:1).

Paul is telling us that believers should eagerly desire the spiritual gifts like prophecy. I remember that when I first read this Scripture, the Holy Spirit began to prompt me to really believe that I should eagerly desire to prophesy. So I read 1 Corinthians 14:1 over and over again until I started to eagerly desire to prophesy. Then I was compelled to ask the Father in heaven for the gift of prophecy. Then a short while later the Lord began to give me visions and dreams, and other prophetic insights for other people. For the Lord Jesus did say,

> Ask and it will be given, seek and you will find, knock and the door will be opened to you… " Jesus then concludes this statement with "…how much more will your Father in heaven give the Holy Spirit to those who ask Him? (Luke 11:9-13).

If you desire to hear from God, and I really think that you should, for Jesus told us in Matthew 7, "…only he who does the will of my Father" will enter the kingdom of heaven (Matt. 7:21). How do you know the Father's will unless He can speak to you? How can you hear His commands in the moment when you need to, unless you can hear His voice? When you hear the Father's commands then that is being prophetic.

Believing believers will ask the Father for the Holy Spirit and for the gift of prophecy, which also comes from the Holy Spirit. The prophet Moses connects these two gifts together: being filled with the Spirit and receiving the gift of prophecy when he said, "I wish that all the Lord's people were prophets, and that the Lord would put His Spirit on them!"(Num. 11:29).

Moses was speaking prophetically about believing believers today, for it is a fact that God desires for all the New Testament believers to be filled with His Spirit and to become a prophetic people (see Acts 2:17-18).

That's why God poured out His Spirit at Pentecost and why He is pouring it out today on all those who ask for it. Do you eagerly desire the spiritual gifts, especially the gift of prophecy? The Heavenly Father wants all His children to ask for the Holy Spirit and to ask for the gifts of the Spirit, like the gift of prophecy.

Jesus said we were to make disciples and teach them to obey everything that Jesus commanded (see Matt. 28:19-20). All Christians are supposed to ask for the Holy Spirit and ask for the gift of prophesy. Those are some of the most important things that the Lord commanded for us to learn. I hope you are finally getting this, as it is crucial for the body of Christ to wake up in this hour and demonstrate who Jesus is to the world around us.

The Fourth Scripture: 1 Timothy 4

The fourth Scripture that supports the belief that all believers can prophesy today is found in 1 Timothy 4 which says,

> Do not neglect your gift, which was given you through a prophetic message when the body of elders laid their hands on you (1 Tim. 4:14).

Paul is reminding Timothy that he should practice the spiritual gift that was given to him by the laying on of hands, which is also known as impartation. When the laying on of hands is practiced the gift of prophecy can be imparted. Those who desire to hear from God can go to someone who can impart the gift of prophecy, and then in faith they can receive the gift of prophecy. But you must not neglect your gift; instead you need to exercise it by practicing it, so you will develop your prophetic gift.

Dr. Paul Cox heads Aslan's Place ministry and teaches on Generational Deliverance and Discernment.[30] The Holy Spirit taught Cox how to discern the gift of prophecy by feeling the flow of the river of God, as it flows through the gift. A seer is a type of prophet who sees visions, and the visions are seen through the seer's eyes. The gift of prophecy is activated through the eyes of the person who has the prophetic gift, and it can be discerned by feeling the river of God flowing through the eyes of the believer who has the prophetic gift.

Cox has demonstrated that believers can discern the river of God that flows through someone's eyes, if the person has the gift of prophecy. You can discern the prophetic gift by placing the palm of your hand about ten centimeters or three inches in front of the believer's eyes. *If you are tuned in to your spiritual discernment gift, and if the person has the gift of prophecy, then you will feel the flow of the river of God as a slight pressure against your hand.* When an impartation occurs for the gift of prophecy, you can feel an increase in the intensity of the flow of the prophetic river through the person's eyes during the impartation.

In summary, I believe I have shown from a Scriptural basis that all believing believers may prophesy today. However, there are some conditions:

- It is Jesus' sheep who hear His voice; those people who belong to God hear his voice. So the condition here is that you belong to God, and you are a follower of Jesus Christ, which means you are following Jesus as a lifestyle, and you have begun to die to following your own will and desires (see Gal. 2:20).

- God pours out His Spirit so sons, daughters, and servants will prophesy, see visions, and have dreams. Again the condition is that you must be a son, daughter, or servant. Each of these depicts that you are in a relationship with Jesus Christ. That relationship is enhanced when you are continually filled by the Holy Spirit. Being filled by the Spirit allows you to be in an active relationship with Jesus and the Father. When that relationship is developed then you will begin to act like a son or a servant, and then you will begin to receive prophetic revelations.

- You most assuredly are going to be able to receive the outpouring of the Spirit, but the condition is that you must ask and then wait for the Spirit to come and fill you. You must also ask for and receive the gift of prophecy.

- You are told to eagerly desire the gift of prophecy. The condition here is that you must believe you are entitled to have the gift of prophecy. Then you need to desire it. And then you need to ask the Father for the gift of prophecy and to receive it by faith.

- You can also receive the spiritual gifts from someone who has the gift of impartation and lays his hands on you. The condition here is that you must believe that the gift of prophecy can be imparted to the believer through the laying on of hands. And you must find someone to lay hands on you to impart the gift. But the gift comes from God, not from the person imparting the gifts. That's why you need faith that it is God's desire to give you the good gift of prophecy.

The Scriptural basis that all believing believers may prophesy today is that the believing believer is to be pursuing God, and is in a relationship with God as a son, daughter, or servant, so that he actually belongs to God and is one of His sheep. Another part of being a pursuer of God is to ask for, wait, and receive the Holy Spirit, and ask for the gift of prophecy. This pursuit displays your desire to have the gift of prophecy.

Another way to pursue the gift of prophecy is to have someone who has the impartation gift to lay his hands on you, and impart the prophetic gift. All believing believers may prophesy today if you are thirsty and hungry, and you want to develop an intimate relationship with the Lord. And also if you are thirsty and hungry for His kingdom and His gifts, and you pursue the gifts so you can receive them, and then you can release the spiritual gifts in your relational networks.

Practice the Gift of Prophecy

We are told to practice the gifts of the Spirit, as they do not develop without practice and without having applied faith. Hebrews 5 speaks of what the mature believers do, for it says,

> …solid food is for the mature who through constant practice have trained themselves to distinguish good from evil (Hebrews 5:14).

You need to practice hearing from God with other believing believers, as having two or three witnesses will help you to confirm what you are hearing. The other believing believers can help you to distinguish the voice of God from other voices. You can practice in home groups or just in informal settings. Constant practice is the way the gift of prophecy will develop and become strong. One reason believing believers need to practice hearing from God is that there are other voices that compete for your hearing. I will briefly teach on those other voices now.

The Voices We Can Hear From

In the Scriptures you will see that Peter demonstrates that you are able to hear from three different voices.

The First Voice is the Heavenly Father's Voice

The first voice that Peter heard from was the Heavenly Father's voice for Peter proclaimed, "You are the Christ, the Son of the living God" (Matthew 16:16). And Jesus tells Peter that this was revealed to him by the Father in heaven. Peter had heard from the Father in heaven and received this word of knowledge, which was a prophetic revelation.

The Second Voice is an Evil Spirit's or Satan's Voice

The second voice that Peter heard from was the voice of an evil spirit or Satan. For in Matthew 16, it says Peter,

> …took Him aside and began to rebuke Him, 'Never Lord!' he said. 'This shall never happen to You!' Jesus turned and said to Peter, 'Get behind Me Satan! You are a stumbling block to Me; you do not have in mind the things of God, but the things of men' (Matt. 16:22-23).

Jesus was speaking to Peter, but indicates the ideas that Peter shared with Jesus were from Satan himself. This indicates that although Peter not only could hear from the Father in heaven, Peter could also hear from Satan. Elsewhere Jesus tells us that Satan is the father of all lies (see John 8:43-44).

The Third Voice is His Own Soul's Voice

The third voice is Peter's own soul. When the angel told the women disciples at the tomb that Jesus had risen, and was going to meet them in Galilee, Peter was not with them. Peter was downcast as his soul was working overtime going over his own failures concerning Jesus Christ's death. Peter was contemplating going back to his old work—fishing. But the angel in Mark 16 tells the disciples,

> 'Don't be alarmed,' he said, 'You are looking for Jesus the Nazarene, who was crucified. He is risen! He is not here. See the place where they laid Him. But go, tell His disciples and Peter, He is going ahead of you into Galilee. There you will see Him, just as He told you' (Mark 16:6-7).

This Scripture notes the specific instructions: "…tell His disciples and Peter." Why "and Peter?" I think the reason was because Peter saw the Lord crucified and buried, and he had denied Him. He was discouraged and his soul told him to go back to his old job, which was fishing. So the Lord had the angel isolate Peter's name, as the Lord wanted Peter to know He had risen, and everything had happened according to God's plan. Jesus wanted Peter to receive inner healing, to transform his thinking, and to be healed from his emotional wounds. In John 21, we read that even after Jesus appeared to the disciples, Peter was still listening to the third voice, his own soul's voice and concludes, "I am going out to fish" (John 21:3).

Peter had decided to go out to fish probably because he still thought his denial of Jesus three times had disqualified him from service. Peter was not able to hear or understand God's call on his life because he was hearing his own soul's voice telling him something like: *You blew it Peter, you let Jesus down. You should go back to fishing because that's the work you know how to do well, so you won't blow it anymore.* Peter was still set to go back to his old ways. However, the gospel of John shows that Jesus had wanted to intervene in Peter's regression. Jesus came and cooked some fish on the fire. Then when the disciples come in, Jesus speaks to Peter and points repeatedly to the fish and says,

> …do you truly love me more than these?
> (John 21:15; 16; 17).

When Jesus pointed to the fish saying "these," He was referring to Peter's fishing career. That was the fall back for Peter as he received his significance and security from his career, which was fishing. But Jesus wanted to transform Peter's soulish ways; so Jesus repeats to Peter "…do you love me?" Then Jesus gives the command to Peter "take care of my sheep." And then finally Jesus says "follow me" (John 21:19b).

Jesus was working on Peter's thinking, emotions, and will, which was his soul. He was doing inner healing on Peter, so Peter could walk out in his birthright. That meant for Peter to change his profession and become the New Testament Church's leader.

Inner healing helps to clear away the ungodly thoughts and feelings from our souls. Peter was not able to hear the Heavenly Father's voice telling him to change his career. Peter had been listening to his own soul's voice instead. Jesus' inner healing work on Peter was successful, for Peter led the disciples and spoke to the crowd after Pentecost, and was one of the key leaders in the early church (see Acts 2:14; 3:1-26; 5:1-16).

The Fourth Voice *Empathetic Defilement*

There is a fourth voice that we can also hear from. Jesus shows us He "… knew what they were thinking…" (Luke 6:8). John Sandford teaches on *empathetic defilement* in his book *Why Do Good People Mess Up.*[31] Sandford explains that in a counseling session or in any other situation where you are listening to a person and you have empathy, then that is when you may be able to pick up the other person's thoughts, like Jesus did. However, the *defilement* occurs when you hear another person's thoughts, but you turn it around to be your own soul's voice. Then you can mistakenly think it is your own idea, or worse, you think it was God speaking to you! That's why you need to practice hearing from God so you can distinguish His voice from the other voices.

We have seen that believing believers are able to hear from four different voices: 1. The Heavenly Father, 2. Evil spirits or Satan, 3. Your own soul, and 4. Another person's thoughts that you pick up. Consequently, learning to walk in the prophetic gifting requires that believing believers need to learn to distinguish between hearing the Heavenly Father's voice and hearing from the other voices. This requires time and practice to mature.

Jesus tells us in Matthew 10:39 that "Whoever finds his life will lose it, and whoever loses his life for my sake will find it." The word "life" in Greek is "*psuche"* and it means your soul: which is your mind, will, and emotions.[32] Maturing in Christ is a process of dying to your own thoughts, will, and emotions, and replacing those with the mind, will, and emotions of Jesus Christ (see Romans 12:2; Ephesians 4:23; Colossians 3:1-4). In Hebrews 5, it tells you that you can mature in your spiritual gifts by constantly using them, in order to train yourself so you can,

> …distinguish good from evil (Hebrews 5:14).

In relation to prophecy, you need to distinguish between the good of hearing the voice of the Father in heaven speaking to you, from the evil of hearing the voice of an evil spirit, Satan, or the evil of hearing your own soul speaking to you, or the evil of hearing another person's thoughts speaking to you. Consequently, you need to practice and learn to distinguish between those different voices, and you may also need to get some inner healing as well.

Guidelines for Prophetic Words

When you exercise your prophetic gift, I suggest that you may want to follow some guidelines that will help you to deliver your prophesies in the most loving and beneficial manner.

Most people who prophesy are not Prophets; they do not function in the office of a Prophet. That means they should stay away from giving prophetic words about sin or correction, and stay away from giving governmental or church body prophecies to name just a few. A Prophet has a level of maturity that allows him to give weightier prophecies, but most other prophetic people are either operating in the gift of prophecy, or they are being trained in the ministry of prophecy, but they are not recognized as prophets, yet.

You are told in 1 Corinthians 14 how your prophecies are to impact those who receive them, for it says, "Follow the way of love" and a little later it says, "Everyone who prophesies speaks to men for their strengthening, encouragement and comfort" (1 Corinthians 14:1-3).

When you prophesy you are told first of all you are to love and that includes among other things having a pleasant facial expression that exudes kindness and gentleness, and you may even smile. Try to be relaxed and without tension or anxiety, as being relaxed will put both you and the person you are prophesying to at ease. Try to be at peace, which can include the volume you use when you share your prophetic word. You are most effective when you use a normal tone of voice. Yelling out your prophecy is normally not appropriate. Most people should give prophetic words with no judgments, calling out of sin, correction, or warnings, and also do not prophesy about babies, marriages, or mates.

When you practice the prophetic exercises, just have the faith that your Father in heaven wants to speak to you and through you. Present what you hear or see tentatively, but with faith and you will be surprised how often you are accurately hearing from the Lord.

Practice Hearing From God at Home

The best place to begin to practice is at home during your prayer time or when you are soaking in the Spirit. Get a journal and a pen, and quiet yourself down. Then just ask the Lord to speak to you, and wait in faith for Him to answer. Then write down whatever you hear or see in your journal. Do not judge it, but write it first, and then look back at it afterwards. Test what you have written by looking in the Scripture to see if what you got correlates or contradicts the Scriptures. Also ask other believing believers to look at what you wrote, and ask them "Would you please try to sense if this journal entry was from the Lord or not?"

When you have practiced enough on your own, and you believe that you are hearing from the Lord, then try to practice hearing from God for other people. Here are five prophetic exercises that you can use with other believers to help you practice your prophetic gifts. These exercises are adapted from trainings that I have attended at *Christian International*, and from Prophet Bill Lackie's book: *Prophetic Activations*, which is a good resource for more prophetic exercises.[33]

Prophetic Exercise #1—Face-to-Face

    a.   Get everyone in your group to partner up. Each person is to stand face-to-face with their partner from a distance of about two feet apart. Pray out loud in tongues for one minute. Ask the Lord to speak to you about your partner, while you are praying in tongues. Try to sense what God might be speaking to you about your partner. He might give you a vision, an impression, some words, or He might remind you of some scene from your past, as a clue about what He wants you to share with your partner. Whatever you receive, remember it so you can ask the Lord to clarify it for you, and give you more information if you need to.

        When a person speaks in tongues it has been shown that her mind shifts from operating from the left brain to the right brain. The right brain is the creative brain, and it makes it easier for you to tune into your spirit. When you are using your right brain it makes it easier for you to hear what the Father is speaking.

        If you do not speak in tongues yet, use some other method to switch to the right brain like smiling, humming a tune, singing a song, dancing, drawing, sketching, or taking a deep breath and just relaxing.[34] If you do not speak in tongues, find a believing believer who can impart the gift of speaking in tongues.

        Paul says that he speaks in tongues more than anyone else, and that you are not to forbid it; therefore, speaking in tongues is another gift that is available to all believers (see 1 Corinthians 14:18; 14:39). It is a very important gift for you use, for when you regularly practice speaking in tongues it builds up your spirit-man.

        After speaking in tongues for about a minute, then stop and listen for about 10 seconds, and receive what the Father in heaven is sharing with you for your partner. Be sure the motives of your heart are set for you to express love to the person, so she is encouraged, strengthened, and comforted. When you begin to share with your partner start by saying, "I sensed that…" and then just share as clearly as you can, what you sensed you had for your partner. When you are done, switch and have the other person share what he got. The other person may want to begin by speaking in tongues for a minute (to get into the right brain in order to hear from God), and then he will share with his partner the revelation that he received.

Record the Prophetic Words

If you can, you should try to record the prophetic words that are given. If you do, then you can give a copy to the person who received the prophetic word, so she can pray into it afterwards and seek God, as to whether it is a valid word from God or not. If you have a portable device to record the audio soundtrack, use it to record the prophetic words, then give a copy of the recording to the person who received the prophetic words, so she can write it out and pray about it.

Prophetic Exercise #2—One-to-One—A Simple Thought from God[35]

b. Have a row of people stand shoulder-to-shoulder. Have three or four people selected to give a simple thought from God for each person in the line. Move down the line in a moderately fast pace and avoid giving long drawn out words.

Prophetic Exercise #3—The Seat of Blessing[36]

c. Have one person sit in a chair in the middle of about five people who will stand facing the chair, and form a semi-circle. Pick someone to go first and then rotate in the order of the semi-circle. Have each person share their prophetic insights from the Lord with the seated person. When the first person has finished prophesying then rotate the semi-circle, so the next person can stand in front of the seated person and begin to speak out his prophetic word.

After each person in the semi-circle has shared a prophetic word, change the person in the chair with one of the persons in the semi-circle, and repeat the process until each person in your group has sat in the chair and received the prophetic words from the other people in your group.

Prophetic Exercise #4—Two Circles

d. Form two circles and the people on the outer circle will prophesy to those on the inner circle. The people on the outer circle will prophesy by going around the circle from person-to-person. Have a timer who will signal when it is time to change to a new person. After everyone on the outer circle has prophesied to everyone on the inner circle, then have the people switch the circles they are in. Repeat the exercise with the inner circle switching places with the people from the outer circle. Then have the new people on the outer circle prophesy to the people on the inner circle.

Prophetic Exercise #5—Single File

e. Make a single file line and have everyone in your group stand facing the same direction. Then have the first person in the line sit in the chair at the end of the line. The person who sits in the chair will receive prophetic words from the other people in the line. Have a leader select the topic for the people to prophesy about, for example: finances, family, health, work, or ministry. When a person reaches the end of the line, that's when she will prophesy to the person seated in the chair. When everyone has prophesied to the seated person, then have the seated person go to the end of the line, and have the first person in the line sit down in the chair. Repeat this procedure until each person has sat in the chair and received their prophetic words from the other people in the line.

These exercises can be used in a home group, or around a table in a coffee shop, or anywhere else you can think of. The important thing to do is to get enough practice hearing from God, so that you can then take your prophetic gift out to other people. When you practice you will begin to build your faith, and you will discover that you really do hear from the

Lord! And that's the key. Then once you have the faith, and you know that the Lord speaks to you, then listen for what He wants to say to the people in your relational networks.

Practice in Your Relational Networks

After you have practiced your prophetic exercises with your Christian friends, and you have gained enough confidence that you really do hear from God, then take the next step and go out to restaurants, shopping malls, coffee shops, or wherever you find yourself, and share your prophetic words. Then just tune into the Lord and ask Him, "Do You have anything that You want to share with me about someone here?"

Keep listening and watching the people around you, and pretty soon you will hear, sense, or see something that you are to share. You need to operate in faith, as often the Lord may only give you a little word, but if you deliver that little word, He can add to it, and He often will. So just step out and be bold, and go up to the person that you have the prophetic word for and share it with them.

Hearing God's Voice

There is a paradox about hearing God's voice. *When you hear the Lord God Almighty's voice, it is known to be a loud voice that even thunders, but I find that it frequently sounds just like one of my own thoughts (see Rev. 16:1; Ps. 29:3-9; 1 Kings 19:12).* There is no booming base voice that reverberates throughout my body. It just comes into my spirit, and then my mind receives a thought. Sometimes it is just an unobtrusive thought. I find that if I am not paying attention, I might miss it.

The Scripture tells us that "…the testimony of Jesus is the Spirit of prophecy" (Rev. 19:10b). When you are witnessing to someone about Jesus, sometimes a prophetic word will appear in your mind, as an unobtrusive thought. The Lord often wants to help you to witness to people about Him, so that's one incidence when you will get a prophetic insight. You may not even be aware that you are being prophetic. But regardless of whether you get a prophetic word when you are witnessing or not, the act of sharing the testimony about Jesus Christ's life, death, and resurrection to someone else means that you are operating under the Spirit of prophecy, whether you are conscious of prophesying or not.

When you receive a vision it sometimes is so quick and faint that you might miss the vision, if you are not paying attention. So when you ask the Lord to speak to you, just wait and listen and watch in faith, and pay attention. The next thing you hear or see is likely to be the Lord speaking to you. So just step out when you get something to share, and share it with the person you are supposed to. Be bold, that way you will also be a blessing.

Use a Tentative Voice When You Deliver Prophetic Words

Try to avoid preceding your prophetic word with, "The Lord God Almighty says…" or "Thus saith the Lord…" as those stylized statements are not appropriate. You may scare the person so he cannot hear your prophetic word. You may also be off with your word. You know there are other voices you can hear from, so being overconfident and in presumption is not appropriate. In Jeremiah 23, the Lord made a comment about this style of delivery:

> If a prophet or a priest or anyone else claims, 'This is the oracle of the Lord' I will punish that man and his household (Jeremiah 23:34).

Just share your prophetic insight by asking a question or you could say, "I was sensing that…" Or say it in some other tentative way like, "I have a feeling…" Remember that even when you are accurate, you only prophecy in part, so it is best to deliver the prophetic word in a tentative and humble way (see 1 Corinthians 13:9). Share the revelation you get in a tentative way, which means you say it with humility.

For example, you may start by saying: "I have the feeling that you are a musician" and then he says, "Yes I am." And you continue, "And you also write your own lyrics." He replies, "As a matter of fact, I just wrote a song this week for my girlfriend, it's our one-month anniversary. How did you pick that up?"

Then you reply, "Jesus Christ is my Lord, and sometimes He shares with me the things that He knows about other people, like you being a musician, and that you write your own lyrics. Do you know who Jesus is?" He might say, "Oh, I am not religious." And you can reply,

> Oh neither am I, but Jesus Christ is the living God, and He is in a relationship with me. He knows all about me and loves me, and guides me in my life. He knows all about you too and He loves you, and He is inviting you to get to know Him. That's why He shared with me that you are a musician, and especially the point that you write your own lyrics, because Jesus knows how much your girlfriend means to you. He was watching you and knows those lyrics are special, as it expresses your heart. May I pray a blessing over you?

He may say, "Yes." And you pray a blessing, and ask the Lord to increase his creativity, and give him more encounters with Jesus Christ.

This exchange actually happened when I was in a restaurant in Bellevue, Washington this past year. I often prefer to start by saying "I have a feeling…" because it is subjective and tentative and less invasive. Then when the next word of knowledge came to me, I could just say it out right, "And you also write your own lyrics." But after that, I did not sense I was supposed to evangelize him anymore that day. I believe I was just supposed to plant the seed that Jesus knows him, and then I was to bless him.

John Wimber made some helpful suggestions about hearing God's voice in his book: *Power Healing*:

> When I speak of listening to God's voice, I mean developing a practice of communion with the Father in which we are constantly asking, 'Lord, what do you want to do now? How do you want to use me? How should I pray? Who do you want me to evangelize? Is there someone that you want to heal?' Sometimes he gives me specific words, pictures in my mind's eye, physical sensations in my body to correspond

> to problems in their bodies. These impressions help me to know who and what to pray for, and how to pray. [37]

Wimber shows us that he had the desire for a relationship with the Father in heaven, and the fruit of that was that he received a variety of prophetic insights. Being able to listen to God's voice allows you to do God's will, so you can touch those people in your relational networks that God directs for you to touch.

Believing believers will develop their relationship with the Father in heaven, so they will commune with Him, communicate with Him, walk out their birthrights, and do the good works the Father has planned for them to do.

But sometimes you may just have a simple word. Try not to judge it, just step out in faith, and share it with the person the Father wants you to share it with, as that's how you will please the Father because,

> ...without faith it is impossible to please God... (Hebrews 11:6).

Step out frequently and you will not only please the Father in heaven, but your gift will grow, and most of all, those people who do not know the love and mercy of our Lord Jesus Christ, can come to know Him, because you took the chance to step out and share what you heard from the Lord with them.

That's what believing believers will do, as they are to be a blessing and share their prophetic gift everywhere they go.

Chapter 3: Discussion Questions

1. The Scripture tells us that Jesus' sheep will hear His voice, and that hearing is not just a onetime hearing, but it is the ability to repeatedly hear the Lord's voice (see John 10:16). Scripture also says those who belong to God can hear God speak (see John 8:47a). Scripture also tells us that in the last days sons, daughters and servants will prophesy, which is hearing from God and speaking out what was heard (see Acts 2:17-18).
   a. How would you describe your current relationship with the Lord?
   b. What do you need to change to become a child or servant of the Lord so you can hear God's voice?
   c. How can you come into a relationship with the Lord and follow like a faithful sheep?

2. God is giving Muslims dreams and they are coming to recognize that Jesus Christ is God.
   a. Since pagans and Muslims receive prophetic visions and dreams, what barriers do you have to receiving prophetic visions and dreams?
   b. Have you asked the Lord to give you prophetic dreams that speak to you?
   c. What is preventing you from asking the Father in heaven for these prophetic gifts?

3. We are to eagerly desire the gift of prophecy (1 Corinthians 14:1).
   a. Have you read this Scripture before? What was your response to being told you were to eagerly desire the gift of prophecy?
   b. Have you ever thought you were to desire it before?
   c. How can you align your will with the Father's will for this Scripture?

4. Moses prophesied that He wished all of the Lord's people were given the Spirit and would become prophets.
   a. Do you think Moses was prophesying about today?
   b. The first two steps of being surprisingly supernatural involve Being Continually Filled with the Holy Spirit and Receiving the

Gift of Prophecy. As a believing believer how important is it to take both of these steps to walk out your birthright in faith?
   c. What hinders you from taking these two steps of faith?
   d. What do you need to do to take these two steps of faith?

5. Jesus said that only he who does the will of the Father enters the kingdom of heaven, so for you to know the will of the Father, you must be able to hear what the Father says.
   a. How important is being able to hear God's voice to enter into the kingdom of God?
   b. Since it is very important to hear the Father's voice to know His will, what do you need to do to learn to hear His voice?

6. Peter demonstrated that believers can hear from the Father, Satan, and their own souls. We need to distinguish between these voices. Do you think it is important to practice hearing from God?
   a. How have you heard from the Father in heaven before?
   b. How have you heard from an evil spirit, from your own soul, or from someone's thoughts before?
   c. How can you distinguish between these voices and learn to clearly recognize the Lord's voice?

CHAPTER 4

SURPRISINGLY SUPERNATURAL STEP #3
HOW TO ASK FOR THE GIFTS OF HEALINGS AND MIRACLES

After you are filled with the Holy Spirit, and you are able to hear God's voice for yourself and for other people, then the third step in becoming a supernatural believing believer is to begin to operate in the gifts of healing. This chapter will teach you the keys that will allow you to heal the sick, so you can do it wherever you go, like Jesus did.

I was exposed to healing and miracles shortly after I was filled by the Holy Spirit; then I was invited to become a trainer for the Healing Rooms ministry, and I also went on many mission trips that helped me to move into higher realms of healing miracles. I also took some courses with Wagner Leadership Institute. One course I took that was taught by Brian Thomson was called the *School of Signs and Wonders*. I listened to it on CDs. Thomson's course helped me to organize my teaching in this chapter on healings and miracles, and many of the points in this chapter are attributed to his course. [38]

As believing believers you need to orientate your perspective on sickness like Jesus had, for the Scripture says,

> The reason the Son of God appeared was to destroy the devil's work (1 John 3:8b).

You may ask, "What are the works of the devil?" Well, here are three Scriptures where Jesus reveals what some of the works of the devil are.

Jesus tells us, "The thief comes only to steal and kill and destroy; I have come that they may have life, and have it to the full" (John 10:10).

Jesus said, "You belong to your father the devil, and you want to carry out your father's desire. He was a murderer from the beginning, not holding to the truth, for there is no truth in him. When he lies, he speaks his native language, for he is a liar and the father of lies" (John 8:44).

Luke tells us in the book of Acts, "...God anointed Jesus of Nazareth with the Holy Spirit and power, and how He went around doing good and healing all who were under the power of the devil, because God was with Him" (Acts 10:38).

Jesus came to destroy the works of the devil, and those works are to steal, kill, destroy, murder, and lie. But Jesus also came so you could have life, and have it to the fullest. I think "full life" sounds like long-life, and I also think it sounds like a life full of love, peace, joy, and excitement, as it is a full life of health: spiritual, physical, mental, emotional, and social health. Paul writes,

> May God Himself, the God of peace, sanctify you through and through. May your whole spirit, soul and body be kept blameless at the coming of our Lord Jesus Christ (1 Thess. 5:23).

The Devil Brings Sickness and Disease, but Jesus Comes Against His Evil Works

The New Testament points out that the devil is the one who assaults people by stealing, killing, destroying, and murdering peoples' bodies, souls, and spirits with sickness—trying to take away the life from people. And the New Testament points out that Jesus came to destroy the devil's work, and He was also to bring full life to people, by bringing healing to all who were under the power of the devil, because God was with Him. *Jesus brings healing and life, but the devil brings sickness and death.*

A Spiritual Attack That Brings on a Sickness

I went to Brasil on a ministry trip a few years ago, and I had a dream the first night I was there. In the dream a woman had a wand in her hand and was steering a tornado in front of her toward my direction. I ran around the building, but she caught up with me. Then she got into the car that was parked there and pulled out a tranquilizing gun, and pointed it at me. The dream ended.

The ministry went well on that trip and many supernatural things occurred as the kingdom of God came with healings, miracles, prophecy, deliverance, and the believers were empowered. When I got home I went to the gym and ran on the treadmill. I checked my heart rate and it was at 180 beats per minute. I was shocked, as it had never been that high before. I went home and I checked my blood pressure, and it was high as well. I discovered I had a cold or the flu, and it took me two weeks to recover. Yet after I recovered, my blood pressure was still high. I made the mistake of worrying about it and with that I bought into the devil's lie.[39] And my blood pressure stayed high and troublesome. About a week later I was led to meditate on Acts 10:38 and I began to repeat it over again in my mind saying,

> ...how He went around doing good, and healing all who were under the power of the devil, because God was with Him (Acts 10:38b).

I then wondered: *Was my sickness due to the power of the devil?* The more I thought about it, the more I realized that something was amiss. I had had a good diet for a long time and I had exercised all my life, so it seemed unnatural for me to have high blood pressure. Then I remembered the dream and that dart gun. I thought: *Maybe that was the key!*

I began to thank God for warning me in the dream about the attack, and I thanked Him for bringing Acts 10:38 to my mind. I decided I needed to get prayer at my church. When the Ministry Team prayed for me, I was surprised when my pastor Mary said, "I see an evil spiritual dart in Neil's back." I received prayer that Sunday and I also got some other believers to pray over the next couple of days with me. Then I had my doctor take some medical tests and all the tests results came back normal. I was in good health. My symptoms had diminished and I was healed.

This brought home to me the reality that many illnesses are the result of people being under the devil's power. I think we need to reform our thinking and begin to realize why the medical field has not been able to find many cures for diseases. They give us drugs to suppress the symptoms of pain or they surgically remove the problem. Now some of their practices are beneficial, but where are the cures?

Medical cures are few and far between. T. Colin Campbell recently reported in his book *The China Study* that "Drugs and surgeries don't cure the diseases that kill most Americans."[40] He recommends a change in diet is necessary; and although I agree that many people need to adjust their diets, I believe that a large contribution to ill health is due to the nature of disease, which is often spiritual.

The truth about the spiritual nature of disease is suppressed by the scientific medical field for two reasons: first, they are not aware of the spiritual issues; and second, they make billions of dollars by surgically removing body parts and selling medications. Even if they were aware of the spiritual causes of disease, they have no motivation whatsoever to explore the spiritual truth about disease. That's why believing believers need to arise today and grab hold of the healing promises that are in the Scriptures and show the world how the devil wants to kill life, but Jesus gives life and heals all diseases.

Believing believers will develop a biblical perspective on disease and healing, and will not embrace our culture's perspective. I prayed with people in a healing center a little over a year ago and my fellow healing ministers would interview the person who came in to receive healing. They would discuss the doctor's diagnosis, the medical insurance, the hospital that they are going to, and the schedule of their medical tests. I felt like these questions continued to give power to the medical model, but failed to encourage the faith in the person that needed the miracle.

My fellow believers appeared to give more homage to the medical model than to God's power to heal. They would eventually pray for healing and see some healings and miracles, but I think this respect for the medical model was misplaced.

Faith in the Lord's power to heal all disease is what believing believers need to promote, for if Jesus healed all who were under the power of the devil, then those of us who are God's children are the only ones on the earth who can bring the Lord's miraculous healing power and come against the devil's power that brings sickness and death. *Believing believers really need to get this revelation that they are THE ONLY ONES who can bring the Lord's power and love that heals all disease and sickness!*

The medical model is limited, as they are not aware of the spiritual nature of disease, nor are they aware of the Lord's power to heal. But as soon as believing believers get out of this acculturated way of thinking, and step into the faith in what the Lord Jesus Christ has provided in the way of miraculous healings and His gift of health, then the world will begin to hear repeatedly that the Lord Jesus Christ is performing miraculous healings today. That was absent during the Enlightenment, and as a result it allowed the devil's lies to permeate the world cultures, but believing believers who arise today will begin to defeat those lies by healing many people with sicknesses in their relational networks.[41]

An Ungodly Power Brings on Sickness

I was visiting a friend who had moved into her mother's home, as her mother was elderly and needed care. Her mother had been falling down a lot. She fell into the sink and onto the floor, and she was tired. I asked if I could pray, but after I prayed a few times she felt no change in her condition. When that has happened before, I usually know there is some kind of evil spirit that is impeding the healing.

I sensed I wanted to test the space in front of her mother, so I moved my hand in front of her mother and I discerned an ungodly spiritual power was in front of her. It appeared to be about three feet tall and there was another one behind her as well. My friend discerned them as well. I prayed for the Father in heaven to release His fire and melt these *ungodly powers* (see Eph. 6:12). I also commanded them to remove anything that they had attached to her mother who we were praying for.

Her daughter reported her mother began to feel better a short while later. Her doctors could try to adjust her medications all they want, but this attack from the devil was not detected by medical tests and was not impacted by medical prescriptions. It was only detected through the power of the Holy Spirit, and by a believing believer who had the gift of discernment and had acquired an awareness of the devil's schemes.

A friend of mine asked for ministry, so after he confessed his ancestor's generational sins and his own sins, I had him sit in a chair and then he told me he had pain in his stomach. I put my hand behind his back and I discerned an evil spirit was there. So I commanded it to go, in Jesus' name. I also broke the curse that had been placed on him by an old associate. Immediately, the pain in his stomach went away. He later reported that the bleeding in his stomach stopped, his anemia was healed, and his energy level returned to normal. He had been having medical treatments for over a year, but in less than half an hour, I was able to minister through the gifts of the Holy Spirit and he was healed, and the devil's works were destroyed.

I am amazed at the amount of illnesses I am witnessing that are the result of evil spirits. In my previous book *Wake Up!* I described how people were healed when I cast evil spirits off their backs.[42] I guess the reason I am amazed at the amount of illness caused by evil spirits is that I failed to really believe the Scriptures that pointed out all the healings that occurred when evil spirits were cast out (see Luke 6:18; 13:32; Matt. 8:16; 17:17: Acts 8:7; 10:38).

Believing believers will read the Scriptures where demons were cast out and people were healed, and they will embrace this worldview and learn to discern demons, cast out evil spirits, and spirits of infirmity, so they can bring healing to people and glory to the Lord. On the book's website: www.suprisinglysupernatural.com in Chapter 4 are two videos that shows two people who were deaf due to being exposed to spinal meningitis at the age of two, and they both were cured when evil spirits were cast out of them, in Jesus' name.

Jesus' mandate was to do good and heal all who were under the power of the devil, because God was with him (see Acts 10:38). So let's look at what Jesus said in Matthew 28. After Jesus' resurrection He said,

> All authority in heaven and on earth has been given to me. Therefore, go and make disciples of all nations, baptizing them in the name of the Father and of the Son and of the Holy Spirit and teaching them to obey everything I have commanded you. And surely I am with you always to the very end of the age (Matt. 28:18-19).

Jesus says that He was given all authority and said "therefore." "Therefore" is a linking word that links the phrase "I am with you always to the very end of the age." Consequently, Jesus is saying something like this: "Go in all my authority and my power and make disciples of all nations, as I will be with you wherever you go" (see Matt. 28:18-19). When you go in Jesus' power and authority you can easily make disciples. As believing believers, you will be empowered to heal every disease and sickness, and the people who are healed will gladly become disciples and want to follow the Divine Healer Jesus.

Therefore, "The Great Commission," which this previous Scripture is referred to, commands you to make disciples and reminds you to do everything Jesus commanded. Healing the sick is one of the commands that Jesus told believers to do. Healing the sick is one of the best ways to bring the good news of the kingdom of God into people's lives.

The Believer's Level of Healing:

Jesus is telling you, "Now it's your turn to destroy the works of the devil and bring healing and full life to others." You have authority to do that when you use the name of Jesus Christ, for Mark 16:17-18 tells us,

> And these signs will accompany those who believe: *In My name* they will drive out demons; they will speak in new tongues; they will pick up snakes with their hands; and when they drink deadly poison, it will not hurt them at all; they will place their hands on sick people, and they will get well" (Mark 16:17-18; emphasis added).

When believing believers use the phrase: "In Jesus' name," it is not just a cliché they close their prayers with. That's because they are full of the

Spirit of God and they commune with the Lord, so those words have weight. They are backed up by the kingdom of God. This is the one of the keys that believing believers need to learn in order to begin to operate in the healing gifts, which is to know that when you carry His Spirit within you, then you carry His power. And when you combine that with your faith, that's what puts the power behind the phrase, "in Jesus' name."

When Brian Thomson was the Director of the Wagner Leadership Institute in Canada, he suggested that believers need to get the healing Scriptures into their souls and spirits. Thomson would read the Scripture from Mark 16, which I just mentioned above, and then asks the believers,[43] "In this Scripture from Mark 16, who does it say gets to drive out demons and heal the sick? Is it the pastor? Is it the elders of the church? Is it the Bible school graduates?"

They respond saying, "No! It's the believer!"

One way you can begin to build your faith is to recognize that believing believers are called to lay hands on the sick. Try to repeat the following round and the responses out loud for a period of time, like for a month. Then you will begin to draw on the faith of that deposit, and you will begin to see people with sicknesses healed when you lay your hands on them. Here is a round and response based on Mark 16:17-18. If you say it like a rap, it makes it kind of fun.

> Round: "Who does Jesus say will lay hands on the sick?"
>
> Response: "Jesus says, believers will lay hands on the sick."
>
> Round: "What happens when believers lay hands on the sick?"
>
> Response: "The sick get well, in Jesus' name."
>
> Round: "The sick get well, in Jesus' name?"
>
> Response: "Yes! The sick get well, in Jesus' name!"

Mark 16:18 tells us that healing the sick is what believers do. This is the believer's level of healing. In Chapter 7 of my book *Wake Up!* I shared how Steve Stewart, who leads the *Impact Nations* ministry, told the story about a Muslim interpreter who was directed to lay his hands on the sick and speak out the healing command, "Be healed, in Jesus' name." And then Jesus healed the sick through his prayers![44] That was the pre-believer's level of healing operating. The Muslim interpreter had seen Jesus working through the *Impact Nations'* team members to heal many other sick people, so the Muslim man had developed some level of faith in Jesus before he prayed. His faith was activated. The sick were healed. He was a believer at some level.

Therefore, if this pre-believing Muslim can see healing occur, then surely all believing believers are given the power to bring life back to sick people by laying their hands on them and commanding the sickness to go, in Jesus' name. I suggest for you to practice this round and the response out loud until it gets into your spirit, for remember the Scripture says,

> ...faith comes by hearing the message, and the message is heard through the word of Christ (Rom. 10:17).

When you hear yourself speaking these Scriptural truths that Jesus Christ declared, that's when they will get deposited into your soul and your spirit. Then the truth can rise up in faith when you begin to exercise the healing gift, as you release the promise that believers do heal the sick. That's what believing believers will do. You will bring healing to others by releasing the kingdom wherever you go.

The Disciple's Level of Healing and Miracles

The disciple's level of healing and miracles is based on Matthew 10, where Jesus says,

> *He called His disciples to Him*, and gave them authority to drive out evil spirits and to heal every disease and sickness (Matt. 10:1; emphasis added).

Did you notice that it said that Jesus "*...called His disciples to Him*"? The disciples were not only called, but they went to Jesus as well. Today, that's what disciples will do when they take *Surprisingly Supernatural Step #1 Be Filled with the Holy Spirit*. All disciples, who are believing believers, will hear Jesus' call, and you will respond to His call by being continually filled by the Holy Spirit. When you allow the Holy Spirit to fill you, you come close to Jesus and you will also abide in Him. Philippians 1 tells us that the Spirit is,

> ...the Spirit of Jesus Christ... (Phil. 1:19).

Jesus always calls His disciples to Himself. When you draw close to Jesus by being continually filled with the Spirit, it is like Jesus called you and you responded to Jesus' desire for you to come close to Him by asking for the Holy Spirit to fill you. That's what believing believers will do because they are disciples; Jesus always calls His disciples to Him. Jesus tells us in John 14 that He comes to us when the Spirit of Truth fills us,

> I will not leave you as orphans; I will come to you (John 14:16-18).

Jesus comes to you when you are filled with the Spirit of Truth, which is the Holy Spirit. Therefore, you simultaneously draw near to Jesus Christ, when you are continually filled with the Holy Spirit. So with that infilling and your obedience to the Lord's commands, the Lord will begin to consider you to be one of His disciples. And then He will give you greater authority, so you can drive out demons and heal every disease and sickness, because that's what disciples do. The second level of healing and miracles is for disciples, as they have walked with Jesus in obedience and are full of the Holy Spirit.

This idea echoes what was taught in the previous chapter on How to Receive the Gift of Prophecy, for I said that you hear God's voice when you belong to God, as a son, daughter, servant, or sheep. You are to be in relationship with God. Then those who are in relationship with God, as a lifestyle, will hear God's voice guiding them and dialoguing with them.

John Wimber demonstrated that he dialogued with the Lord, as he had a close relationship with the Lord. Wimber communed with the Lord.

Wimber saw healings, miracles, and demons fleeing from people, and many people came to a saving faith in Jesus Christ, because Wimber had become a disciple.

That's the same situation with the disciple's level of healing. When you draw near to Jesus, you are obeying by being continually filled by the Holy Spirit, and it is as if you are placing your head on Jesus' chest, and you are learning how to listen for His heart. That's being in communion with the Lord. And you are also inviting Him to transform you and to sanctify you through His Spirit.

When you are called to Jesus, His supernatural power and authority is transferred to you, and then you will walk out with the power over all disease and sickness. You will begin to see miracles happen regularly, and you will bring healing to the sick people who are around you. This is the fruit of being a disciple of Jesus Christ. You are in a close relationship with Him, which is also the fruit of being a believing believer.

Healing level one is the believer's level. On the first day you believe in Jesus, you can pray for the sick in Jesus' name and the sick will get well—that's healing. Sometimes it is gradual, sometimes it will be immediate, but that's the believer's promise that they will see healings when they lay their hands on the sick. We can define healing as a gradual miracle that uses the laying on of hands and the healing commands to bring the healing to the sick person. Healing may take hours, days, weeks or longer.

Healing level two is the disciple's level. The disciples have authority over every disease and sickness—authority means miracles will happen and at other times, there will be healings. But the miracles will be more frequent over time. Miracles are instantaneous healings and they occur when you are declaring a healing command and then Ka Boom!—all of a sudden the pain is gone, the tumor disappears, the blind now see or the deaf now hear. It's a miracle because it was impacted by the kingdom of God. The sickness had to go and health arrived in the next moment.

I find that quite often miracles are hardly noticed. Often times the change comes without fanfare; the miracle happens, but if you don't pay attention, you might miss it. On the book's website: under Chapter 4 is a video called

Demonstration of Five Healing Miracles by Jesus Christ.[45] When you watch it, you will see that the last miraculous healing on that video was when the lady's detached retina was reattached. She began to see light out of the eye that was totally dark before. It was a miracle! But when the miracle occurred, the lady only had a bit of a smile. She did not really appear to notice the miracle.[46]

As a believing believer you sometimes will need to capture the moment when the person is miraculously healed. You will need to get the person to acknowledge what Jesus has done right away. You need to encourage the recipient of the miracle to celebrate it with praise and worship over what the Lord Jesus has done when He displayed His goodness, love, and His miraculous power to heal.

Whether you are a believer or a disciple who is a believing believer, you are called to heal the sick and you are given that power and authority, in Jesus' name to do it. Believing believers are called to heal the sick, but they are also called to grow up and become disciples by being filled with the Word of God and being continually filled with the Holy Spirit (see John 15:7). Then they will learn to be obedient in everything that the Lord tells them to do, because the believing believers are in relationship with the Lord. Then they will mature and move onto higher levels of authority. Then they will learn to heal every disease and sickness, and frequently they will demonstrate miracles, because Jesus calls His believing believers, who are His disciples, to Him (see Matt. 10:1).

You are Commanded to Heal the Sick and Tell Them the Kingdom of God is Near!

In Luke 10 we read,

> Heal the sick who are there and tell them, 'The kingdom of God is near you' (Luke 10:9).

This is a command, "heal the sick." You are not asked if you want to do it. The disciple is told to do it. You are also told to tell them "The kingdom of God is near you." That is also a command.

That is the essence of the *Surprisingly Supernatural Step #3: How to Ask for the Gifts of Healings and Miracles, as* you will tell them "The kingdom of God is near you!" Then you will heal them, and remind them "The kingdom of God came, that's why you got healed." Implicitly, you are telling them there is a King. So naturally you tell them who the King is: "It is King Jesus Christ! He was the one who healed you!" (see 1 Sam. 8:7; Luke 23:3; Rev. 19:16).

I ministered in Brasilia, Brasil at a supernatural school a few years ago, and when I came back to my host's home, a dance with the Spirit began when someone said, "Neil, you should pray for the boy, he has asthma." I looked over and saw the boy getting out of the car, and I also saw the maid, so I said, "Okay, bring the maid in too." They said, "Oh, she is not a believer." I got excited in my spirit and said, "Just bring her in, so she can see what Jesus does."

I put my hands on the boy's chest and rebuked the asthma and commanded the lungs to open up; and as I did that the boy's breathing got deeper and deeper. I asked him how he felt and he said, "better." I told him to "go do something that you could not do before, and then come back and tell us." He went away; when he came back, he said: "I am healed." When he said that, I suddenly felt sore muscles on the left side of my neck, and I recognized it was a word of knowledge. So I asked the maid "Is the left side of your neck sore?" She said it was. I asked her if we could pray for her, and she said, "Yes."

We laid our hands on her neck and commanded the pain to go, in Jesus' name. In less than five minutes we checked it out and she said her sore neck was healed. I then asked her, "Would you like to know how I knew about your sore neck?" She said, "Yes I would." Then I asked her, "Would you like to know who healed your sore neck?" She said, "Yes I would." I told her,

> The kingdom of God came and the King healed your sore neck. It was King Jesus Christ who healed you! Jesus told me about your sore neck, because He loves you and he wants you to know that He knows everything about you. That's why He got us to bring His kingdom to you today,

so you would be healed. Do you see how much He loves you? He not only told us about your pain, but Jesus healed you as well!

She nodded. Then I asked her, "Since Jesus loves you so much, would you like to ask Him into your life to be your Lord and Savior?" She said "Yes" and then she prayed and received Jesus, asked to be forgiven for her sins, and she received the Holy Spirit.

That's being a supernatural believing believer who releases the kingdom of God with healing, words of knowledge, and telling them who the king is—"It was King Jesus Christ!" Then you invite them to be saved. It's really fun to release the kingdom of God, and when you do that you will make an eternal difference in people's lives. Healing really is the good news of the gospel of Christ. Believing believers will learn to release healing and miracles everywhere they go.

More Keys to Accessing the Gifts of Healings and Miracles

Like I mentioned in the last chapter on prophecy, how badly do you want the gifts of the Spirit? People do not move in the gifts of the Spirit, because they do not go after it. In 1 Corinthians 12 it says,

> But eagerly desire the greater gifts (1 Cor. 12: 31).

And in 1 Corinthians 12:28 it says there are gifts of miracles and healings, and a little later in that chapter it calls for believing believers to eagerly desire the greater gifts (see 1 Cor. 12:31). Believing believers will pursue the greater gifts of miracles and healings. This is one of the keys to moving in the gifts of miracles and healings, and that is to build up your desire for the greater gifts.

Another key is to memorize the Scriptures on healing. I suggest that you can begin with the ones I have already mentioned like Mark 16:17-18, Matthew 10:1-2, and Luke 10:9, to mention only a few. Look in your Bible's concordance under "heal," "healing" and "miracles" and then look up those Scriptures and read them. Then try to memorize as many of the healing Scriptures as you can. It is good for you to read them out loud, that way you will get them into your soul and your spirit. *Then you will build up your faith to the point where you will begin to start speaking out the Scriptures as healing commands, and you will tell the sicknesses to leave the bodies of those who are sick, so they will receive their healing.*

On the book's website: www.surprisinglysupernatural.com is the *Surprisingly Supernatural Step #3: How to Ask For the Gifts of Healing and Miracles* card. This card uses the healing Scriptures to help believing believers to learn to ask for the healing gifts by personalizing the Scriptures that speak about healing. Use this Surprisingly Supernatural Card, as it will be helpful for you to get the healing Scriptures into your soul and spirit, so those gifts can later be expressed through you when you are in your relational networks. You can go to the website and download the Surprisingly Supernatural Cards for free.

Knowing your identity in Christ and then walking out your identity in Christ is another key for believing believers to learn to walk out, so they can demonstrate the gifts of healings and miracles. In my book: *Wake Up!* I cover the practices of Daniel and his friends, and the practices of the first disciples, and I share many other aspects of our identity in Christ.[47] The basic idea is that you need to know in your heart that our Father in heaven has blessed you in the heavenly realms with every spiritual blessing in Jesus Christ (see Eph. 1:3). You have every spiritual blessing, so nothing is withheld from the believing believer. If you believe it, you will get it!

The first step of releasing the gifts of the Spirit is to be continually filled with the Holy Spirit. John 15:5 tells you that if you abide in Jesus, you will be fruitful and that can mean that when you pray for healing, you will see the healing manifest as the fruit of abiding in Jesus. But if you do not abide in Him, then you can do nothing. Believing believers will recognize their need to be filled with the Spirit continuously in order to see the fruit of healings and miracles consistently manifest. When believing believers are continuously filled by the Spirit until they are overflowing with the Spirit, that's when they will be abiding in Jesus and He will be abiding in them (see John 15:5).[48]

In this chapter, I discussed earlier that a disciple can draw on the promises in Matthew 10:1 that states that disciples are given authority over all disease and sickness. Disciples will learn to obey whatever they hear God speak, and then when they hear the Word of the Lord, they will declare it! That's when the miracle will manifest.

Another key is to keep praying for the sick and do not give up. Francis MacNutt found that persistent prayer over longer periods of time brings greater levels of healing to the sick.[49] Take more time when you pray, and pray at different times, like each day or over several days or perhaps weekly. You will begin to see your authority grow, as you pursue the kingdom of God. Then you will see it released in your relational networks, as you demonstrate that Jesus really is the Eternal King.

The final key for a believing believer is to demonstrate the gifts of healings and miracles in your relational networks. Inevitably you will encounter nonbelievers in your relational networks that need healing. You can ask them if you can bring healing to them, and then you can lay your hands on them. Frequently, when you lay hands on nonbelievers you will see more healings and even greater miracles will happen than you will see when you pray for believers. When you administer healing to nonbelievers it allows the Lord to demonstrate His power and love for the person, so they can come to know Him through the sign of the healing miracles.

Nonbelievers Bring Out Miracles

Another dance with the Holy Spirit started at work when a client of mine told me her knee was hurt. I offered to pray for her, and after a couple of minutes her knee was healed. Then she said, "My shoulder has been bothering me." Again I prayed, and a few minutes later the shoulder was healed. It had bothered her for quite a while so she proclaimed, "It's a miracle!"

I was invited out to dinner and at the table was another couple who were *Buddhists*, as was my client. During the dinner conversation, I asked my client to tell her friends what happened when I prayed in Jesus' name. She said, "Neil prayed for my knee, in Jesus' name, and it was healed!" Then I said, "How about your shoulder?" And she said, "Oh yeah, my shoulder got prayer too, it was a miracle!" When a nonbeliever testifies to other nonbelievers it can be a powerful testimony time that plants seeds, which can be harvested later.

The Holy Spirit had me sit next to Guy on the flight from Seattle, Washington to Houston, Texas. Guy told me he was formerly a Catholic from Venezuela, but was now an agnostic. I testified to Guy that Jesus had been healing the sick through me over the last few years. He asked, "What kind of diseases have you seen healed?" When I finished the list, Guy asked, "How about ankles?" I said, "Sure, Jesus can heal ankles too." Guy explained he had sore ankles, and asked me if I could pray for them.

Guy crossed his leg, so I could lay my hands on the ankle closest to me, and I prayed, "Lord, although I am only touching one ankle, I ask that you would heal them both at the same time." After a few minutes he tested them and they were both healed. So after he was healed I asked him if he could feel the anointing that flowed out of my fingers. He felt it, but when I pulled away He told me, "The sensation is diminishing." The Holy Spirit left, as it did not want to stay with Guy. Then I told Guy what Jesus said in John 14,

> And I will ask the Father, and He will give you another Counselor to be with you forever—the Spirit of truth. The world cannot accept Him, because it neither sees Him nor knows Him. But you know Him, for He lives with you and will be in you (John 14:16-17).

I explained to Guy that although he had felt the Holy Spirit, it did not want to stay with him, because he was still part of the world. He had never given his heart to Jesus, and he had not invited Jesus to come into his life. I said, "Jesus just healed your ankles, so I would suggest you pray to receive Him now." Guy agreed and prayed.

I tested him afterwards and he felt the anointing again, but this time when I pulled away Guy said, "I think it's there." I questioned him again, and again he said, "I think it's there." I then assured him it was there. He was now born again and was brought into God's family. Bringing healing to nonbelievers and then bringing them to Jesus is what believing believers are to do.

If you practice the keys I suggested on the pages from **73 to 80,** then you will begin to receive the gifts of healing and miracles.

Healing People Brings Other People to Jesus

Jesus is the One who you are to model yourself after, so what does the Scripture say about our Lord in Matthew 4?

> Jesus went through Galilee teaching in their synagogues, preaching the good news of the kingdom, and healing every disease and sickness among the people. News about Him spread all over…and people were brought to Him… and He healed them (Matt. 4:23-24).

This Scripture is one of the theme Scriptures for believing believers, for it says that when people were healed, news about Jesus spread all over, and other people were brought to Him. That's what believing believers are to do. People who are ill with various diseases will come to the believing believers, and Jesus will heal them through you. Then news will spread all over, and other people will be brought to Jesus, first to be healed, and then to be saved.

When Jesus heals people through you, the good news about Jesus Christ will spread all over, and then more people will be brought to Jesus to be healed, and then to be saved. Healing works the same today as it did in Jesus' day. The miracles and healing gifts are great tools for believing believers to use; healing gifts make it very easy to bring people into a relationship with Jesus, once they are healed. That's why the gospel means "The Good News." When the gospel of the kingdom is preached with healing, Jesus does what medical doctors and drugs cannot do—Jesus heals all disease and sicknesses.

Matthew 4:23-24 also says that all the people who were demon-possessed were healed by Jesus. The result was that more people were brought to Jesus. This is what I mentioned earlier in this chapter, there are evil spirits out there and they are trying to steal, kill, and destroy people's lives and especially since the medical model does not believe in *spirits of infirmity*. These demons have a field day as they cannot be stopped by medicine.

Believing believers will begin to realize the extent of evil spirits that bring disease, and then they will begin to destroy the devil's works and as a result, more people will be brought to Jesus. And Jesus will heal them all. When people were healed, other people were brought to Jesus first to be healed, and then they were saved, as they will receive Him as their Lord and Savior. That is what believing believers will learn to do with *Surprisingly Supernatural Step #3: How to Ask for the Gifts of Healings and Miracles*, as this step will allow other people to hear that Jesus heals the sick through you. When the people with sicknesses are brought to you, you will heal them, and then you will bring them to Jesus to be saved. Paul echoes this idea,

> I will not venture to speak of anything except what Christ has accomplished through me in leading the Gentiles to obey God by what I have said and done—by the power of signs and miracles, through the power of the Spirit…I have fully preached the gospel of Christ (Rom. 15:19).

As a believing believer, you need to fully preach the gospel of Christ, and you will do that with the power of signs and wonders, and with miracles and prophetic words. That was what Paul said he was doing when he said, "leading the Gentiles to obey God by what I have said." Paul "said" prophetic words that revealed God's heart to people and God's knowledge. Paul's prophetic words also revealed what was in other peoples' hearts (see 1 Sam 9:19). And Paul also taught the Scriptures.

Paul also administered the power gifts and brought miraculous healing to people. Paul implies that his goal was to lead the Gentiles to Christ with prophetic words, miraculous healings, and anything else that helped him to fully preach the gospel of Christ. If Paul's goal was to fully preach the gospel, then that should be your goal too. Paul's desire is the same as the believing believers' desire, for we all want to be like our older brother Jesus Christ and be empowered to destroy the works of the devil.

Faith, Thirst, Hunger, and Childlikeness

The currencies of heaven are faith, thirst, hunger, and childlikeness. You have a greater chance of accessing the kingdom of God if you have faith, thirst, hunger, and childlikeness. The greatest healing evangelists accessed the kingdom when they read the New Testament in faith and believed it. Then miracles began to happen around them.

They locked onto Mark 16:18 and believed that if they placed their hands on sick people, then the sick will get well. They also believed 1 Peter 2 that states by Jesus' wounds you have been healed (see 1 Peter 2:24b). They believed that all sicknesses were to be left at the foot of the cross. If they found any sickness, they knew they just needed to put it back on the cross, as Jesus took all the sicknesses by His stripes. They also believed Matthew 10 where Jesus gave His disciples,

> ...authority to drive out evil spirits and to heal every disease and sickness (Matt. 10:1).

The healing evangelists read the gospels and believed they were called to do what Jesus had done. They developed faith. Faith occurs when you hear the *rhema* word of God, which means the now word of God, that is breathed into your spirit in the moment you need it. When you take in the *rhema* word and act appropriately on it in obedience, then the healing will happen. This is explained in Romans 10:17 and Hebrews 11:6 which says,

> ...without faith it is impossible to please God...
> (Heb. 11:6).

Believing believers will do what the great healing evangelists did; they will take the Scriptural promises and read them out loud, and then they will repeatedly hear the Word of God until it drops from their heads into their spirits. This is like you did earlier in this chapter when you chanted the round: "Do believers lay hands on the sick and the sick get well?" And the response was, "Yes, believers lay hands on the sick and the sick get well!" When these verses are repeated out loud, it will help to get the Word and the faith into your soul and spirit. Then it will bubble up in faith when you begin to lay hands on the sick, and then the sick will get healed! Hearing the Scripture and believing it builds faith, and faith will give you access to the Lord's healing power.

Hunger and thirst comes when you see the need for the kingdom of God to be released in your relational networks, because you see all the sick people who have no hope outside of Jesus. Then you will recall what the Scripture calls the believing believer to do; it declares you are to bring healing to them. That's when hunger and thirst builds up inside of the believing believer. Then healings will start to flow. The believing believer will begin to notice all the healings that are needed that only Jesus can heal. Then you will begin to develop a hunger and thirst for the healing gifts, so Jesus' healing power can be released through you, so all the sick will receive their healing.

Childlikeness occurs when the believing believer realizes that she cannot do the healing, as she does not have the power to heal. It is only Jesus who has the power, so the believing believer gives Jesus permission to use her body to flow His healing power through her. And the believing believer obediently follows the directions of the Lord, as to when the healing is to be released and to whom. Childlikeness is having faith and trust in the Lord, and it is also realizing that you do not have the power to heal. So your heart waits humbly for the Lord's directions. Childlikeness is trusting that the Lord will move through you with His healing power, as you know that you are dependent on Him to do it, as you do not have that power.

Jesus Never Prayed For the Sick

Jesus never prayed for the sick. Here are seven examples of Scriptures for you to read that will help you see how Jesus ministered to the sick.

> 'But that you may know that the Son of Man has authority on earth to forgive sins...' He said to the paralytic, 'I tell you, get up, take up your mat and go home' (Mark 2:10-11).

> ...Jesus put His finger into the man's ears. Then He spit and touched the man's tongue. He looked up to heaven and with a deep sigh, said to him 'Ephphatha!' (that word means 'Be opened!). At this, the man's ears were opened, his tongue was loosened and he began to speak plainly (Mark 7:33-35).

He rebuked the evil spirit. 'You deaf and dumb spirit' He said, 'I command you, come out of him and never enter him again' (Mark 9:25).

Jesus reached out His hand and touched the man, 'I am willing' He said, 'Be clean!' Immediately He was cured of leprosy (Matthew 8:3).

...He rebuked the winds and waves, and it was completely calm (Matthew 8:26).

Jesus had compassion on them and touched their eyes. Immediately they received their sight and followed Him (Matthew 20:34).

When Jesus saw her, He called her forward and said to her, 'Woman, you are free from your infirmity,' He put His hands on her, and immediately she straightened up and praised God (Luke 13:12-13).

Jesus never healed the sick by praying to the Father. But He did do three key steps:

First Step: Jesus Asked the Father in Heaven What He Should Do

Jesus asked the Father what He should do,

> I tell you the truth, the Son can do nothing by Himself; He can only do what He sees His Father doing, because whatever the Father does the Son also does. For the Father loves the Son and shows Him all that He does (John 5:19-20).

Jesus may have talked with the Father the night before on the mountain top, or just before He met the person that He was going to heal. He heard from the Father in the unique way the Father wanted to bring the healing to the sick person. That's why Jesus says one time: "pick up your mat and go home;" another time, "He spit and touched the man's tongue;" and another time, "Jesus reached out his hand and touched the man" (Mark 2:11; 7:33; Matt. 8:3). Jesus never healed the same way, but He always healed the right way. And He was always at the right time; because Jesus first listened to the Father tell Him what He was to do.

The Second Step: Jesus Stepped into Faith and Was Surrounded by the Power of God

Jesus stepped into the faith and the authority He was given over all disease and sickness, and over all demonic oppression.

> The Spirit of the Lord is on Me, because He has anointed Me to preach good news to the poor. He has sent Me to proclaim freedom for the prisoners and recovery of sight for the blind, to release the oppressed, to proclaim the year of the Lord's favor...Today this Scripture is fulfilled in your hearing (Luke 4:18-19, 21b).

With the Spirit upon Him, Jesus knew that God was with Him. Jesus did not have to actually step into faith, as much as He did in that moment when He had just finished being tempted by the devil in the desert. Having stepped into faith, Jesus then returned in the power of the Spirit (see Luke 4:14). Then Jesus stepped into faith each and every day by walking in the surrounding power of the Holy Spirit. You will see that this story witnesses to the surrounding power of the Holy Spirit that Jesus walked in.

> 'If I just touch His clothes, I will be healed.' Immediately her bleeding stopped and she felt in her body that she was freed from her suffering. At once Jesus realized that power had gone out from Him. He turned around in the crowd and asked, 'Who touched My clothes?' (Mark 5:28b-31).

The second step that Jesus took was stepping into faith because He walked in the presence of God; He knew He could release it wherever He went. And sometimes, Jesus was not in control over when it was released. It just happened.

SURPRISINGLY SUPERNATURAL

The Third Step: Jesus Acted Verbally and Physically Against the Sickness

Jesus acted directly against the sickness. He spoke directly to the ailment and commanded the sickness to go:

- Jesus might say, "...You deaf and mute spirit" he said, "I command you to come out of him and never enter him again!" (Mark 9:25b).
- Jesus might say, "You spirit of infirmity, get out now!"
- Jesus might say, "Be clean" (Matt. 8:3b).

Jesus first asked the Father, and then He stepped into faith, and finally He acted against the sickness by issuing commands with words and actions. You would be *wise* to follow Jesus' ways.

Do Not Pray to the Father or to Jesus to Heal the Sick!

The only Scripture where it appears that a disciple prays before healing is found in Acts 9 which says,

> Peter sent them all out of the room; then he got down on his knees and prayed (Acts 9:40).

Many people pray to the Father in heaven or to Jesus to heal the person, but neither Jesus nor His disciples prayed to the Father asking Him to heal. Peter was not doing that here.

Peter sent the unwanted people out of the room, so he could hear from the Father, just like Jesus did. Peter got on his knees and asked the Father something like: "What do want me to do now?" Peter apparently had heard correctly, because when he got up he said,

> Tabitha, get up! (Acts 9:40c).

And Tabitha opened her eyes and rose from the dead.

Peter took the disciple's three-step approach: he asked the Father what He wanted to do, then he stepped into the faith and the authority he was given, and then he acted in faith and spoke out the command: "Tabitha, get up," and the miracle happened, Tabitha rose from the dead. Believing believers are to copy what Jesus and the first disciples did. You are not to pray to the Father or to Jesus for them to heal the sick person. Instead, you will take disciple's three-step approach and command the healing to come.

The Disciple's First Step

Jesus' disciples have the same mandate that Jesus had. You are to first hear from the Father about what you are to do. That's why you need the gift of prophecy, and you need to be a son or a daughter or a servant who belongs to God. Then you will hear what God says. Once you hear what the Father tells you to do for the person's healing, then you can go on to the second step. But you not only need to hear, you need to listen to what the Father tells you as well. You need to develop the habit of asking for revelation and waiting in faith and listening for the answer.

The Disciple's Second Step

The second step is to step into the faith where the Scripture tells you about your identity in Christ, as a believing believer, and tells you about the authority and power you have been given through Jesus Christ. You literally step into Jesus Christ, when you are continually filled by the Spirit to the point of overflowing, and then you will believe what Jesus said, in Matthew 10,

> He called His twelve disciples to Him and gave them authority to drive out evil spirits and to heal every disease and sickness (Matt. 10:1).

As a believing believer you will claim this Scripture by faith and believe that Jesus has already given you the authority over evil spirits, and the authority and power to heal every disease and sickness, because He is with you.

You can also claim by faith the Scripture in John 15 and say, "Lord, if I remain in You, and You remain in me, there will be much fruit, without You I can do nothing" (see John 15:5). Then you can say, "Lord, you promised there will be much fruit; therefore, since I am Your disciple who has the Spirit of God in me and upon me; I will be fruitful. So I receive your promises by faith. I receive Your authority to drive out evil spirits and to heal every disease and sickness" (see Matt. 10:1).

Jesus assured you that He would be with you always to the very end of the age (see Matt. 28:20). Since believing believers regularly practice being continually filled by the Spirit, you know that Jesus is actually literally with you every day. Therefore, with that understanding, you will have faith that the Scripture from John 15:5 will apply to you, as your life will bear much fruit! You can also combine that Scripture with your faith concerning this next Scripture that speaks about how Jesus ministered,

> …and He drove out the spirits with a word and healed all the sick (Matt. 8:16b).

Then you can declare in faith: "Thank you Lord Jesus, since you are with me always, my words will also drive out evil spirits and heal all the sick. So Lord, in faith, I declare the words I speak will be Your words, and they will bring healing to the sick and will drive out demons."

Faith is a big component of stepping into these promises for healing, but an even bigger component is to be filled by the Holy Spirit continually. You can say "Thank You Jesus for always being with me" but if you do not take the time to be continually filled by the Spirit; your words might only be words. But if you are continually filled, then you will be walking in the presence of God every day of your life, just like Jesus did; and you will be remaining in Him, and He will be remaining in you; that's what will give life to your faith. You will know that you are empowered by God, and you will be fruitful, for Jesus will be with you. The words you declare will bring about the healing that is required.

The Disciple's Third Step

Then the third step is to put your faith into action with what you say and do. For example, you could say,

- "I command all back pain to go now, in Jesus' name."
- "Spirit of infirmity, I command you, in Jesus' name, to get out of him now. Leave and never come back."
- "Spirit of deafness, leave her now, in Jesus' name."
- "Be healed!" And then you extend your hand to help her up, and when she stands, her legs straighten and strengthen.

Additional Practices That Help to Bring Healing

Laying your hands on the sick person increases the effectiveness of the healing, as the Holy Spirit can flow through your hands and into the sick person to drive out the disease and heal them. You may take communion as an act of faith and acknowledge that healing is in the blood of Jesus. You can personally claim, "By Jesus' wounds, I have been healed," which is adapted from 1 Peter 2:24.

When communion is taken, believing believers can paraphrase the Scripture from John 6 and declare, "Jesus you said…unless I eat the flesh of the Son of Man and drink His blood; I will have no life in me. Lord, I want to have Your life in me, so I choose to eat Your flesh and drink Your blood which are represented by these communion elements, so I can receive Your life. I receive Your life into my body for healing" (see John 6:53). Faith in what Jesus did, which is represented by the communion elements can bring healing to the believer's body.

As a believing believer, you will hear what the Father says about the sick person's problem. Then you will need to step into faith, and into the Scriptural promises that the disciples have on healing. And then you will speak and take actions in faith, so you will bring healing to the sick. When you practice praying for the sick your faith will increase, as God will use you to bring healing to more and more people, because you will be walking out in faith and in obedience, as you practice bringing healing to the sick.

One healing clue I use is that if I have prayed for someone three times to be healed, and there is no change at all, I am pretty sure an evil spirit needs to be cast out.

Healing Issues Concerning Believers

I suggest that you may want to practice the laying on of hands for healing with your friends who are believers, family members, and yourself first; until you gain your confidence and build up your faith. That is until you realize that God's power regularly flows through you to heal the sick. Consequently, because you may work with believers, I am going to briefly mention some of the barriers to healing that believers may have.

My experience has shown me that believers often need to confess their sins and iniquities, especially if that was the reason for the illness to attack them, before they can be healed. Nonbelievers are not under the same criteria, as they often get healed right away. But it seems like the Father wants His children to be, His children. The Heavenly Father wants His children to know how sin and iniquities opens up the door, so sicknesses can enter and assail them. It would be prudent and obedient for them to stop sinning, and to be free from their ancestor's iniquities, so they could receive their healing.

Barriers to Healing:

Jesus clearly showed He was willing to heal the sick (see Matt. 8:3). And Jesus apparently at times healed all the sick that were brought to Him (see Matt. 8:3; 8:16; Luke 6:18-19). However, it is unlikely that believing believers will always see the people they lay their hands on healed. Believing believers first of all need to develop faith. They also need to operate in the keys to healing miracles that were mentioned earlier in this chapter from page **73-83**.

I have found that more people get healed now, than not; but before only a few would get healed. That's because I lacked the faith, and I did not understand the kingdom keys that would allow me to regularly see healing miracles manifest. When you build up your faith, and you understand the healing keys, and you apply them, then healing miracles will occur more consistently.

When a person does not get healed I am not disturbed, because I know the enemy wants to hinder all healings. So I just need to find the key for the person's healing. Henry W. Wright wrote the book: *A More Excellent Way*, and in it he compiled the spiritual roots of disease.[50] Wright has outlined a number of healing keys in his book; consequently, Wright's book is an excellent resource to have in your healing library.

When the healing key is found, the healing comes. Sometimes the key is that the person has to want to be healed. If their identity is wrapped up in their illness, then they are not likely to receive their healing. The person may need to have faith that the Lord can heal her, and she needs to believe that she would be better off without the sickness.

Believing believers are called to lay hands on the sick, but it is God's power that heals. Believing believers need to lay hands in faith, but also in humility, as they know they need the healing key before they can break off the sickness from the person. Those keys only come from the Lord, so the believing believer needs to ask for the healing revelation from the Lord, and then he needs to listen for it, receive it, and then apply it. Sometimes the barrier to the healing is due to sin.

Un-confessed Sins

Sins are often doorways for sickness and disease to enter into a person's body. The Scripture does say,

> Is anyone of you sick?…Confess your sins to each other
> and pray for each other so that you may be healed
> (James 5:14-16).

Sins such as: unforgiveness, fear, sexual immorality, occult practices, witchcraft, excessive anger, judgments, lack of faith, unbelief and other sins are often responsible for the sicknesses that take hold of people. Other barriers are generational sins (iniquities), as they bring sicknesses into the believer's life from familial spirits. These spirits of infirmity can carry generational illnesses into the believer's body. All these sins need to be confessed to the Lord, and forgiveness needs to be received, before the healing usually comes.

Clean Out the Evil Spirits or Change Locations So You Can Heal the Sick

However, when you pray for nonbelievers the barriers to healing often do not impede the healing power. It appears that Jesus just wants to give them a sign that the kingdom of God is near. So Jesus just heals the nonbeliever. But sometimes you will pray for nonbelievers (or believers) when the atmosphere has too many demonic spirits present. Those evil spirits can impede the power for the healing. Jesus may have encountered something like that here in Mark 6,

> …And they took offense at him. Jesus said to them, 'Only in his hometown, among his relatives and in his own house is a prophet without honor.' He could not do any miracles there, except lay his hands on a few sick people and heal them. And he was amazed at their lack of faith (Mark 6:3c-6).

I believe the offensive attitudes and their lack of faith directed toward Jesus opened the door for demonic spirits to come into the area. Then those demonic spirits managed to inhibit the flow of the kingdom of God into that area. That's why it says, "He could not do any miracles there" (Mark 6:5).

When you want to bring healing to people, sometimes you will need to drive the evil spirits out of the area first, before the healing can come. Worship is one way to clear the area of evil spirits. Another choice is to move the sick person to another location, where you can minister healing to him with fewer demonic spirits present.

The Key is to Ask the Holy Spirit

The key is to ask the Holy Spirit what you are to do. Do what He says. If you do not get the key from the Holy Spirit for the healing barrier or from the interview with the sick person, you may still pray, but if healing does not come, you will need to get the key. So bless the person and tell her to ask God to reveal the missing keys for her healing, and then invite her to come back again to receive healing prayer another time.

Believing believers are disciples who are given authority to lay hands on the sick and see healings and miracles manifest. So all believing believers just need to be continually filled with the Holy Spirit, listen to the Father, and have the faith to know that you have been given the authority to heal the sick. Then just go out and ask people "Would you like to be healed?" Then lay your hands on them and heal them.

Bringing healing to people is fun, and it really represents the good news of the gospel of Jesus Christ. When you pray for people and they are healed, ask them, "How long have you had the sickness and the pain in your body?" You will be astounded at the length of time people have carried their pain and diseases in their bodies. Especially since it only took five minutes for the believing believer to release the gifts of the Spirit, so the healing could manifest and the sickness could leave. This should put a fire in your spirit once you find out how long people have had their sickness and pain. Frequently, they report they have had their sickness for years.

Believing believers will discover that Jesus' power can work through you to heal all those people who are under the devil's power in minutes. You need to get going as a believing believer and heal all the hurting people who live around you every day, so you can bring glory to the Lord Jesus, and at the same time destroy the works of the devil.

Activations to Practice Healing the Sick

Get a few believers together and ask if anyone has any pain or sickness in their body.

Take the Disciples Three Steps:

1. Ask the Father what He wants you to do and how He wants to bring healing to the people who are sick.

a. You may receive revelation about the sickness and its root cause. If the person is a believer, and the root cause was sin, you will need to lead her in a prayer to repent for her own sins and her generational sins.

2. Step into faith in Jesus by asking for the Holy Spirit to come, and asking the Lord to send His *Healing Angels* to help with the healing task. And remember the Scriptural promises that believing believers can draw on in faith, so you can bring the Lord's healing power to the sick.

3. Then lay your hands on the person and issue commands with words and actions that will bring healing to the sick person.

After you bring healing to the sick share your testimonies with the people in your larger group, or with anyone else who will be blessed from hearing the testimony. Tell them how good the Lord Jesus was to have poured His healing power through you to heal the sick. Then share the highlights from the healing you participated in.

The *Surprisingly Supernatural Step #3: How to Ask For the Gifts of Healing and Miracles* card is on the book's website. Download the card for free and use this Surprisingly Supernatural Card to get the Scriptures for healings and miracles into your soul and spirit, so those gifts can be expressed through you when you are in your relational networks. Use the Surprisingly Supernatural Card regularly until you see the gifts of healings and miracles manifest in your life.

Chapter 4: Discussion Questions

1. Jesus went around destroying the devil's works (1 John 3:8). And the devil comes to steal, kill, destroy, murder, and lie. These are some of the clues that will help believers to know what they are called to destroy.
   a. How have you been aware of the evil spirits that are in, on or around people that are stealing, killing and destroying their lives?

2. Medical Science gives drugs for disease or does surgery, but cures are few and far between, as they are in it for the profit. The devil is out destroying people's health; but because few people think the devil is real, they just ignore the evidence that he might be involved in the sickness.
   a. What can you do to help destroy the devil's work in relation to healing needs?
   b. What do you need to do to begin to discern if an evil spirit is causing problems?

3. Memorize the Scriptures on healing and get them into your spirit so you can begin to walk out and lay your hands on the sick and see them recover (see Mark 16:17-18).
   a. Look in the New Testament and find five healing Scriptures that you will begin to memorize.

4. For the believer's level of healing it means that all believers, as long as they have some level of faith, are able to lay hands on people and see the sick healed, in Jesus' name. The second level of healing is the disciple's level as disciples are given authority over all sickness and disease (see Mark 16:17-18; Matt. 10:1-2).
   a. If you are a believer, you are called to heal the sick; what is hindering you from doing that?
   b. If you are a disciple you will operate in miracles; what is required for you to become a disciple?

5. Believing believers will bring healing to people who do not know Jesus' love and power, but they will demonstrate it by healing them and then bringing them to receive Jesus Christ as their Lord and Savior.

a. Keep your eyes open for the people you can bring this dynamic witnessing opportunity to.

6. Disciples are to take the same three steps Jesus did to minister in healing. They are to ask the Father what He wants to do, they are to step into faith knowing that Jesus has empowered them and is with them, and then they are to command the sickness to go.
    a. What do you have to do to acquire these three steps?
    b. Try to find people in your church or home group who you can practice on.

CHAPTER 5

SURPRISINGLY SUPERNATURAL STEP #4A ASKING FOR THE GIFT OF DISCERNMENT

This chapter on "Asking for the Gift of Discernment" precedes the next chapter on binding evil spirits and driving out demons, as the gift of discerning of spirits helps the believing believer to identify evil spirits when they are present, which you must know first, before you can cast them out. Therefore, you need to have the gift of discernment operating to be able to detect demons. I have already mentioned in the last chapter how I have discerned some evil spirits; so in this chapter, I will explain a few more details about how you can begin to receive the gift of discerning of spirits, and how you can practice it.

Due to the lies of the devil many people are either unaware of evil spirits or they would prefer just to ignore them. *However, being unaware or ignoring the reality of the demonic spirits leaves those people in jeopardy, as the demons can assail them with sickness, sin, and deception.* I believe this is a very important time for believing believers to recognize that evil spirits are intent on acting against believers in an attempt to hold them back from their birthrights. Therefore, it is crucial for believing believers to begin to discern evil spirits and educate the people in your relational networks about demons, and their negative impact on the world in which you live.

Discern or discernment is translated by the King James Version (KJV) from the Greek word *diakrisis*. I think the meaning of "discern" closely describes what we do when we try to determine if an evil spirit is in, on, or around someone else, or if there is an ungodly defilement present. Discern means: "to see or notice something unclear, to understand something not immediately obvious, and to distinguish that is to tell between two or more things."[51] When we try to discern evil spirits they are usually not obvious, because they are deceptive. They try to hide and make it unclear as to where they are, so they can avoid being detected. That's why we need to have the gift of discernment developed.

The definition of discernment appears to describe some of the process we use when we try to uncover the demons that live around us or the defilement they leave behind. The NIV translated *diakrisis* with "distinguish," which means: "to differentiate, tell apart, or tell between."[52] I do not think the definition of "distinguish" describes the process of detecting evil spirits, as well as the definition of "discern" does. Consequently, I will use the terms "discern" "discerning" and "discernment" when describing this spiritual gift.

Ask For the Gift of Discerning of Spirits to Identify Demons

Paul makes this statement in 1 Corinthians 12, just before he discusses the gifts of the Spirit, which includes the gift of discerning of spirits,

> Now about spiritual gifts, brothers, I do not want you to be ignorant. You know that when you were pagans, somehow or other you were influenced and led astray to mute idols (1 Cor. 12:1-2).

If being led astray by mute idols was a problem in those days, then in our day, with the people in our culture, they are also susceptible to the same problem. Revelation 9 tells us that nonbelievers in the end of the end-times did not stop their worship of demons. Behind their idols are the demons that they worship (see Rev. 9:20b). It appears that Paul is implying that the spiritual gifts listed in 1 Corinthians 12:7-11 and 27-31 are to help equip believing believers, so they can avoid being ignorant of idols, demons, and demonic structures that are in the world around us. Therefore, you need to have all the gifts mentioned in 1 Corinthians 12 to battle against these demonic forces.

That's what believing believers will do, for they will release all the gifts of the Spirit in their relational networks to battle against those demonic forces and demonstrate that Jesus Christ is the Most High God. Therefore, on the palette of gifts that believing believers will use is the particularly useful gift of discernment.

> Now there are diversities of gifts, but the same Spirit…to another discerning of spirits… (1 Cor. 12:4, 10; KJV).

The gift of discerning of spirits (discernment) is also used to test the spirits, which 1 John 4 encourages you to do (see 1 John 4:1). Therefore, all believing believers will desire the gift of discerning of spirits and ask the Father for it, as it is one of the greater gifts that you are told to desire (see 1 Cor. 12:31). I suggest for you to pray the prayer in the activation section at the end of this chapter (page **97**), and ask the Father for the gift of discernment.

Lust to Discern With Your Five Physical Senses

The only thing believers are allowed to lust after is all the gifts of the spirit. But right now I encourage you to lust after the gift of discernment. One thing that I noticed was once I had begun to soak in the presence of the Lord for extended periods of time, the discernment gifts just started to operate in me. First, I began to smell an evil spirit that came to attack me. Then as I continued to minister, another discernment sense came to me, and then another sense came to me, until I had discerned with all five of my physical senses. Some people think that using our physical senses is New Age or is an occult practice, but they do not understand the implications of the language associated with the phrase "to distinguish good from evil." This phrase is found in both the Old Testament and the New Testament, and in Hebrews 5 it says,

> But strong meat belongeth to them that are of full age, even those who by reason of use have their senses exercised to *discern* both good from evil (Heb. 5:14; KJV; emphasis added).

The English word "discern" is translated from the Greek word: *diakrisis* by the KJV. *Diakrisis* means: "to discriminate, discern, doubt, judge, etc…"[53] You have all been trained to discriminate or discern your world ever since you were a young child. Perhaps you did not like the *taste* of beets, but you liked the *feel* of your blanket; you disliked it when you *heard* someone scream at you or when you *smelled* someone smoking a cigar; but you enjoyed *seeing* someone smile at you. Without anyone else telling you what you were to like, you learned to have your own unique interpretations of the stimulus that was brought to your five physical senses that you either accepted or rejected. This training to discriminate and discern is helpful to see why the Old Testament expresses the concept of discernment in the Hebrew language with the word "*Bene.*"

Besides Hebrews 5:14 describing the task of distinguishing good from evil, it is also found in 1 Kings 3:9 where Solomon prays,

> Give therefore thy servant an understanding heart to judge thy people, that I may discern between good and bad [evil] … (1 Kings 3:9; KJV).

The English word "discern" in the previous Scripture is translated from the Hebrew word: *Bene.*

Bene means: "feel, perceive, view," and it also means "to separate mentally or distinguish, understand: - attend, consider, discern, etc…"[54]

Bene is also the Hebrew word that is translated with the English word "discern" in Job 6:30,

> Is there iniquity in my tongue? Cannot my taste discern perverse things? (Job 6:30; KJV).

Bene's definition ties into what Solomon did when he discerned between "good and bad [evil]," and what Job did when he discerned perverse things or malice, which are types of evil that he discerned with his sense of taste.

Both Solomon and Job appear to imply that they used their physical senses when they discerned. *They used physical senses such as: feeling, seeing, hearing, smelling or tasting to discern.* The Scripture is showing you that the five physical senses are used to discern good from evil.[55] Some scholars believe that the most accurate way to translate "discern" for Hebrews 5:14, 1 King 3:9, and Job 6:30 is to discern good from evil by using the five physical senses.[56]

That's what happened with me. The Holy Spirit taught me to discern evil spirits, evil structures, and evil defilement through my five physical senses. Here are some examples of how the Holy Spirit has taught me to experience the gift of discernment, so I could discern evil spirits and evil defilement. I have also discerned Godly powers with my five physical senses, but for this chapter I will focus on discerning evil spirits and evil defilements, so we can take our stand against the devil's schemes (see Eph. 6:11b).

Discerning Evil Spirits: By Smell

The first time I discerned was when I became aware that an evil spirit was trying to attack me, the Lord opened up my nose to smell its foul smell, so I could awaken to my authority in Christ and tell it to leave.

On a side note, the NIV translates the Greek word "*akarthotos*" with "evil spirit" (Mark 1:23). But the meaning of "*akarthotos*" is "impure, morally lewd, specifically demonic, *foul or unclean.*"[57] Demons often smell foul or unclean. This past year when I was doing altar ministry at my church, I was praying for a woman, and I called out "I command! All ungodly spirits must leave now!" Coincidentally, I was toward the end of a long fast, and I immediately smelled a foul smell waft past my nose, as a demon left this woman (see Mark 9:29). Believing believers can discern evil and evil spirits with the sense of smell.

Discerning Evil Spirits: By Feel

I have already described in Chapter 4 how I discerned an evil spirit on a fellow's back by feeling it with my hand. I also mentioned in my book *Wake Up!* how I was led to discern evil spirits that were on the backs of people by placing my hand behind them and then feeling the ungodly spirit by discerning it in my throat as a cough or a tickle.

I said this manifestation of demons on people's backs correlated to Rick Joyner's vision in his book: *The Final Quest.* Joyner's book described an upcoming *move of God* that is going to occur, but evil spirits want to try to stop it by riding on Christians' backs.[58] I think we are very quickly approaching that *move of God,* and that's why believing believers need to develop their discernment gifts today!

I know of other believers who have felt an upset stomach when they discerned evil, other believers have felt coolness on their hands, and others have felt a buzz on their heads. The Lord will give you your own unique signal to feel when you discern, if you ask Him for the gift of discernment. I have also felt witchcraft as a pressure on my temple. I have also written in Chapter 3 how I felt the ungodly power that was in front and behind an elderly lady. I have held an ungodly piece of jewelry depicting the third eye from Hinduism, which I discerned by feeling the ungodly defilement it had on it. I have touched books and statues, and I felt ungodly defilement on them by feeling the defilement as a cough or a tickle in my throat. Believing believers can discern ungodly defilement and evil spirits with the sense of feeling.

Discerning Evil Spirits: By Sight

I have seen evil spirits when the Lord has opened my spiritual eyes. I saw an evil spirit looking out of the eyes of the person who sat across from me at lunch. The evil spirit had red irises and vertical black pupils; they were shaped like the eyes of a snake. I saw a demon that looked like a small grey cloud in my hotel room at the top of the wall near the ceiling. I saw another demon next to my bed with green almost florescent skin and red eyes. Sometimes, I can discern visually without actually seeing. For example, I have sensed that some people have veils over their eyes due to praying to idols. I have seen other things on people without really seeing them. I just get an impression. Believing believers can discern evil and evil spirits with the sense of sight.

Discerning Evil Spirits: By Taste

In 2008, I was ministering to a man and I began to taste nicotine in my mouth and I asked him "Do you smoke or did you?" He said, "Yes, and that's why I have throat cancer." Job speaks about how he discerned by tasting iniquity and perverse things in his mouth (see Job 6:30). After I realized that Job did this, I wanted to explore this idea of tasting ungodly words in my mouth. I will try to explore if I can taste in my mouth another person's malice towards me. Believing believers can discern evil and evil spirits with the sense of taste.

Discerning Evil Spirits: By Hearing

In Chapter 6, you will read how the Lord told me that the person I was talking with had an evil spirit in her stomach, which was subsequently stirred up by the Holy Spirit. In the same chapter, you will read how the Lord gave me the names of the specific spirits that were in the guys next to me on an airplane. Consequently, the gift of prophecy is one of the keys to discerning of spirits, as you can hear from the Lord directly the names of the evil spirits that are in people.

Although the Lord has told me the names of the evil spirits that are in people or when an evil spirit is present, I have not heard an evil spirit, at least to my knowledge, like Philip did when he heard the shrieks of evil spirits, as they came out of people (see Acts 8:7). Some deliverance ministers have heard demons speak through people. I have not heard that yet. But I expect that I will hear demons shriek or talk sometime in the future, as all believing believers can discern evil and evil spirits with the sense of hearing.

Believing Believers Need a Mentor to Train With and They Need to Train Themselves

In Hebrews 5:14 it says,

> …by constant use have trained themselves to distinguish good from evil (Heb. 5:14; NIV).

I have practiced using the gift of discernment by finding something that is defiled. Then I try to feel the defilement, so I could train myself to discern good from evil. To learn to discern, I suggest you get a mentor that you trust who can accurately discern evil. I run training classes and teach discernment classes where I get people to feel an evil spirit or an ungodly spiritual line (a leyline) or a defiled object like a piece of jewelry. Here are some suggestions on how you can begin to practice to discern something with the sense of feeling.

Activation: Practicing to Learn to Discern Good from Evil

1. Pray and ask the Father in heaven for the gift of discernment, so you will be enabled to discern between good and evil (see 1 Cor. 12:10; Heb. 5:14).

Pray this Prayer Out Loud and in Faith:

I thank you Heavenly Father that You give good gifts to Your children who ask for them. Heavenly Father, I now ask You for the good gift of discernment. I want to be able to know when evil spirits are in me, on me, or around me; or when other people have evil spirits in them, on them, or around them; so I can either bind those evil spirits or cast them out. I want to wake up and take my stand against the devil's schemes; so please give me the gift of discernment so I will be able to discern evil spirits. In faith, I choose to receive the gift of discernment from You now Father, thank you.

After you have prayed this prayer, give praise and worship to the Father for giving you that good gift of discernment. Then try to sense what the Father will be showing you. It may come through your physical senses or from a word of knowledge or in a dream, so pay attention to the clues that you will now start to receive.

2. Find something that is defiled or find a demon.

3. Place your hand next to it or touch the defiled object, and try to discover the signal that your body receives that indicates an ungodly defilement is present. The believing believer can tune into her body and sense the signal she is receiving, and then discover if the object is an evil spirit or is a defiled object. The believing believer can discover the unique way that God has given her to know how she is to discern evil spirits and defiled objects. Some people may see in the spirit and see demons and other spiritual things, but if you do not have that seer gift, you can develop your discernment gift as another option.

4. Take your hand away from the evil spirit or the defiled object once you discerned it is evil, and determine if your discernment signal goes away. If you are away from the evil spirit or the defiled object, you should not be signaled by your discernment gift being activated. You should feel neutral or good, and have no sense of your discernment gift being activated.

5. Repeat the last two steps (3. and 4.) once more and try to discern the evil spirit or the defiled object again. You are now trying to confirm that you are getting the same signal. If you get the same signal in your body, you now have identified how God has equipped you to discern evil.

6. Now find a different evil spirit or a defiled object, and start again.

As you practice these steps you can also ask the Holy Spirit to teach you. If you operate in the gift of prophecy you can just ask the Lord for the names of the evil spirits. But notice how Hebrews 5:14 says "they trained themselves," this means there is an application to discipline and regular practice is required in order for you to learn to discern between good and evil.

Sometimes I go into a bookstore or into a store that sells games, and I try to practice discerning good from evil. You can practice your discernment gift with books and games. There are books on the occult and games based on the occult that have evil defilement on them that will help you practice your discernment gift when you touch the object or by placing your hand next to it. Then you can determine if your discernment gift is activated or not.

Not all "supposedly evil" books or games have evil defilement on them. You will be required to practice your discernment skills to sharpen them up, so you can determine what items have defilement on them and what items are not defiled.

People who see in the spirit tend to be less sensitive to the sense of touch. It seems that when you use one sense, the other sense may become less sensitive. But you can still develop the gift of discernment with practice. All believing believers will develop their discernment gifts, so they can identify the ungodly spirits in the world that are in, on, or around other people. I find I have a regular job of discerning and cleaning people off from the demons that are hanging on their backs that try to hold them back from participating in the upcoming *move of God*.

My hope is that believing believers will practice their spiritual gifts and develop their abilities to discern evil spirits on other people. Freeing people from demonic attacks is a loving and compassionate gesture, and you are doing the Lord's will; when you do that you will be destroying the devil's work. I would love to see more believing believers develop their discernment gifts and start to destroy the devil's work wherever they find evil is present.

The devil has lied to everyone in our culture, so now many people do not accept that evil spirits exist, including many believers. Believing believers will need to take the responsibility to make sure this lie is destroyed by revealing how evil spirits are a very present reality in their relational networks. When you discern an evil spirit is present, you can immediately draw on the authority Jesus Christ has given you over all evil spirits, so you can bind it, stir it up, or command it to leave (see Luke 10:19). Many people will be healed due to the believing believers who will begin to discern evil spirits and then cast them out.

The gift of discerning of evil spirits is also helpful to clear up property that has been defiled, as you can discern defilement on property and land. Once you have discerned there is an evil presence, you have the power in Jesus Christ's blood to cleanse the property and the land.

Believing believers will need to awaken to the gift of discerning of evil spirits, so you can assist in advancing the coming *move of God* by destroying the devil's works. You also need to awaken to this gift now and learn to discern defilement on property and land, and then learn how to cleanse it. Those are some of the practices that the sons of God who will be revealed at the end of the end-times will do. The sons of God will be commissioned to cleanse the land (see Rom. 8:18-21). This is an exciting time for the believing believers, for you get to awaken to the call Jesus Christ has on your lives, as you begin to operate in all of the gifts of the Spirit.

Chapter 5: Discussion Questions

1. Since Revelation tells us people will not stop worshipping idols and demons in the end-times, how important do you think it is to develop the discernment of evil spirits?
    a. Have you asked the Father for the gift of discerning of spirits?
    b. If not, why not?

2. Moses thinks all believers should have the gift of prophecy and the Holy Spirit.
    a. Can you explain why someone might think that the prophet Moses was speaking the Father's heart when he said all believers should have the gift of prophecy and have the Holy Spirit upon them?
    b. Could Moses' intention mean that having the Holy Spirit meant that believers would have other gifts of the Spirit beside prophecy, as well?
    c. What do you need to do to acquire these spiritual gifts?

3. The Hebrew word *Bene* means to discern with the five physical senses.
    a. Did you have a prejudice against using the physical senses?
    b. Have you shut down in any of your physical senses?
    c. How can you activate your physical senses to become active?

4. Can you describe how you have sensed something spiritual with:
    a. Your eyes?
    b. Your nose?
    c. Your hearing?
    d. Your taste?
    e. Your touch?
    f. Discuss what and how was it sensed?

5. Who do you know who could help you by confirming when you discern good from evil?
    a. Where can you go to learn to discern good from evil?
    b. How important is it for you to learn?
    c. If you don't know the devil is there, how will you know his schemes?

CHAPTER 6

SURPRISINGLY SUPERNATURAL STEP #4B HOW TO ASK FOR THE AUTHORITY TO BIND EVIL SPIRITS AND DRIVE OUT DEMONS

The next step for you to take to become a supernatural believing believer is the *Surprisingly Supernatural Step #4B: How to Ask for the Authority to Bind Evil Spirits and Drive Out Demons*. In this step you will learn how you can stir up, bind, or drive out demons from nonbelievers so they can hear the gospel message and receive Jesus Christ.

When you stir up, bind, or drive out demons from a person you are not setting the person completely free from evil spirits. No, your goal with this step is to prevent the evil spirits from blocking a person from hearing the gospel message. *When you bind or cast out a demon, it helps the person to be free to hear the gospel message, and it also demonstrates that Jesus Christ is the King of kings and the Lord of lords.* The experience the person can have when the evil spirit leaves his body can be helpful, as the person may feel the demon moving around in his body just before exiting. This experience of feeling the demon exiting when it is commanded to leave, in Jesus' name, helps to demonstrate that Jesus Christ is the Lord of all.

Stirring Up a Demon

I was having coffee with a woman who was an Iranian Muslim, and she asked about the book I was writing so I suggested, "Why don't I show you a DVD that I am using to illustrate my book, so you can see what it's about." I played the DVD for her called: *Demonstration of Five Healing Miracles by Jesus Christ*. (This video is uploaded onto the book's website:

www.surprisinglysupernatural.com; it is listed under Chapter 4). After seeing the video, I asked her if she could feel the anointing coming from my hands, and she said she could. She then commented, "You are a real believer!" I wondered: *Has she met other Christians before, but has she never seen Christians pray for the sick, so the sick get healed?* I did not tell her what I was thinking.

We discussed the view that Muslims have about God, which is that they think He is singular. I compared that idea with what is found in the Bible, where God is referred to in the plural. I showed her an example from Genesis that uses the Hebrew word *Elohim* for God, and I told her that *Elohim* is in the plural form.

Then I read where God says, "Let *us* make man in *our* own image, in *our* likeness…" (Genesis 1:1, 26; emphasis added). Once again, I pointed out that this Scripture shows that the Creator God uses plural pronouns to describe Himself. Then I explained to her what Deuteronomy 6 means where it says,

> Hear, O Israel: The Lord our God, the Lord is *one"* (Deut. 6:4; emphasis added).

I told her, "the word '*one*' from Deuteronomy 6:4 in Hebrew means '*united*;' it does not refer to the numeral one, and it does not imply a singular meaning."[59] Then I turned to the gospel of John and read,

> In the beginning was the Word, and the Word was with God, and the Word was God. He was with God in the beginning (John 1:1-2).

We continued to discuss our views about God, and I showed her in John 1:17-18 where it identifies the Word, who was God, as Jesus Christ. I explained that the plurality meant the Holy Trinity: the Father, the Son of God—Jesus Christ, and the Holy Spirit.

Then the Lord told me, "Impart into her for a period of time, as she has an evil spirit in her stomach that will be stirred up by the impartation."

I asked her to extend her hands to me and to let me impart to her for a while, as we continued to talk. She extended her hands to me, and I imparted the Holy Spirit.

She questioned the validity of the Bible. So I discussed with her the details about the manuscript evidence and the Dead Sea Scrolls that affirm the evidence of the Bible. After about ten minutes I asked her, "Is your stomach feeling upset?" She replied, "It was upset just a little while ago." I said, "Okay, we can stop the impartation now." Then I told her "The Lord told me that I was to demonstrate by imparting the Holy Spirit to show how the Holy Spirit would stir up the evil spirit that was in your stomach. That's why your stomach was upset."

We talked a bit more and then I asked her, "May I point the tips of my fingers directly to your stomach and see if the evil spirit will be stirred up?" She replied, "Okay." Pointing the flow of the Spirit to her stomach, I said, "I command all ungodly spirits to come up and out on the breath." Then I asked her, "Is the spirit moving up?" She replied, "No, it's going down!" I stopped and explained, "I should not cast it out anyways unless you receive Jesus Christ first, for it will only come back and bring other evil spirits with it if I did" (see Luke 11:24-26).

She was significantly touched and then she asked me, "Do I have to give up everything?" I responded, "Being submitted to God and praying are both good practices. But you need to receive Jesus Christ as your Lord and Savior, and direct your submission and your prayers to Him." I explained how she could pray to receive Jesus. She told me, "I am not prepared to pray today," but she said she was going to read the New Testament that I had given her, and pray to see if she could understand if she needed to change her path.

Once again, ever since I got filled with the Holy Spirit to the point of overflowing I could release the gifts of the Spirit, and the result was this Muslim woman moved several steps closer to knowing that Jesus Christ is more than just a prophet that the Muslims teach. All believing believers are called to stir up evil spirits that are in, on, or around nonbelievers to demonstrate that Jesus Christ is supreme over all.

Binding Demons

When I speak about binding evil spirits, some people may think this is a controversial topic, so I want to share a story with you to demonstrate that believing believers have the authority to bind evil spirits in the people who are within your realms of influence. Jesus said in Matthew 18,

> ...whatever you bind on earth will be bound in heaven, and whatever you loose on earth will be loosed in heaven (Matt. 16:19).

Now some scholars think this verse is only relevant to the preceding context of church discipline. The context shows that binding and loosening pertains to a person's relationship to the church. But I suggest that the kingdom context of the verse Matthew 16:19 that refers to "binding," may have a broader context than being limited to church discipline.

In the following story you will hear how the Lord told me to bind the evil spirits that were in the men who were sitting next to me on an aircraft. These men were living here on the earth, and the result of binding the evil spirits that were in them, on them and around them, resulted in impeding those evil spirits from operating in the earthly realm.

I believe that the binding may also have impacted the ruling spirits that controlled those evil spirits, as this binding may also have impeded the communication between the ruling demonic powers in the second heaven, and the lesser evil spirits associated with them that were affecting the men that I wanted to share the gospel with. [60] The Scripture does say what you "bind on earth will be bound in heaven" and that probably means binding evil spiritual powers in the second heaven (see Matt. 16:19).

Although binding the evil spirits here on the earth may impede their communication with the ruling demonic spirits, you are usually not supposed to address or confront those ruling spirits directly, for Jude writes,

> In the very same way, these dreamers pollute their own bodies, reject authority and slander celestial beings. But

even the archangel Michael, when he was disputing with the devil about the body of Moses, did not dare to bring a slanderous accusation against him but said, 'The Lord rebuke you!' (Jude 8-10).

Unless you are specifically called by the Lord to confront these ruling demons or corporate strongholds, you should avoid doing that, as you would be stepping out of your realm of authority. As believing believers, you can approach the dismantling of these ruling corporate strongholds by dealing with the evil spirits that operate here on earth, and dealing with the sin issues that are associated with those ruling demonic strongholds.

One such demonic power could be the corporate stronghold called "gay rights." There is a ruling spirit who controls the demons associated with the gay issues and all homosexual practices. It may have been one of the demonic powers that was bound in this story.

Binding Evil Spirits in Nonbelievers so They Can Hear the Gospel

I was on a trip from Belem to Forteleza, Brasil and my seat assignment was changed. I was moved to sit on an aisle seat next to two men. As I greeted them, I discerned they were homosexuals. I asked the Lord, "Lord, what can I do? I would like to share with these guys about You." Jesus then told me to "bind the *spirit of lust*, the *spirit of homosexuality*, the *spirit of rebellion*, and the *spirit of unbelief*" and a few other spirits.

Then I asked Jesus for a word of knowledge to give to them. Jesus said, "They were down here at gay dance clubs, dancing, drinking, and entering private rooms for sex." I wrote it all down in my prayer journal. And then I bound the spirits the Lord told me to bind by speaking the commands out in my mind. I did not speak the commands out loud, as I did not want the men sitting next to me to hear me.

After lunch I asked them, "I would like to share with you some of the great things I have experienced here in Brasil. Would you allow me to tell you about them?" They agreed, and I began to tell them "I have seen many miraculous healings, in Jesus' name." I explained, "The reason we see healing is that Jesus died for not only the sins of all mankind, but He also died for our healing." Then I referenced 1 Peter 2:24 "By his stripes we have been healed," and I explained, "When we accept that by faith, then we can receive the healing because of what Jesus did and the healings will just come." I told them, "We have seen blind eyes healed, cataracts dissolved, deafness healed, HIV healed, sore backs healed, and tumors disappeared, all in Jesus' name." I ended up telling them a bit more and I covered the basic gospel message in a few minutes.

When I was finished sharing, the guy next to me responded and said, "Well, we were down here dancing, drinking, and having a great time ourselves!" Then he turned to his friend, and they both laughed. I replied, "I know!" And then I showed him my prayer journal. He asked, "What's that?" I told him, "It's my prayer journal, and the Lord Jesus told me you were down here 'dancing, drinking, and entering private rooms for sex.'" He picked up my prayer journal and read it, and then he was silent for a while.

After a few minutes, we began an in depth discussion about many topics that lasted the remainder of the trip. The topics included many spiritual topics, but after twenty minutes into our discussion his partner leaned over and said, "He normally would have cut you off after ten minutes into that conversation." The guy I was talking with turned to his partner and said, "Yeah!" But he turned back to me, and we resumed our discussion for two more hours until the plane landed.

He had been raised in a Seventh Day Adventist church. He felt the power of God flow from my hands, and we talked about different healing forms. I shared my view that the other forms of healing like *Reiki* Healing were probably frauds, as they are performed by evil spirits. We also talked about the tendency for men to become homosexuals due to family dynamics and generational sins. He let me pray and impart to him before we deplaned.

He was brought closer to God because I bound the spirits that were operating in him and around him that would normally have prevented him from hearing the gospel message. His partner's statement appeared to confirm that's what had happened, as he did say, "He normally would have cut you off…" But he didn't cut me off because the evil spirits were bound. All believing believers can bind evil spirits when you are in another person's company, and those evil spirits must submit to your authority, in Jesus' name.

When I saw this guy in the airport his eyes would rivet onto mine, and I could tell he was significantly touched from our exchange, because it was Jesus' Spirit that was flowing into him when I prayed for him. All believing believers have the authority to bind evil spirits that are in, on, or around the people you want to share the gospel with.

Believing Believers Are Given Authority Over Scorpions

Jesus tells you in Luke 10 that,

> I have given you authority to trample on snakes and *scorpions* and to overcome all the power of the enemy; nothing will harm you (Luke 10:19; emphasis added).

I find it interesting that Revelation 9 speaks about the demonic powers that will be released from the Abyss, and it describes them as having *power like that of scorpions*, and they will inflict people with the "sting of a scorpion" (Rev. 9:3-6; emphasis added). These demonic powers *will not attack believers who have God's seal on their foreheads*, but these demonic powers *will attack nonbelievers who are without God's protection* (see Rev. 7:3; 9:4b).

Could the Lord want to alert believing believers to the authority He has given you over *scorpions* for the time that you are now coming into? I wonder: *Will nonbelievers soon be attacked by the scorpion's sting?* I believe that the demonstration of God's power over the demonic spirits will become an increasingly popular way to bring the kingdom of God to nonbelievers, as we move further into the last of the last days. During these last of the last days believing believers will demonstrate to nonbelievers that Jesus Christ is the Lord over all by demonstrating that He has given the believing believers His authority over all the demonic spirits that attack nonbelievers.

Jesus gave the seventy-two disciples authority over the enemy's power (see Luke 10:19). What do you think the reason was for Jesus giving them that authority? I think John 10:10 gives us the answer, as it implies there are evil spirits who want to: steal, kill, and destroy other people's lives. *Believing believers are called to receive the authority that Jesus has already given you over the power of the devil, and you are to come against the devil's work and bring those people who are under the devil's power, out from it. And then you are to bring them into the abundant life in Jesus Christ and into His kingdom.*

Saint Antony Describes the Enemy's Tactics and the Believers' Authority

Saint Antony lived in the 5th Century and was one of the desert fathers who operated as a believing believer. Antony had visions, cast out demons, healed the sick, and encouraged other believers to have faith to stand against the enemy and demons. This is an excerpt from Robert Myer's translation of *Athanasius Life of St Antony*, where Antony speaks about the enemy's tactics.

> Since the Lord dwelt with us, the enemy has fallen and his powers have declined. Therefore, he can do nothing; still, though he is fallen, like a tyrant he does not keep quiet, but threatens even if his threats are but words. And let each one of you bear this in mind [that as believers you] …can despise the demons. Now, if they were bound to such…they can enter in spite of locked doors, and seeing they are present everywhere in the air…Including their leader the Devil…nevertheless, we live and live our lives in defiance of him, it is plain that they are without any power…Indeed, if it were within their power, they would not let one of us Christians live, for the service of God is an abomination to the sinner. And since they can do nothing, it is rather themselves they hurt, for they cannot carry out any of their threats. We must fear God alone, and despise those beings and not fear them at all. [61]

Antony suggests that believers should go to their homes without any fear, as the demons will only make fools of themselves. He also informs us of their tactics: demons first try to deceive the heart by unclean pleasure, and giving people unclean thoughts. If that does not work, they can show up as: a visible incorporeal spirit like a ghost, a phantom, or an apparition in order to frighten people.

They can transform themselves into women, beasts, reptiles, bodies of huge size, and hordes of warriors. They may also prophesy and foretell future events or quote from Scripture or repeat and echo what you have read. They may also rouse believers to prayers, and thus preventing their sleep.[62]

However, Antony clearly testifies that the Lord has given us all the power over the enemy and nothing will harm us (see Luke 10:19). Antony also says that making the sign of the cross is effective to ward off their attacks. As believing believers, you need to grab hold of the faith and the authority over the enemy to walk out and destroy the devil's works.

The Surprisingly Supernatural Step #4B: How to Ask for the Authority to Bind Evil Spirits and Drive Out Demons card is one of the first steps you will use to bring people into the abundant life in Jesus Christ by learning how to release His kingdom upon other people and setting them free from demonic powers. You can get this card from the book's website www.surprisinglysupernatual.com, as it is a free download.

You Need Authority and Discernment

Since Antony testifies that evil spirits are "present everywhere in the air," you not only need to exercise your authority in Jesus Christ, but you also need to discern if demons are there.[63] Which is what we taught in the previous chapter concerning the topic of "discerning of spirits" (KJV). God gives you the gift of discernment so you can know if a person has an evil spirit. Then when you know it is there: you can bind it, stir it up, or cast out the evil spirit from that person.

Many people command demons to go, and they assume they go. But you need discernment to know if the person is free from the evil spirits or not. One of the main ploys of demons is to deceive. The demon is happy to play quiet in hopes that you think it has left. Demons deceive—so you need discernment.

If you believe the Scripture that says you have been given authority over all the power of the enemy, as it does in Luke 10:19; then you can stand and declare that the demons must leave, but you need both the discernment and the authority to deliver people from demons.

I encourage you to use *the Surprisingly Supernatural Step #4B How to Ask for the Authority to Bind Evil Spirits and Drive Out Demons* card that you can download from the book's website. Then you can ask the Father in heaven for the gift of discernment and also for the authority and power to stir up, bind, or command evil spirits to go.

Sometimes you need the person's cooperation by expressing their will and stating that they want the evil spirit to leave. This may include having the person confess the sin that permitted the evil spirit to come into the person's life. But if it is a nonbeliever that confession may not be necessary, but it will always be necessary for believers to confess their sin before a demon can be driven out, especially if the sin was the doorway for the demon to enter into the person. James 5:16 tells us that if you have sinned, you should confess your sins to each other, and then you may be healed. Oftentimes after the sin is confessed, the evil spirit can be cast out, and then the healing will come.

In this Scripture you will read how Paul gives an example where he shows that believing believers can cast out a demon from a nonbeliever even when the nonbeliever has not given you permission to cast it out. In Acts 16, Paul turned to the slave girl, who had a *spirit of fortune telling* in her, and said,

> 'In the name of Jesus Christ I command you to come out of her!' At that moment the spirit left her (Acts 16:18b).

This is an example of a believing believer who released the gifts of the Spirit to drive out a demon. Paul showed that he had discerned the evil spirit was there. He also showed he had authority over that evil spirit, as he drove it out of her. He demonstrated that the name of Jesus Christ was powerful. This Scripture shows that believing believers are given the authority to command evil spirits out of nonbelievers, even if the nonbeliever has not given you permission to cast out the evil spirit.

The lie the Western world has believed is that "demons do not exist" and that lie is partly attributed to demons that block people's understanding from knowing that there are demons in, on, and around you in your world. I discussed in my book *Wake Up!* how Daniel showed there are both Godly and ungodly powers in the world that influence the human kingdoms.[65] Many people in the third world have experienced the demonic realm, but many people in the Western hemisphere think that those people are just ignorant and uneducated. That's because many of the people who live in the Western hemisphere have been influenced by evil spirits that persuaded them to deny the existence of demons.

Having participated in ministry for a few years now, I have observed that most people are unaware that they have an evil spirit who is living within them. Most people are seldom aware of how the evil spirit has been influencing them. It is only when a believing believer releases the power of God that they awaken to the reality that a demon has been living within them. Frequently they are shocked when they feel the evil spirit moving about and then leaving them.

Believing believers, who follow Jesus Christ, are given the power over all these evil spirits that block people's thinking. Believing believers need to begin to exercise your authority and power over all the power of the enemy and either bind or cast out these evil spirits that block nonbelievers' thinking (see Luke 10:19). *Surprisingly Supernatural Step #4B* is learning about how you can stir up, bind, or drive out evil spirits, so nonbelievers can hear the gospel message and receive Jesus Christ.

Imparting the Holy Spirit and Then Spontaneously Stirring Up a Demon

Since the Holy Spirit began flowing out from my hands I have seen spontaneous healings, deliverances, and evangelism because of it. This story is about having the gift of discernment and releasing the overflow of the Holy Spirit where I spontaneously stirred up a demon and demonstrated that Jesus Christ is more powerful than all the false gods.

I was in a restaurant in Seattle and I saw my waitress had a tattoo on her arm. I asked her about it and she said it was a Hindu symbol. I asked her,

"Is that your religion?" She said "No, I am more *Buddhist*." I immediately felt compelled to tell her about the *Buddhist* woman who had a demon cast out of her.

Then I asked her to point her fingers toward mine and I asked her if she could feel the anointing. She said she could and she said "That's the '*Chi*.'" I responded, "No, it's the Holy Spirit who I had invited to fill me over many months, and then the flow reversed and began to flow out of me. Then the people I prayed for began to get healed, in Jesus' name."

I then shared with her the word of knowledge and said, "Oh, the anointing is travelling up your arm and into your body." She responded with a strained expression on her face and said, "Yes, that's very interesting." Then she pulled away. Just then I had another word of knowledge that her stomach was upset, and immediately I thought it was due to a demon. I then reflected on how I had spontaneously told her about the former *Buddhist* that had an evil spirit cast out of her. I realized that story may have been inspired too.

After the meal ended, I asked the waitress about the word of knowledge that I had, and I said, "I sensed your stomach was upset right after I imparted the Holy Spirit. Was I accurate in what I sensed?" She said, "Yes, my stomach felt nauseous." She had shared with me earlier that she was formerly a Christian, so I told her "I suggest you read the New Testament again and notice how Jesus often dealt with sickness by casting evil spirits out of people. You may find it interesting, as I think your stomach was upset, because an evil spirit was upset when the Holy Spirit was flowing out of my hand and into your body." She thanked me for that information.

Being continually filled with the Holy Spirit has allowed me to impart to some people who get healed, others are delivered from evil spirits, and others have evil spirits that are stirred up. Having the gift of discernment helped me to know the demon was there. I heard God's voice, which helped me to pursue the question and ask if her stomach was really upset. Her confirmation allowed me to share with her how Jesus healed people by casting out evil spirits. That was all I needed to do for this evangelistic encounter. I knew I had completed my assignment, because I had a great deal of peace and satisfaction that came over me after I shared all that I was called to share.

Sometimes you are to plant seeds, and other times you are to harvest. It is such a pleasure to serve the Lord Jesus Christ and bring His kingdom into other people's lives. Believing believers are now needed to arise, because many people in our cultures have opened themselves up to evil spirits. Therefore, believing believers have the opportunity to show them that Jesus Christ is Lord over all, and He has given you authority over all the evil spirits that are in them, on them, and around them.

Surprisingly Supernatural Step #4B: How to Ask for the Authority to Bind Evil Spirits and Drive Out Demons is an important tool for the believing believers to wield as we go about proclaiming the kingdom of God and demonstrating that Jesus Christ is more powerful than Buddha, more powerful than all the Hindu gods, more powerful than Allah, and more powerful than all other false gods. Jesus Christ is the King of kings and the Lord of lords, and He reigns supreme (see Rev. 17:14; 19:16). Jesus is calling His believing believers to demonstrate His supremacy over all those evil spiritual beings and false gods (see Matt. 24:14).

Let the Post-Modern Nonbeliever Experience the Demon

Seizing our authority and power over all the power of the enemy is very important in the post-modern world, for one of the values of the post-modern world is that everyone has an equal voice. You can say,

> Jesus is the way, the truth and the life, no one comes to the Father' except through Jesus (see John 14:6)

But they can reply, "That's your opinion!" Our words do not carry the weight they once did. But Paul says that "For the kingdom of God is not a matter of talk, but of power" (1 Cor. 4:20).

If you have faith and utilize the power you are given over the enemy, then you will demonstrate the kingdom of God in power, and you can give the post-modern nonbeliever an experience of a demon moving in her body or leaving her. Then she will have a personal testimony of the power of Jesus Christ that words cannot refute.

Some people object to subjective experiences and claim that they are invalid. That was Descartes' view as he claimed theology lapsed into subjectivism, and that only the objectivism of natural science is valid. This set up the false dichotomy between "I know" and "I believe." However, Michael Polanyi comments on objectivism and writes "knowledge is neither purely objective nor purely subjective, but as that which is available to the person who is personally and responsibly committed to seeking the truth and publicly stating his findings."[66]

If the post-modern nonbeliever is committed to seeking the truth, she can draw on both the objective and subjective personal experiences to find the truth. Therefore, experience is an important value in post-modernism. If the believing believer can give the nonbeliever an experience of her own that she cannot deny, like having an experience of an evil spirit moving within her or leaving her body; then when she notices the change in her body or her soul from the evil spirit leaving her, that experience can become an open door. When that happens, then you can come along side of her experience, and share how the kingdom of God came to her. That may naturally lead you to share with her who the King is: "It's Jesus Christ, He's the King!"

Surprisingly Supernatural Step #4B: Is Not Full Deliverance

Surprisingly Supernatural Step #4B: How to Ask for the Authority to Bind Evil Spirits and Drive Out Demons is not full deliverance. It is dangerous to do a full deliverance on nonbelievers, if they have not received Christ and His Holy Spirit first, for you are told in Luke 11 that,

> When an evil spirit comes out of a man, it goes through arid places seeking rest and does not find it. Then it says, 'I will return to the house I left.' When it arrives, it finds the house swept clean and put in order. Then it goes and takes seven other spirits more wicked than itself, and they go in and live there. And the condition of that man is worse than the first (Luke 11:24-26).

Surprisingly Supernatural Step #4B: How to Ask for the Authority to Bind Evil Spirits and Drive Out Demons teaches you to use the authority you have in Jesus Christ to stir up, bind, or drive out demons to help the person realize the truth you are sharing about Jesus Christ. You do not sweep it clean and put the person in order before he receives Christ. But you do need to do that after he has accepted Jesus Christ.

One person who was a secular humanist heard my stories of healing, and then she said "I have pain over my left eyebrow. Why don't you pray for it?" I put my finger tips on her left eyebrow and commanded the pain to go. She then said "Oh, it moved over to my right eyebrow." I said, "I am sorry, but I don't think pain moves like that, do you?" She said, "No." I informed her it was an unwanted visitor, some sort of an evil spirit. Feeling the demon move within her was the open door that allowed this secular humanist to become a believer.

Jesus Christ is the Way, the Truth and the Life, and He is the Exclusive Way to the Father

Whether you stir up a demon in a nonbeliever so they feel it moving in their body like that waitress did, that Muslim did, or that secular humanist did, or if you bind the spirits that operate in and around nonbelievers like I did with the homosexuals on the airplane, or if you drive out demons from a person like I did with that *Buddhist* woman, then you are operating in *Surprisingly Supernatural Step #4B How to Ask for the Authority to Bind Evil Spirits and Drive Out Demons*. When you take this step your faith will grow tremendously, as you will prove that the Lord Jesus Christ is more powerful than all the evil spirits that are behind all the other religions that are not Christian, and over *spirits of homosexuality*, and over all other evil spirits.

Jesus is the way, the truth and the life and only through Jesus can you come into a relationship with the Father in heaven (see John 14:6). *But you do not have to talk about Jesus being the way, the truth and the life, and being the exclusive way to the Father before you have first demonstrated that by releasing the gifts of the Spirit.* If you bind, stir up, or drive out a demon from a nonbeliever, so he can feel it move in his body and recognize how the demon has influenced him, then you can talk to him about Jesus Christ from that perspective; that way the nonbeliever will learn who Jesus really is, and learn that He has all the authority and power over the enemy.

Jesus Christ has delegated all His power and authority over the enemy to the believing believers, so that nothing at all will harm you (see Luke 10:19). In Matthew 28:18 Jesus said,

> All authority in heaven and earth has been given to me. Therefore go and make disciples of all nations... (Matt. 28:18b-19).

Jesus is saying something like "you have all the power over the enemy and nothing will harm you—because I promise to be with you until the very end of the age, so go and make disciples with the power that I will pour through you" (see Matt. 28:18-19).

Believing believers have an obligation to go out in His authority and "destroy the devil's work" (1 John 3:8b). You are charged to bring in the harvest, and you do that with the power of the Holy Spirit being inside of you, so you can release prophetic words, heal the sick, and stir up, bind, or drive out demons. Whatever method you use, you are proclaiming the kingdom of God is near, and then you can easily tell them that Jesus Christ is the Eternal King.

Avoid Pursuing the Gifts Outside of an Intimate Relationship with the Father and Jesus Christ

I will suggest for the gift of discernment and driving out demons, like I did with healing and prophecy, that you must avoid pursuing the gifts of the Spirit outside of an intimate relationship with the Heavenly Father and the Lord Jesus Christ, as it can be dangerous for you. You may open yourself up to spiritual attacks.

However, if you are truly abiding in Jesus Christ, and you have a close relationship with Him, then you are given authority and protection, so you can tell the demons in, on, or around people to go. And they must leave. Becoming a son, daughter, child, sheep, or servant is imperative for you to be able to walk out in the Lord's power and authority, as having an intimate relationship with the Lord enables you to know His will and to obey it.

I also suggest that you may want to practice on believers who can help you to grow in your faith, until you know that demons submit to you, because you have received the authority of Jesus Christ. So I encourage you to practice *Surprisingly Supernatural Step #4B How to Ask for the Authority to Bind Evil Spirits and Drive Out Demons* with other believers.

You can download the Surprisingly Supernatural Card from the book's website, and then you can ask the Father in heaven for the gift of discernment, and also for the authority and power to stir up, bind, or command evil spirits to go. Be sure to use this card to decree and declare to the Father in heaven that you want the gift of discernment, and you want the authority to drive out evil spirits. For Paul does tell us to,

...eagerly desire the greater gifts (1 Cor. 12: 31).

Use the Surprisingly Supernatural Cards regularly to help you to practice asking the Father for the gifts of the Spirit until you see discernment and the authority and the power to drive out demons regularly operating in your life.

Believing Believers Will Become Aware of Our Polluted Environment

I suggest that all believing believers will need to practice using their gift of discernment, and practice doing deliverance in this coming season. Since I have had my discernment gifts awakened, it feels as if we live in a polluted environment. Earlier in 2010, I sat at a table in a restaurant with a friend eating, when I felt something that was defiled land on my face, so I cast it off. Then I leaned back and tested the space in front of me, and I discerned it was defiled.

The Scripture indicates there are different ways of travel: "The highway of the upright avoids evil" (Prov. 16:17); "And a highway will be there; it will be called the way of holiness" (Isa. 35:8); "He had a dream in which he saw a stairway resting on earth, with its top reaching heaven, and the angels of God were ascending and descending on it" (Gen. 28:12). These Scriptures show us there are highways of the upright, ways of holiness, and stairways to heaven. I wonder: *Is the inverse from what these Scriptures have shown us also true? Are there travel ways for demons to travel on as well?*

Since there are horizontal highways of holiness, ways of holiness, and vertical stairways to heaven and ladders where angels of God ascend and descend and transverse across the earth, could the enemy have corrupted some of these travel ways and defiled them? (see Gen. 28:12; John 1:51; Matt. 4:8). Some Christian leaders teach that leylines are spiritual highways that evil spirits use to travel across the earth.

Like my experience at this restaurant table, I have encountered these defiled passageways not only in a number of public places like restaurants, but I also have encountered them in many churches and in Christians' homes. I think these lines of defilement are highways of travel for spiritual beings. Since Satan still controls the kingdoms of the world; these evil spirits move across the earth using these leylines and they leave their ungodly defilement on them (see Matt 4:8-9).

One pastor wanted me to check his bedroom for defilement. When I checked it, I felt an ungodly leyline running across the place where their pillows were placed on their bed. And another ungodly line was moving up the length of the bed on his wife's side. As soon as the pastor heard me declare this he exclaimed, "My wife has nightmares every night!"

I believe those defiled highways allowed demons to run up and down her body and across her head, and they gave her the substance of her nightmares. We live in a polluted environment due to unclean spirits. Believing believers are called to wake up and to begin to clean up the polluted spiritual environment. Believing believers need to become aware of the devil's schemes (see 2 Cor. 2:11; Eph. 6:11).

Believing believers can ask the Father in heaven to bring His angels and fire to cleanse these defiled leylines. We can also cleanse defiled objects, but objects that are dedicated to evil cannot be cleansed; therefore, they should be destroyed. The Scripture does say, "He who is caught with devoted things shall be destroyed by fire, along with all that belongs to him" (Josh. 7:15). I believe evil spirits leave a defiled residue in the spiritual realm that marks both the dedicated objects and the people that belong to those evil spirits.

Defiled Residue Can Mark You!

I was going to conduct a discernment test with *Harry Potter* books and contrast them with other books like the Bible, because J.D. Rowlings wrote that some Christians believe her books are evil, but in response to that she wrote, "That objection is utterly unfounded."[67] However, *I found out that I could discern there was an ungodly defilement on Harry Potter books.*

I acquired some *Harry Potter* books and put them on a stand by my door. I left them there for a month. But then I realized I should move them outside, because every time I passed them, I could sense the ungodly defilement that was attached to them. So I put the books outside. But then when I went past that stand again, even with the books outside, and to my surprise, I still discerned the stand had ungodly defilement on it. The ungodly defilement from the *Harry Potter* books had leaked onto the stand by my door!

The devil deceives and he may use his defilement to mark the people and the objects that belong to him. I believe the leylines are created by God, but they have been defiled by evil spirits; consequently, believing believers need to learn to clean them off. But objects that are dedicated to false gods or dedicated for evil purposes, like *Harry Potter* books, should be destroyed.

I find that if I ask the Father in heaven to bring His fire to cleanse the defiled object a few times, but if it still has defilement on it, then I just discard the defiled object and destroy it. It may have been created and dedicated to a false god or was created to serve evil; consequently, it cannot be cleansed. I do not want it to touch me or infect me with its ungodly defilement, so that it will signal to evil spirits that I belong to them.

I want to be solely set apart for the Lord's purposes, and solely belong to the Lord (see John 8:47). Being set apart is one of the definitions of being holy. Believing believers need to clean their environment from the ungodly defilement and walk in holiness themselves.

Believing Believers Must Alert Other People about the Devil's Schemes

Demons deceive, but it is time for believing believers to arise and break the deception off the minds of the people in your relational networks. Because the demonic realm has been ignored for so long, many people do not think it exists; many do not even know that these lines of defilement are strewn across the world in which we live. But the biblical view says it does exist, and if you have discernment, you will feel it exists. If you ignore it, the demonic realm will not go away, you will just be unaware of the devil's schemes (see 2 Cor. 2:11; Eph. 6:11).

Many of us are like the infant who plays in the mud and gets all covered in dirt and mud. The infant does not think anything is wrong with playing in the mud. He is unaware that dog feces are mixed in with the mud he is playing in. The infant not only gets dirty, but he may also get sick from the unclean feces that are mixed up in the mud he is playing in.

Believing believers will realize they are required to grow up and reach maturity in order to learn to extricate themselves and other people from the filth of the spiritual defilement that is around us, due to the foul and unclean spirits that pollute our environment. Many people in our relational networks do not realize their world is polluted by ungodly defilement. And they don't even know Saint Antony reported that demons, ". . . are present everywhere in the air. . ."[68] Therefore, the task for all believing believers is to expose the demonic realm, cleanse your defiled environment of it, and educate other people about the reality of the demonic realm and its influence on their world.[69]

I have already mentioned that Jesus states that believers will drive out demons and heal the sick (see Matt. 10:5-8; Mark 16:17-18). If you do not do that, what does that imply? Consequently, believing believers will be required to practice their healing gifts, their discernment gifts, and their authority to drive out demons.

Believing believers also need to begin to educate people in your relational networks that evil spirits do exist. And that evil spirits are intent on trying to destroy your lives. Believing believers need to overcome the stigma that comes from thinking that "demons are not polite topics of conversation in the educated society."[70] Instead, you need to educate others by bringing healing and freedom to the people who are attacked by demonic spirits, that way you will let them know that Jesus Christ is the Lord God Almighty.

On the book's website www.surprisinglysupernatural.com under Chapter 6 is a video titled: *Get off my Back Demon! In Jesus' name!* This video shows believers who describe the demonic attacks they experienced. The people on this video are Christian believers who experienced attacks from evil spirits. Believing believers need to be aware of these spiritual attacks, and then learn to drive out the demons whenever you discern them.

Practice Discernment Gifts and Deliverance

Believing believers can practice doing deliverance on their homes and on hotel rooms, as this is one way you will help people by driving out the darkness, and bringing in the light of God. You will need to clean out your home regularly, and your hotel room every night before you go to sleep. You do not know what sins took place in your hotel room before you stayed there, and you do not know what evil spirits may have been invited into that room; therefore, you will need to discern the evil spirits that are there.

I was on a ministry trip a few years ago, and I was in my hotel room resting on the bed when the Lord opened my eyes to see a gray blob at the top of the wall between the ceiling and the wall. It looked like a small gray cloud. I knew it was a demon waiting for an entry point (a sinful act) to come into me. I immediately commanded that evil spirit out of the room, in Jesus' name, and it left.

How to Do Deliverance on Rooms

You can do deliverance on rooms. When I do that, I like to take five steps to do it.

Step one is to step into Jesus, which you do when you are continually filled by the Holy Spirit to the point of overflowing.

The second step is to ask the Lord for the names of evil spirits present in the room. Then wait in faith for the names of those spirits to come to your mind. Another way you can see if evil spirits are in your room is to use the gift of discernment by walking around the room and trying to sense or see if an evil spirit is there.

The third step is to command the evil spirits to go. Sometimes, I ask the Father to send His angels to capture the demons and to take them away.

However, I prefer to incapacitate the demons so they cannot return. I did an experiment where I first discerned that evil spirits were in a room, and then I gave a global command for all of them to leave. I went back and I was able to discern that all of the evil spirits were still there. Global commands may not work. What I now do is to ensure that each demon I discern is individually cast out of the room.

What I also do is that once I remembered I had received a spiritual sword, I learned to strike at the demons on the wall with the spiritual sword. When I do that they usually fall down to the floor. Then I ask God to send His angels and take the remains of the demons that are on the floor away. The following end-note has a reference for you to learn a bit more about incapacitating demons. [71]

The fourth step is to ask the Father to send His angels into the room to guard it and keep the demons out.

Finally, the fifth step is to pray for the blood of Jesus to cover over every doorway, wall, ceiling, floor, window, and any other entry way. However, Saint Antony says, "They can enter in spite of locked doors" so you still need to be diligent and discern if a demon enters again, even after you have prayed.[72] And when you have discerned a demon has come back, just command it to leave, or incapacitate the demons and then ask the Lord to send His angels to remove the debris of the demons from the floor. You can ask the Lord to send His fire to cleanse all the defilement that was left behind by the evil spirit as well.

Practice Exercise: Self-Deliverance or Deliverance on Someone Else

You can practice self-deliverance, which is deliverance you do on yourself. This is the same model that you would use when you do deliverance on another person, who is a believer. But do not attempt to do deliverance on nonbelievers, as their condition will only get worse (see Luke 11:24-26). You may practice this method of deliverance on yourself or with another believer. If you do it with another believer, ask him to give you permission for you to practice with him, and ask him ahead of time to forgive you for any mistakes you might make.

Remember that you are to operate in love when you do deliverance, and you are to operate like you did when you practiced prophesying by being: encouraging, strengthening, and comforting. Try to refrain from being judgmental or making accusational comments directed to the person you are working with. Instead, allow the love and the peace of God to flow through you as you minister to the person during the deliverance session. Try the following steps to help you to practice ministering deliverance on yourself or with another believer.

1. Ask for the Holy Spirit to fill you and to overshadow you. Ask for the Holy Spirit to come and fill the room, and ask for the Lord to send His angels to help with the deliverance session.

2. Ask the Lord to remind you of any sins or ungodly practices in your life (or in the life of the person you are ministering to)—be open to receive words of knowledge and any other revelation that the Lord may reveal about these issues and the sinful practices.

3. List the names of the offenses (sins); those names will function as the names you will associate with the demons. (For example: if the offense (sin) was "fear," you will address the evil spirit and call it: "*spirit of fear.*"

4. Confess the sin, repent, and vow not to practice it again. Ask for God to give you His grace to help with the needed change in your behavior.

5. Then stand on the Scriptures from Matthew 10:1; 10:8; 18:18; and Luke 10:19 by believing them, and then command the evil spirit to be silent and not to manifest in any way (by throwing up, or affecting the person's body, etc…).

   Then command the evil spirits by name. Use their functional names, and command them to come up and out on the breath, in Jesus' name. Breathe out regularly from your mouth and say, "I command all ungodly spirits to get out now!"

   You may also want to state the specific name of the evil spirit. For example say, "*Spirit of fear*, I command you to leave now! Get out! In Jesus' name. I don't want you, I don't need you, get out now! Come up and out on the breath." Then continue to breathe out from your mouth and try to sense if you feel the evil spirit moving up and out of you.

6. Sometimes having an attitude is useful, as you can speak to the evil spirit, as if you are scolding a bad dog. Speak to the evil spirit with the authority you have in Christ, and you can display a bit of attitude. But attitude does not have to be confused with volume. You can exhibit an attitude and your authority with a normal tone of voice. Be sure you tell the person you are ministering to that you are not speaking to her, but clarify that you are addressing the evil spirit.

7. Determine if you sense any movement in your body as you command the spirit to leave. Also determine if there are any changes in your body, mind, or emotions during or after the deliverance. That change can be an indication that the evil spirit has left.

8. Continue until you feel the change within yourself or when you receive the faith that the evil spirit has left you. If not, go back to point 1 above, and receive more revelation from the Lord.

9. Give praise and worship to the Lord after the deliverance session and celebrate your new freedom.

10. Post-Deliverance: evil spirits will often want to come back. So stand guard! Be aware if you are being tempted by the same sinful thoughts or actions that the departed evil spirit had influenced you with before. If you do sense the evil spirit has returned, determine if you sinned. If you did, immediately confess the sin and get it covered by the Lord's blood. Then command the evil spirit to leave again, in Jesus' name.

11. If you cannot do self-deliverance and maintain freedom, then you probably need to get another believing believer who can do deliverance sessions with you.

You can practice doing deliverance on rooms, on yourself, or with other people; as this practice will help to train you to walk out as a believing believer. You are all called to destroy the devil's works and drive out demons (see Mark 16:17). One of the sure ways you can destroy the devil's works is to command evil spirits out of people, or at least to bind them, so people can hear the gospel message clearly. With my gift of discernment activated, I have been able to sense ungodly powers and spirits, and then by standing in the authority Christ has given me, I command them to go.

One easy way to practice deliverance, which believing believers should try to learn, is to discern evil spirits that are on people's backs and then cast them off. I shared how I did that in this chapter, and also in Chapter 3 of my book *Wake Up!* I intimated it was a prophetic warning that these demons are trying to hinder believers from walking out in their birthrights, and they are trying to stop believers from participating in the *move of God* that will soon be here.[73] There are lots of opportunities these days for you to bring healing and freedom to people, if you begin to exercise these simple deliverance practices.

Christians Regularly Need Deliverance

I believe it is unwise for a Christian to go without receiving deliverance ministry at least once a year.

Deliverance is an ongoing need for believing believers. You are in a battle and you need deliverance, especially if you are actually advancing the kingdom of God. If you do that, you will be susceptible to the attacks of the enemy. So it is good to know how to do self-deliverance, but you should also know some people in your relational networks that will be able to do a deliverance session with you, when it's needed. Jesus did not say we will not be attacked, He said,

> I have given you authority to trample on snakes and scorpions and to overcome all the power of the enemy; *nothing will harm you"* (Luke 10:19; emphasis added).

You can overcome the power of the enemy, and the enemy *will not harm you!* But Jesus did not say the enemy will not attack you. They will attack you, and if you are wise, you will discern when demons attack you, and then you will rebuke them. But Prophet Rick Joyner wrote about the hordes of demons that will be coming and will try to stop the upcoming *move of God* that will bring many nonbelievers into a relationship with Jesus Christ and His church body. The demons will jump onto the backs of Christians, and if you agree with their tactics they will get bigger and exert greater control over you.[74] I have discerned over a thousand demons on people's backs these past few years. This demonic activity is real and it needs a response from the believing believers.

I think it's a mistake to think you are absolutely free from demonic attacks. They can be in you, on you, or around you. You are not to fear them, but you are to become aware of them, as they are looking for an opening (a sinful thought, an ungodly emotional reaction, or an ungodly action), so they can enter you.

I mentioned earlier in this chapter how an evil spirit was hanging out watching me from the crack between the wall and the ceiling in the hotel room. It was just looking for an opening. It was waiting for me to sin, so it could enter me. If you think, feel, or act sinfully they will capture you for sure. I shared the story in the Chapter 3 where I was hit by an evil dart, because I was releasing the kingdom of God and doing ministry. So even if you release the kingdom of God, you may become a target for an attack.

Just because you shine your light you may be attacked. There are witches who can see your spiritual light, and then they can place a curse on you that puts witchcraft rings around you. Regardless of the cause, you sometimes may not even be aware of when you have been assailed by a demonic attack. But you are not to be ignorant of the devil's schemes, so I recommend that you should go regularly for deliverance ministry to be cleansed from evil spirits that attack you, so "nothing will harm you" (Luke 10:19) (see 2 Cor. 2:11; Eph. 6:11).

Living a Holy Life

Living a holy life is a good antidote for demons if you have any around you, on you, or in you. You cannot receive deliverance and still practice the same sin and expect to remain free. Demons will come back through any door that was opened by your sin.

- Discipleship is important.
- Reading God's Word out loud and with faith is important.
- Worshipping the Lord with a full heart is important.
- Being in an accountable relationship is also an important way for you to stay clear of evil influences. This relationship includes the honest confession of sins and receiving forgiveness.
- Taking communion regularly is also another component of keeping yourself clean and holy.

When Does a Person Need Deliverance?

If the symptoms are evident and they inhibit the person's life, for example: fear, worry, anger, illness, or they hear voices in their head, or they are unable to walk out their birthright, then those symptoms are frequently the result of an evil spirit being present.

If a person feels an inward pressure to do something: to drink, to smoke, to gamble, to lust, or to have immoral sex, worry, fears, anger, and if the drive is coming from inside of you, then it often means those inward pressures are probably coming from a demonic source.

When you pray for healing several times and the symptoms of the sickness have no change that usually indicates that an evil spirit is present.

When you discern an evil spirit is in another person, you probably need the person's permission before you can drive out the evil spirit during the deliverance ministry.

If you believe the Scripture that says you have authority over all the power of the enemy, then you can stand and declare that the demon must leave; but you also need discernment, as well as the authority to deliver people from their demons (see Luke 10:19).

The *Surprisingly Supernatural Step #4B How to Ask for the Gift of Discernment, and the Authority to Bind Evil Spirits and Drive Out Demons* card is a tool that will help the reader to get the Scriptures associated with binding evil spirits, driving out demons, and having discernment of evil spirits into your soul and spirit. I suggest that you download this card from the website for free, so you can build up your faith and your spirit to the point where you will begin to seize opportunities to bind spirits or drive out demons whenever they present themselves.

Although I covered deliverance from a broader basis, the point is that all believing believers, who are continually filled with the Holy Spirit have the mandate that Jesus Christ gave to you that you are to drive out demons (see Mark 16:17). When you drive out demons you bring the kingdom of God in to do it. Remember Jesus told the disciples to pray like this,

> Our Father in heaven, hallowed be your name, your kingdom come, your will be done (Matt. 6:9-10).

I was ministering in Sao Paulo, Brasil in a home group, and I sensed the Lord wanted me to invite Godly spiritual hosts into the room. So I specifically asked Him to send an angel and a power into the room. I did not sense the power, but I had asked the Lord of Hosts to send His kingdom into the room. I confirmed what my interpreter sensed that an angel had come into the room. I discerned it was the *angel of fire*. (Powers are one kind of spiritual beings, and they are different from angels. Like angels, "powers" can be both Godly and ungodly powers (see Eph. 6:12)).

We conducted a very short fire tunnel, where everyone in the home group took turns walking into the *angel of fire*, and then each person stood in the presence of the angel's fire for several minutes. While they did that the angel's fire caused deliverance to occur. It was the purifying fire of God. We could feel and smell the sin, the iniquities, and the evil spirits leaving the people, as they stood in the *angel of fire*.

What was interesting was that we had prayed for the Father to send His kingdom, and have His will done. I realized afterwards that the Father had brought His kingdom, which was represented by the *angel of fire*. He also performed His will that night, which was to have a deliverance session that brought more freedom to those believers.

When you bring the kingdom in to drive out demons you are doing it because that's the Father's will (Matt. 6:10). You need to keep your eyes open, and be awake for the future society will develop this phenomenon,

> Because of the increased in wickedness, the love of most will grow cold… (Matt. 24:12).

This prophecy will occur as you approach deeper into the end of the end-times, and that means evil spirits will have easier access to people, especially to nonbelievers. The three woes from Revelation 8 indicate that attacks will be released upon the earth at the end of the end-times. One of those attacks we read about in Revelation 9 is that God's angels will release demons that were trapped in the Abyss, and then they will come upon the earth (see Rev. 9:2-5). That means more and more nonbelievers will be afflicted by evil spirits that will cause sicknesses and other maladies that will assail them during this time.

Believing believers in contrast will be continually filled more and more by the Holy Spirit, and will be given more of God's power and authority to drive out demons or bind evil spirits. And the believing believers will preach the gospel of the kingdom and set people free by bringing them to Jesus Christ.

I think it is now the time for the true believing believers to wake up and recognize these demons want to destroy your lives, so you need to put them on notice. Therefore, I suggest you read this notice out loud and in faith:

> "Demons, I will no longer allow you to operate out of secrecy and deception. I am now going to discern you, and I will become aware of the devil's schemes. I will no longer believe your lies, for I know you are really my enemy. Instead, I am going to be continually filled with the Holy Spirit and the power of God, and drive you out of people, cast you off of people, and ban your demonic structures from influencing my relational networks. Because Jesus Christ is my Lord, and He has promised that He will be with me till the very end of the age. Consequently, I will go out in His authority and power and trample on snakes and scorpions and overcome all the power of the enemy, and nothing will harm me" (see Luke 10:19; Matt. 28:18-20).

That's what *Surprisingly Supernatural Step #4B How to Ask for the Authority to Bind Evil Spirits and Drive Out Demons* is all about. So take the challenge and walk out in your birthright, and begin to discern demons, bind them, stir them up, or cast them out of people.

Then begin to educate other people that evil spirits, demons, and the devil are real spiritual beings that do exist. And teach them that these demons want to destroy their lives and inhibit their ability to know the Only True God and Jesus Christ's mercy toward them, and His willingness to forgive them for all of their sins. Then you can invite them to receive the Lord Jesus Christ and be saved.

Chapter 6: Discussion Questions

1. When we inhibit the evil spirits that are in, on, or around people from influencing them, we are allowing the nonbelievers to be free so they can hear the gospel message.
    a. Can you describe how you have tried to share your faith with someone, but you were unable to get your message across?
    b. How do you think evil spirits have been blocking the people from hearing the gospel message?

2. The gift of discernment helps to know if evil spirits have left the person or not.
    a. How have you noticed someone might have an evil spirit?
    b. How were you able to discern the evil spirit being in, on or around the person?
    c. We need to ask the Lord for the gift of discerning of spirits. What is preventing you from asking Him in faith for this gift?

3. Believing believers may command evil spirits off of people's minds or out of their bodies to help the person know Jesus is Lord and to help the person hear the gospel message.
    a. How can you begin to learn to bind evil spirits and cast out demons, so other people can hear the gospel message?
    b. How can you begin to experiment with the gift of discernment and then begin to bind or cast off evil spirits?

4. The secular society thinks that evil spirits are a myth from the Middle-Ages.
    a. How can you be an advocate to educate people that evil spirits are real?
    b. As we enter into the end-times the encounters with evil spirits will grow. Are you willing to quit ignoring their reality and begin to stand in your authority in Christ and command evil spirits to leave people?

5. The Bible says that in the end-times evil spirits will be released to torment nonbelievers.

      a. Do you see why the Lord will want to demonstrate His power through believing believers who can discern evil spirits, bind evil spirits, and cast them out?
      b. How can you grow in these gifts so when nonbelievers are tormented by evil spirits, you will bind them or cast them out and then you can bring them to the Lord Jesus Christ to be saved?

6. Jesus is the King of kings and Lord of lords and He is supreme over all other gods associated with other false religions.
      a. How can you be willing to be prepared to confront people in false religions and show them that evil spirits live in them because they worship false gods?

7. Jesus told the disciples who tried to cast out a demon, but were unsuccessful, that they were perverse and unbelieving. What do you think Jesus would say to believers who do not even attempt to cast out demons? True believing believers need to begin to practice driving out demons.
      a. What do you need to do in order for you to begin to practice deliverance?
      b. Mark 16: 17 tells us believers will drive out demons, I said earlier if you do not drive out demons are you a nonbeliever? The true believers who want to follow and obey the Lord Jesus Christ need to rise up in this hour. All believing believers need to arise.

CHAPTER 7

PRACTICING THE RELEASE OF THE GIFTS OF THE SPIRIT

In this book, we have discussed how believing believers are able to be continually filled with the Holy Spirit, have the ability to hear the Father's voice, are able to heal the sick, and are able to discern evil spirits, and then bind them or cast them out. These abilities come from being in relationship with the Father through your faith in Jesus Christ and having His Holy Spirit in you and upon you, and thus making you into a believing believer.

I hope you do not think that being a believing believer who operates by releasing the supernatural gifts as something strange now. I hope that you do not think of yourself as being surprisingly supernatural. I say that because our Lord Jesus implied that His sheep will hear His voice (see John 10:16). And those who believe in His name will drive out demons, and lay their hands on sick people, who will get well (see Mark 16:17-18; Matt. 10:8).

Prophecy, deliverance, and healing are the portions for all true followers of Jesus Christ, once they have been continually filled by the Holy Spirit. That's why I call them believing believers. When you believe that Jesus Christ has given you every spiritual blessing, and you begin to ask regularly for the Holy Spirit to fill you, and you ask for the gifts of the Spirit, then your life will be transformed; and you will walk out in your birthright *in Jesus Christ* (see Eph. 1:3). Then it will be very easy for you to witness on Jesus Christ's behalf.

When a believing believer is in a relationship with the Heavenly Father, the Lord Jesus, and the Holy Spirit then you are given access to all the spiritual gifts and that means you will be able to do what Paul says in Romans 15,

> ...I have proclaimed fully the gospel of Christ (Rom 15:19b).

To begin with you do not have to be operating in all the spiritual gifts to begin to preach the gospel of Christ. You can start by operating in only one of the gifts, like healing for example. When you witness to nonbelievers with the gift of healing, and you lay your hands on them and they get healed; that's when you can invite them to ask Jesus Christ for His mercy and to save them. The gospel means "The Good News." When the nonbeliever gets healed, he can easily see the good news of the gospel of Christ.

But eventually, as a believing believer, you will fully preach the gospel of Christ, and that means you will demonstrate the kingdom fully with healing, prophecy, deliverance, as well as, with love, peace, joy, caring for the poor, and you will help those who are in need of justice. When you become a believing believer, you release the gifts of the Spirit as your approach to preaching the gospel, and it aligns to what Paul shared in 1 Corinthians 2,

> My message and my preaching were not wise and persuasive words, but with a demonstration of the Spirit's power, so that your faith should not rest on men's wisdom, but on God's power (1 Cor. 2:4).

Paul did not solely operate in the Spirit's power. He occasionally reasoned with people trying to convince them of the truth about the gospel of Christ (see Acts 18:4; 28:23). And he also cared for the poor (see 2 Cor. 8:19-21). So if you follow Paul's example, at times you will care for the poor's practical needs, and at other times you will witness to nonbelievers by reasoning with them about the truth of the gospel of Christ.

Although reasoning is not the way you win a person's heart. Sometimes reasoning can deal with their mental objections; when they are overcome, then they may permit you to access their heart and their felt needs, which are always fulfilled in Christ. In addition to sharing the power of God to witness to people, there are some other considerations to be included in your witnessing approach.

Engle's Scale of Evangelism to Access Evangelism Success

Many believers are now being trained throughout the body of Christ to release the gifts of the Spirit. But the release of the gifts of the Spirit approach is different from many of the standard evangelistic approaches in the recent past. Therefore, I want to help you to see how effective releasing the gifts of the Spirit is as an evangelistic method. It will be helpful for you to understand "The Engle's Scale of Evangelism."

"The Engle's Scale of Evangelism" was developed by James F. Engle and Wilbur Norton to help demonstrate the process of how people come to Christ. Briefly, they said that people come from a deficit position, which may start at negative 10, and then they need to be brought up the ladder to Zero, which is the point of conversion where they receive Jesus Christ as their Lord and Savior. The scale starts at negative 10 and moves to 0, which is conversion to Christ. And then it continues upward to +8, which is learning to become a disciple, who eventually will become a believing believer.[75]

Descriptions for the Levels of the Engle's Scale of Evangelism

- **-10:** A person with no awareness of the super-natural and is a complete atheist.
- **-9:** No knowledge of Christianity.
- **-8:** Initial awareness of Christianity.
- **-7:** Has some interest in Christianity.
- **-6:** Aware of the basic facts of Christianity.
- **-5:** Starting to grasp the implications of Christianity.
- **-4:** A positive attitude toward Christianity.
- **-3:** Has awareness of his or her personal needs.
- **-2:** Challenged to act.
- **-1:** Repentance and faith.
- **0:** Conversion: A disciple is born!
- **1:** Evaluation of the decision.

2: Becoming a part of the body.
3: Involved in ministry.
4-7: Growing in faith and maturity.
8: Making other disciples—a disciple is matured and becomes a believing believer.

When a believing believer releases the gifts of the Spirit, you will demonstrate that the kingdom of God is near, and then you can tell the nonbeliever who the King is: "It's King Jesus Christ!" Releasing the gifts of the Spirit can take a person from negative 10 with no awareness of the supernatural and can move him up several steps on the Engle's Scale. Some people may move from negative 10 to 0 (conversion) in one encounter. Here are some examples when I released the gifts of the Spirit, and the result was nonbelievers had sudden conversion experiences that moved them up several levels on the Engle's Scale.

A Word of Knowledge Helps to Move a Nonbeliever from Negative 6 to 0 on the *Engel's Scale*

I was flying to Los Angeles and I sat next to an Asian student from Western Washington College. She was going to visit her parents in Texas. They were *Buddhists*. I did the impartation test and she felt the power of God flow from my hands. Then I shared a brief gospel message about who Jesus was, and I shared why she should receive Him as her Lord and Savior. She indicated that she had heard a little bit about Jesus before, because her boyfriend was a Christian, and she had gone to church with his family.

I asked her what her name was and she said, "Gloria." I told her, "Your name is prophetic, because it's symbolic of what the Lord wants to do through you. I believe the Lord Jesus wants you to release His healing power to touch other people, so you will bring Him glory. That's why your name is Gloria!" Then I received a word of knowledge and asked her, "Does your mother have inflammation in her joints?" Gloria said, "Yes, she has arthritis in her knees." Gloria's eyes grew bigger, because she knew Jesus knew her mother's situation.

I told Gloria that "in Mark 16:18 it says that believers lay hands on the sick and the sick get well. If you receive Jesus Christ today you can go as a believer and in Jesus' name, you can lay your hands on your mother's inflammation, and she will get well. Would you like to pray to receive Jesus now?" She said, "Yes." Gloria prayed and asked Jesus to be her Lord and Savior, and then I imparted the Holy Spirit and the gifts of healing to her. Gloria moved from about a negative 6 to 0 in the span of a half hour during a flight from Seattle to Los Angles, because the gifts of the Spirit were released.

In Chapter 7 of my book: *Wake Up!*, I wrote that "Believing in Jesus is the first step into the doorway of the kingdom, but even with that first little step through the doorway of the kingdom, the believer can lay hands on the sick and they will get well."[76] I believe that is especially true in this case since I had the word of knowledge about Gloria's mother's inflammation. And I also imparted the gifts of healing to Gloria, and I know the Scripture is true that believers lay hands on the sick and they get well (see Mark 16:18). I had no doubt that her mother could be healed if Gloria touched her and prayed "Be healed! In Jesus' name!" When you operate in the gifts of the Spirit yourself, you will operate in faith and you are enabled to encourage others to step out in faith too. That's what I did with Gloria.

Gloria was one of those sudden conversions that we frequently get when we release the gifts of the Spirit.[77] Evangelism should not be separated from discipleship, as the new believer should be in a continuous process of transformation.[78] This is ideal, but it will not always happen.

I gave Gloria my e-mail address, but she has not contacted me, so I was not able to see if she was discipled or not. However, I do carry discipleship material around with me like Surprisingly Supernatural Cards, Bibles, and other pieces of writing that I can give to new converts, so they can begin to walk out the process of transformation without initially being discipled by another believer.

A new convert who does not get into a discipleship relationship right away is not ideal, but believing believers are compelled to be merciful and snatch nonbelievers from the fire and save them (see Jude 22). You are also to trust that the Lord can lead the person in the appropriate steps of faith.

I have prayed for Gloria, and I also trust that God will bring her into relationships with other believers who can help to disciple her. One Surprisingly Supernatural Card that is on the book's website: www.surprisinglysupernatural.com and is listed under Chapter 7 is a card that helps nonbelievers to pray and ask Jesus to be their Lord and Savior. It is called: *How to Ask Jesus Christ to Be Your Lord and Savior."* It is also a free download.

I believe the percentage of sudden conversions are going to grow to a much higher percent, once believing believers get a hold of this vision that all believers can learn to release the gifts of the Spirit and touch people with healing, deliverance, and prophecy. When God really pours out His Spirit, it will result in numerous salvations when miracles are released in plazas, in public malls and on public transit. The believing believers need to get ready by immediately being continually filled by the Spirit, and by learning how to release the gifts of the Spirit today, as this outpouring is going to come in a very short time from now.

Muslims Come to Christ When the Gifts of the Spirit are Released

I befriended a Muslim businessman whom I will call Ali (not his real name). He started to witness the transformation that was occurring in my life since I became filled with the Holy Spirit. A few years ago I told him how Jesus was healing people through me. Then he shared how he had a problem with an internal organ and he asked for prayer.

We sat in my car and I asked if I could touch his hand when I prayed for him, and he said "Yes." When I prayed, the Spirit's power was released and an electrical current flowed into Ali's hand. Ali was shocked by a bolt of God's electricity! He immediately opened the car door and declared, "I have to go!" My friend had a personal subjective experience that day that came from his friend who follows Jesus Christ, and he could not deny its reality.

I laid my hands on him over subsequent visits, and he could feel the anointing of the Holy Spirit on his internal organ each time I prayed for him. Then the Lord told me that "when Ali's father dies, he will become a believer." The next year his father died, and I came to visit him five months later. Again I prayed for his internal organ, but this time I felt compelled to ask Ali, "Do you want to receive Jesus as your Lord?" And he said, "Yes." So he prayed to receive Jesus Christ as his Lord and Savior, and then I did a deliverance session with him, and he felt the evil spirits moving within his stomach area before I commanded them to leave. He was born again into Jesus Christ that day.

Persuading people from different religions is not easy, but when you first release the kingdom of God, then you can tell them that Jesus Christ is the Eternal King, and that makes it is much easier. I have seen Ali occasionally and I have shared my faith with him, and I have encouraged him in his faith. He required a few touches over a couple of years, but it was only five or six visits in total and then he came to the Lord. That was because the gifts of the Spirit were released each time enabling Ali to move up several levels on the Engel's Scale.

I was in Starbucks and a Muslim woman asked me about my book. I shared a few of the supernatural stories in the book with her, and then I tested her with the impartation of the Holy Spirit. She felt it in her fingers, but it left her fingers when I pulled away. I had her read the card *You Experienced a World Test*, and she read that Jesus said that the Holy Spirit would not be with the world (see John 14:16-17).

I asked her if she knew anything about Jesus. And she said they had some exposure to Jesus as a child. I explained a little more that Jesus was the Creator God, and He came as a sacrifice for our sins. I told her how Islam was a throwback to the law, but through Jesus Christ we not only have forgiveness, but we also have righteousness, as the Holy Spirit makes us holy, and He can also heal us.

I told her if she prayed to receive Jesus she would then feel the Spirit flow into her body and remain. She wanted to pray, so we prayed a sinner's prayer. And then I imparted the Holy Spirit and she felt the Spirit rush up into her torso, and she reported that it went all the way down to her feet. I then had her confess worshipping a false god and I cast out a *spirit of false religion* from her.[79] She felt it move up her torso and then up through her throat, and then it came out of her mouth as she breathed out. Then I prayed for her eyes and they were healed. She moved up six levels on the Engel's Scale just because I released the kingdom of God.

Release the Good News of the Gospel and Do What Doctors and Drugs Can't

When you share the gospel of the kingdom today, it means you must demonstrate the Spirit's power. That gives them a personal subjective experience. The gospel of Jesus Christ is also called the "Good News." When people get healed, it is a personal and subjective experience for them, as they feel better. Some people even cry when they are healed, because what doctors and drugs could not do, Jesus Christ can—Jesus heals the sick! That's the good news of the gospel. Their tears are tears of joy and relief.[80]

In today's post-modern world everybody has an equal opportunity to share their point of view. Your opinion about Jesus is not any more valid than their opinion is about *Buddha*, or *Allah*, or whoever their god is. But when you give them their own experience with the power from the kingdom of God, they will retain a memory of that experience. Then that can open up the doorway into their heart, which allows you to share your faith about Jesus with them. Then you can ask them if they want to receive Jesus Christ as their Lord and Savior.

In this post-modern era you can give them a supernatural experience that will shift their current frame of reference; because when they have a personal experience, it is true for them! Then you can refer to their experience later on, and you can continue to share with them about Jesus Christ from that perspective. Releasing the kingdom of God with all the gifts of the Spirit flowing out of you will open the doors of nonbelievers' hearts so they can receive Jesus Christ.

The Muslims' Goal and the Believing Believers' Goal

In Chapter 3, I listed three videos that showed Muslims were having visions, dreams or encounters with Jesus Christ, and then they became believers. Jesus is working at evangelizing the Muslims. However, another video on the website under Chapter 7 is called: *Muslim Demographics*. This video reveals that the Muslims intend to take over the Western nations by having large families, and they plan to become the majority population in the democratic nations, due to the low average birthrates in those European nations (1.3 children per couple). Consequently, the Muslims will just vote in their Islamic law (Sharia Law) once they become the majority population in those Western European nations.[81]

One key strategy is for believing believers to release the gifts of the Spirit en masse among the Muslims, and show them that Jesus Christ can heal their diseases and drive out their demons. Many Muslims tend to be argumentative, so it can be difficult to discuss with them why they should accept Jesus Christ. But when they are healed or a demon is stirred up or cast out, then they can begin to understand that Jesus is God (see John 1:1-2, 17-18). Then they may be willing to listen to you. Releasing the gifts of the Spirit will be one of the best ways to win over many Muslims and other nonbelievers in the years to come.

I believe that the Lord is going to pour out His Spirit in great waves in North America during the coming years and beyond. And I also believe that being a believing believer, who releases the gifts of the Spirit, is what the whole church is called to do today. And that role will continue to last until the very end of the age. Every single believer who wants to glorify the Lord Jesus Christ can be continually filled with the Holy Spirit, and then they can walk out and demonstrate the kingdom of God in their relational network.

Fruit From Releasing the Gifts of the Spirit

When I began this book project, I started to keep a record of the ministry that I was involved in. During a two year period, I witnessed to over 375 people with the power of the Holy Spirit. Many believers were brought into a deeper understanding of the Lord Jesus Christ and His Spirit. These believers heard about His call on their lives for them to become believing believers, and they heard His invitation for them to be continually filled by His Holy Spirit. Many of them received miraculous healings or had demons driven out of them or cast off of them.

Of the over 375 people that I witnessed to over that period, 169 of them were nonbelievers. Over three dozen of these nonbelievers became born again believers, as they prayed and asked Jesus Christ to be their Lord and Savior. And they also received an impartation of the Holy Spirit. Most of these people only had a single encounter with the Holy Spirit. But once I released the gifts of the Spirit, I just shared a few words about Jesus Christ with them, and they were convinced that Jesus was God, and they wanted to ask Him to be their Lord and Savior.

All of these new born again believers were offered help so they could connect with the body of Christ, and receive fellowship and discipleship in some way. It's important for believing believers once the gifts of the Spirit are released and nonbelievers accept Jesus Christ, that you point these new converts in a direction so they are able to grow in Christ.

Evangelism should be linked to discipleship, which means the new convert must be connected with someone or some material that will help them to take the next few steps in Christ. However, the believing believer does not know the future, only God knows that. The believing believer is compelled to respond to the promptings and leadings of the Spirit of God, and release the gifts when they are called to release them. Then the nonbeliever may be willing to accept Jesus Christ's salvation and His Spirit, so he becomes born again (see John 3:3-5).

The Lord knows what each person needs and when they need it. If He has given you the grace to win someone over to Him, He has His reasons. Maybe the person will die soon, and you were there just in the nick of time. Receiving Jesus Christ and receiving His Holy Spirit brings people into a new journey in life. They are born again and then they belong to God. Therefore, God will see to it that they will grow.

Believing believers need to seize all the opportunities to win people over, so they will receive eternal life in Jesus Christ. With some of the new converts the believing believer will be able to disciple them themselves, but for other new converts, God will provide different discipleship opportunities so they can grow. But the believing believers are called to win souls, whenever the Lord provides that opportunity.

The witnessing opportunities I have had over that two year period, has been the most fruitful time in my life for ministry. Once I was clothed in Christ, I became fruitful (see John 15:5). When I minister, I just follow the leading of the Lord. I am not obsessive about going out to witness, but the only thing I try to be obsessive about is being obedient to the Lord, and listening to what He is asking me to do.

The witnessing opportunities I have had over this two year period occurred not because I went out looking for them. I just went out being aware that the presence of God was with me, and I knew that meant that I could touch someone with God's power whenever and wherever I was called to do that. Walking with the presence of God around me has created the lifestyle for me of walking in the Spirit. Consequently, when I meet people in my daily rounds, I would just pay attention to what the Lord asks me to do. Sometimes, I am not aware of His leading, but I am led anyway.

I went to a prophetic school offered by *The Elijah House* in Spokane, Washington. One day at lunch time I sensed I was supposed to go to lunch by myself. So I got in my car and drove out toward the street. At the street, I sensed the dance had begun and I was supposed to follow by making a turn to the right. I turned right, and then at the next corner, I sensed I was to turn right again (see Isa. 30:21). But I thought: *All the restaurants are to the left, I wonder where I am going?*

I drove, and then I noticed the *Iron Horse Bar and Grill*, and I sensed I was to turn into their parking lot. As I entered the building the lady behind the bar said something to me, but I could not hear it. So I asked, "Are you the waitress?" And she said, "I am the everything!" Then the Lord spoke into my mind: "I am the all in all." I knew that this was a set up.

She sat me at a table by the deck and I observed that she was pregnant. I ordered lunch and ate it. When she came to see if I wanted to have anything else, I felt compelled to test her sensitivity to the Holy Spirit, so I asked her to point her fingers toward mine. After a few seconds, I asked if she felt anything and she said "I feel a tingling like electricity." I asked her, "Do you know who is touching you?" She said, "No, I have no clue." I said, "The Lord Jesus Christ is touching you with His Holy Spirit. Do you know Jesus Christ?" She responded, "I know about Jesus." Then I said, "You had better know more than just about Him, because the son you are going to give birth to has a call on his life. He is called to be a prophet."

She began to cry as she knew there was no way I would know she was going to have a son. I had never seen her before in my life. I asked her, "Would you like to pray to receive Jesus now?" She said, "Yes." And we prayed and then I imparted to her some gifts of the Spirit, and as I was finishing imparting to her she let out a little scream and said, "He jumped in my stomach!" And I responded, "Just like John the Baptist" (see Luke 1:41).

When you give yourself to the Lord for His purposes, He sometimes will speak to you, and sometimes you are led by the Spirit. Scripture tells us that those who are led by the Spirit are the sons of God (see Rom. 8:14b). When you are led, it means you respond to the promptings of the Spirit, you may not know the whole plan, but you follow like a sheep would, as you are just trusting that the Lord is leading you.

As sons and daughters of the King you are called to operate in rest and peace as you go about your days carrying the presence of God with you. Jesus did not heal everyone He met who was sick. He just healed or cast out demons when He was instructed to do that by the Father in heaven. That's the plan for all believing believers, who are to learn to respond to the leading of the Spirit, and learn to respond to the Father's voice. You do not have to rescue everyone, but you do have to reach those people that He places in front of you and tells you to touch. Then you get to touch them with His power and His love.

If 5,000 believers capture the vision in this book and become believing believers, who will operate by walking in the presence of God as a lifestyle, then as you go through your daily life, you will just release the kingdom of God. Then each of you will see three nonbelievers every two months who will ask Jesus Christ to be their Lord and Savior, so they will become born again.

If 5,000 believers in my city of Bellevue, Washington with a population of about 115,000 get a hold of this vision and become believing believers, then the whole city will be transformed in just over fifteen months (5000 x 1.5 converts x 15mths = 112,500). You can do all things through Jesus Christ who strengthens you, for it is not by might, nor by power, *but it is by Jesus Christ's Spirit* (see Phil. 4:13; Zech. 4:6). What about your city? What about your nation? Do you want to take your city for God? If you capture this vision and you become a believing believer who can release the gifts of the Spirit, then you will.

Personally writing a book on empowering believers to learn to become sons and daughters of the King, so they can release the gifts of the Spirit, and the result will be that the Lord Jesus is glorified was an awesome responsibility. But when I look at my stats, I have to remain humble. I am doing okay, but there have not been multitudes saved at any one stop, yet. But I have to remember that is not the goal.

The goal is for each and every believing believer is to be continually filled by the Spirit of God, and then to follow the promptings the Lord gives the believing believers throughout their day. In the Preface, I wrote that the Lord told me "You are going to be part of a new movement…" that God is going to bring about. "'It is going to involve individual believers who will release the gifts of the Spirit right where they live, work, and play.' Then I began to see that God was leading me to lay my hands on people and I witnessed healings and miracles performed right before my eyes. I was in shock that God was working through me! I began to understand that this new movement was for the ordinary saints like me."

It was for all believers who wanted to believe for more of God in their lives. So no rallies, but I am just trying to encourage each and every believer to embrace the truth that the Lord Jesus Christ wants to breathe on you, so you can go out like He was sent, as a believing believer who is full of the Holy Spirit (see John 20:21-22).

It is really fun to release the kingdom of God and all the gifts of the Spirit flowing out from you, so you can bless people with healing, words of knowledge, or driving out evil spirits. But most of all you are able to extend to people the invitation to accept Jesus Christ as their Savior, and allow them to become born again. It is such an honor to be given the opportunity to bless people with the best gift in the world: the forgiveness of their sins in Jesus' blood, and being able to start a relationship with the Only True God.

That gift will last forever, as it is eternal. It is the most precious gift that anyone can receive. That's the mandate for believing believers, who the Scripture considers to be *wise* from a number of Scriptural perspectives (see Dan. 4:18; 12:3, 10; Prov. 11:30; Matt. 25:1-13). You walk in the Spirit because you are being continually filled by the Holy Spirit, then you will begin to operate with ease as you release the gifts of the Spirit and you will bring nonbelievers to faith in Jesus Christ.

I suggest that you use the Surprisingly Supernatural Cards regularly until you are able to release the gifts of the Spirit wherever you go. That may take weeks, months or even longer. But practice, be patient, and persevere until you become the believing believer that the Lord wanted you to become.

We are approaching the end of the end-times and Jesus asked "when the Son of Man comes, will He find faith on earth?" (Luke 18:8). Jesus wants to see His followers, the believing believers, to walk out with great faith and to be able to demonstrate the kingdom of God among all the nations of the world (see Matt. 24:14). We need to have faith when Jesus comes back because He knew the little horn would empower the Illuminati to propose the New World Order and the One World Religion, and they want to destroy Christianity, Christians, and depopulate the world (see Rev. 13:7-10). The Godly solution is that believing believers need to arise in this hour *en masse!*[82]

The *wise* virgins from Matthew 25:10-13 are the saints who have the oil for their lamps and they represent believers who honor the Lord Jesus Christ by loving Him and obeying Him, and becoming a home for Jesus and the Heavenly Father (see John 14:23). The *wise* virgins have oil. Therefore, they are clothed in the armor of light and clothed in Jesus Christ Himself; consequently, they will have very fruitful lives, and they will lead many nonbelievers into a relationship with Jesus Christ (see Rom. 13:12-14; Dan. 12:1-3).

The *wise* virgins will be invited to the wedding banquet at the end of the age, and they will become the Bride of Christ (see Matt. 25:10). Now is the time for you to respond to this message and become a believing believer who can release the gifts of the Spirit, so you can glorify the Lord

Jesus Christ in the world around you by walking in the Spirit, as He is calling the Bride of Christ to arise.

I believe my next book will be called: *The Joy of Walking in the Spirit*. I hope you will join in on the journey with me, and become a believing believer who is full of faith and is full of the Holy Spirit of God. This next book will show some of the next steps of faith that believing believers will be encouraged to take, as we continue to release the gifts of the Spirit and demonstrate the kingdom of God to glorify the Lord Jesus Christ.

Chapter 7: Discussion Questions

1. Is it now a bit of a surprise that you are surprisingly supernatural?
    a. Or did you kind of always think you were surprisingly supernatural?
    b. What kind of changes do you need to make to become surprisingly supernatural?

2. Did you realize that the Lord Jesus wants His sheep to hear His voice, drive out demons, and lay their hands on sick people who will get well (see John 10:16; Mark 16:17-18; Matt. 10:8)?
    a. What do you have to do to transform your thinking and begin to do those practices?

3. Do you see how releasing the gifts of the Spirit can bring nonbelievers to sudden conversion experiences that moved them up several levels on the Engle's Scale?
    a. How does the Engle's Scale help to indicate that releasing the gifts of the Spirit is a great way to bring in the lost?

4. Do you see how releasing the gifts of the Spirit is critical now, as we are in post-modernism and all the voices are valid?
    a. Do you believe *Buddha, Allah* and all the other false gods will bow to the power of Jesus Christ as He works through you?
    b. Do you see it is time for you to become a believing believer who can release the gifts everywhere you go?
    c. With the New World Order and the One World Religion being actively promoted by the Illuminati, how does that create the need for the believing believers to arise today?[83]

5. If you capture this book's vision then you will be able to transform the city you live in, and transform your nation.
    a. What are you waiting for?
    b. Do you see the urgency of the call to be continually filled by the Spirit of God and to learn how to release the gifts of the Spirit in this hour?
    c. Get the vision and walk out in your birthright.

Note: There are two more Step Cards that relate to releasing the gifts of the Spirit for evangelism and there is also a booklet called: *Congratulations on Your New Life in Jesus Christ*. This booklet is an invitation to new converts to step into the supernatural blessings that all believers can have in Jesus Christ. They are all posted to the webpage: www.surprisinglysupernatural.com and are listed under Chapter 7:

- *Surprisingly Supernatural Step Card #5: How to be a Witness of Jesus Christ*
- *Surprisingly Supernatural Step Card #6: Intercession for Evangelism*
- The booklet: *Congratulations on Your New Life in Jesus Christ*

These Step Cards will help you to ask the Lord for the gifts of the Spirit to witness and to intercede, and they are free downloads from the website.

CHAPTER 8

BECOMING THE BRIDE OF CHRIST

The body of Christ is entering into the final period of the end-times; consequently, I have realized that this three book series that the Spirit led me to write was intended to help believers to become the Bride of Christ.[84] Therefore, we need to know what the Lord wants us to do as His body on earth just before He comes back.

Much of this book has taught aspects of what the Bride of Christ is supposed to do at the very end of the end-times. And that is to release the gifts of the Spirit and bring glory to the Lord by bringing nonbelievers to faith, so they can become children of God themselves. This chapter will show some of the reasons why I think the body of Christ needs to be continually filled by the Holy Spirit, and why they need to learn to release the gifts of the Spirit, so they will become the Bride of Christ.

Jesus tells us,

> Behold, I come like a thief! Blessed is he who stays awake and keeps his clothes with him, so that he may not go naked and be shamefully exposed (Rev. 16:15).

This is a prophetic warning for those who live at the end of the end-times. Jesus declares we need to keep our clothes with us. When you are naked, you will expose your sinfulness from your life to the Holy God. That's why you need to be clothed in Jesus Christ, as His righteousness will cover your sinfulness. My first book is called "*Transformed by the Power of God: Learning to be Clothed in Jesus Christ,*" but I had wanted it to be called *The Designer's Clothes,* because the revelation was about being clothed in Jesus Christ, who is The Designer (see Rom. 13:14).

My second book is called *Wake Up! Preparing for the End-Times Outpouring*, and it alerted believers to a number of spiritual hindrances that they need to wake up to. It also covers the character issues believing believers need to develop, so they will be effective ministers when they release the gifts of the Spirit.

Releasing the gifts of the Spirit to bring in the harvest is what this third book *Surprisingly Supernatural* has taught.

These books cover the basis of what Jesus wants believers who live at the end of the end-times to do. You need to wake up, get dressed in your spiritual clothes, release the gifts of the Spirit, bring in the harvest, and glorify the Lord. Once you are awakened and you have your spiritual clothes on, then you can easily glorify the Lord.

The end-times parable in Matthew 25 speaks of the *wise* virgins who had oil, which implies they had gotten dressed (see Matt. 25:1-13). I believe the *wise* virgins had gotten dressed, and then they glorified the Lord, as they went about living their lives on the earth at the very end of the age. You will be *wise* if you follow these *wise* virgins' practices, and be continually filled by the Holy Spirit, so you are clothed in Jesus Christ, as they were believers for they had lamps; but their lamps were also full of the oil of the Holy Spirit. Those *wise* virgins were the only believers who lived at the end of the end-times who got to enter into the wedding banquet at the very end of the age (see Matt. 25:1-13).

Another end-times parable teaches about the talents we are given and we are supposed to use them (see Matt. 25:14-30). This third book *Surprisingly Supernatural* teaches you how to do the things the Bride of Christ is supposed to do at the very end of the end-times, which is to use your talents. Your talents are the spiritual gifts that you have been given. *The Bride of Christ is supposed to use her talents by releasing the gifts of the Spirit into the world around her, so she can bring glory to the Lord.*

My hope is you will take these prophetic words seriously and know that the Lord wants His children to be faithful followers at the very end of the age. Jesus did ask,

> ...when the Son of Man comes, will He find faith on the earth? (Luke 18:8b).

Having faith when Jesus comes back means that you really believe that the Father in heaven wants to clothe you in power! (see Matt. 6:30b; Luke 24:49). Having faith means that you not only believe the Father wants to clothe you in power, but you will act on your faith and ask Him to clothe you.

Great faith means that you are absolutely certain, which means you really believe that the Lord wants to work through you to bring miracles into other people's lives (see Matt. 8:6-13). But bringing miracles into other people's lives requires that you have Jesus with you (see John 15:5; Rom. 13:14). When you have Jesus with you, what was impossible before becomes possible. But do you really have the faith for that reality or not? (see Luke 18:27; Matt. 17:20). Believing believers will have faith, great faith!

When Jesus asks if there will be faith on earth when He returns, He is wondering if there will be any believers who will walk out in great faith and demonstrate who He is to other people in their relational networks. Believing believers will have great faith and will demonstrate the reality of miracles.

Here are some of the prophetic words that point to the responsibility and the participation of believing believers who are assigned to live at the very end of the end-times, as they are slated to become the Bride of Christ (see Acts 17:26-28).

The Bride Belongs to the Bridegroom

John the Baptist was a prophet who Jesus said, "...there has not risen anyone greater than John the Baptist..." (Matt. 11:11b). Jesus clearly had respect for John the Baptist and this was one of John's prophetic utterances: "The bride belongs to the bridegroom" (John 3:29). The Bride of Christ is to belong to the Lord Jesus Christ, who is the bridegroom. I wrote in Chapter 3:

> "Jesus supports this idea about the believer who is in a close relationship with God, is able to hear God speak when He said,

> He who belongs to God hears what God says (John 8:47a).
>
> This verse implies that those people who belong to God, who are His possession, are the people who will hear His voice…"

It is not coincidental that the Father in heaven has poured out His Spirit since Acts 2 on all people hoping that they will receive the Spirit and become the children of God, who actually belong to God. When they become God's possession, then they will be able to hear what the Lord says, and will be able to prophesy that to other people as well (see Acts 2:17-18). This coincides with what Jesus said, "He who belongs to God hears what God says" (John 8:47a). The Bride of Christ is to belong to the Lord, and will have an intimate relationship with the Lord, and will be in communion with the Lord.

We have read throughout this book how we are to belong to the Lord. And that begins by asking Jesus to become our Lord and Savior, and then by being continually filled by the Holy Spirit, and then we will learn to demonstrate that we are God's children by releasing the gifts of the Spirit. And we will bring glory to the Lord. There are a few prophetic Scriptures that indicate believers who live at the end of the end-times will be continually filled by the Holy Spirit and they will bring glory to the Lord.

The Wise Will Understand

The *wise* we are told from Daniel will *shine* like the Stars in Heaven, will *lead many* to righteousness, and they will *understand*. The book of Daniel ends with this,

> Those who are *wise* will shine like the brightness of the heavens, and those who *lead many to righteousness*, like the stars for ever and ever (Dan. 12:3; emphasis added).

Daniel describes believing believers that live at the end of the age, and he prophesies that they are *wise*, as they will lead many to righteousness.

Leading people to righteousness is leading them into a relationship with Jesus Christ, so they become sanctified, purified by His blood, His Spirit, and His Word. Then those new born again believers can demonstrate that they are the children of God, just like the believing believers who lead them to Jesus Christ, as they will learn to release the gifts of the Spirit as well. Daniel also says,

> …the words are closed up and sealed until the time of the end…None of the wicked will understand, but *those who are wise will understand* (Dan. 12:9-10; emphasis added).

The words have been sealed up, but now we are at the end of the end-times and the *wise* will understand them. Remember that Matthew 25:1-13 also talks about the *wise* virgins in a parable that speaks about the end of the end-times? There is a connection between the *wise* from Daniel 12, who understand that they are to lead people to righteousness at the end of the age, and the *wise* virgins whose containers are full of oil (see Dan. 12:3, 10; Matt. 25:4). They both represent the Bride of Christ, who is *wise*, as she is full of the oil of the Spirit, so she can demonstrate the gifts of the Spirit and lead many to righteousness, which is leading them to Jesus Christ. They are the believing believers who will arise in this hour for they will be *wise* and understand that they are to be continually filled by the Holy Spirit, which is being filled with oil, until they shine like the stars; and then they will be able to lead many nonbelievers to Christ, as that's what the Bride of Christ will do (see Prov. 11:30).

What the Wise Servants Will Do

In Matthew 24, it states that believers must keep watch, and then it says,

> So you also must be ready, because the Son of Man will come at an hour when you do not expect him (Matt. 24:44).

Believing believers must be ready for the Lord's return and must be *wise*, as Matthew 24 states,

> Who then is the faithful and *wise servant*, whom the master has put in charge of the servants in his household *to give them their food at the proper time*? (Matt. 24:45; emphasis added).

What *food* is Jesus referring to here? Well, Jesus speaks about *His food* in John 4 and says,

> *'My food,'* said Jesus, *'is to do the will of Him who sent Me and to finish His work*. Do you not say, 'Four months more and then the harvest?' I tell you, open your eyes and look at the fields! They are *ripe for the harvest* (John 4:34-36; emphasis added).

The faithful and *wise* servant is called to give the other servants their *food* (see Matt. 24:45). In context, the *food* is *doing the Father's will*, and that is *to bring in the harvest and to glorify the Lord.* (see John 4:34-36).

This book: *Surprisingly Supernatural* and the Surprisingly Supernatural Training Schools teach believers to get the good food of doing the Father's will. The goal is that you will not only learn to release the gifts of the Spirit, but you will bring in the harvest. And then you will disciple the new believers and teach them about the time that we are in; how they need to be continually filled by the Spirit, and they need to learn to release the gifts of the Spirit to glorify the Lord by bringing in the harvest themselves. That's what the faithful and *wise* servants of the Lord will be involved in at this time.

A Prophetic Word on Training the Saints Today

Ann Ott is a prophet, and she operates a ministry called: *In His Presence* (IHP). Ann's ministry teaches believers to prophesy and to heal the sick. Then she takes them out on outreaches to bring in the harvest and glorify the Lord. Ann emailed the author (8/27/2011) the following:

> "A Word to Ann from the Lord concerning IHP. The reason IHP exists is because of these ministries who refused to let their people be trained or step out and do the things God told them to do. They're sitting there in agony because they know they're called. No option for them. He is saying we

exist because of that. We're going to open the flood gate. This is why we're going to grow so unbelievably. I saw God crying because His churches have done this and haven't allowed the people to be trained or have not encouraged them to step out in their gifting. God is upset."

There has never been a more urgent need for the saints to be trained to do the works of ministry than the time that we are now in (see Eph. 4:12). We need to keep watch, but we also need the *food* of doing God's will. This is the goal for all of the saints to learn *to bring in the harvest* at this time. The faithful and *wise* servants of the Lord will teach and empower the saints to do the work of ministry until the saints will become the Bride of Christ.

The Bride of Christ is the Army of God

The Song of Songs depicts a relationship between the Bridegroom and the Bride. And in Chapter 6 it describes a bride, which appears to be the Bride of Christ for it says,

> You are beautiful, my darling, as Tirzah, lovely as Jerusalem, majestic as *troops with banners* (Song of Songs 6:4; emphasis added).

Here the Bride of Christ is described as beautiful, lovely and is like an *army with banners*. What is significant is that *Adonai* is described in Exodus 17 as *Adonai-Nissi*, which means: "The Lord is my banner" (see Exod. 17:15). The Bride of Christ will become the army of God, and she will be clothed in Jesus Christ, and He will also be our banner.

The Bride of Christ is to become a great army at the very end of the end-times, the Lord will be her banner, and He will also clothe her in His glory. Then she will bring glory to the Lord. The verse in Song of Songs continues with her friends describing the Bride of Christ, for they say,

> Who is this that appears like the dawn, fair as the moon, bright as the sun, majestic as the stars in procession (Song of Songs 6:10).

This sounds like the description in Daniel 12 that tells us the Bride of Christ is bright like the heavens and shines like the stars, as this verse describes the Bride of Christ is shining bright as the sun, and is majestic as stars (see Daniel 12:3). Being bright like the heavens and shining like stars is only because the Bride of Christ is to be clothed in the armor of light (see Rom. 13:12; Luke 11:36). That's what makes her beautiful, lovely and majestic in the Lord's eyes, because when she is clothed in the armor of light, then she can demonstrate who Jesus Christ is to the world around her.

The Believing Believers' Allotted Inheritance

Daniel closes with this statement,

> …at the end of the days you will rise to receive your allotted inheritance (Dan. 12:13).

I believe the *wise* will receive their allotted inheritance in two portions. The first portion of their inheritance is receiving the fullness of the kingdom of God in this life. And that's what the Lord spoke to Aaron about,

> The Lord said to Aaron, 'You will have no inheritance in their land, nor will you have any share among them; I am your share and your inheritance among the Israelites' (Num. 18:20).

Those who are *wise* will know that having the Lord Himself as their inheritance is a great honor. Only Aaron and the other priests could come close to God's Tent of Meeting, but the other Israelites were banned from going to the Tent of Meeting, and they were unable to have true intimacy with the Lord (see Num. 18:22). But Aaron and the priests could go before the Lord and be intimate with Him, as they performed their acts of worship.

The *wise* generation of believers that will live at the end of the end-times will be willing to have the Lord for their inheritance, who is Spirit; because of that they will have great intimacy with the Lord (see John 4:24). They will also have great exploits, because they will have the Holy Spirit as their inheritance in this life.

The believing believers will also be the Lord's Inheritance, as 1 Samuel 10 implies that when it says,

> ...Has not the Lord anointed you leader over *His inheritance*
> (1 Sam. 10:1b; emphasis added)

The Lord is the believing believers' inheritance and the believing believers are the Lord's inheritance (see Ex. 34:29). With the knowledge of this, the believing believers will worship the Lord in Spirit and truth, and out of that intimacy the love and power of God will flow through the believing believers.

The result is that the believing believers who have continually received the Holy Spirit will have the Holy Spirit as their inheritance in this life. Then they will walk out in obedience and bring glory to the Lord in their relational networks demonstrating: healing, miracles, deliverance, prophecy, and signs and wonders. That's how the *wise* will recognize that they have the Lord Himself as their inheritance in this life. Consequently, they will walk out their birthrights by demonstrating the Lord's spiritual gifts.

That's the first portion of their inheritance in this life, which is intimacy with the Holy Spirit and obeying the Lord by releasing His power and love. That's the believing believer's inheritance in this life. The fruit of which will be that many will come into a relationship with Jesus Christ and receive His forgiveness for their sins and His righteousness, as they will lead them to righteousness (see Dan. 12:3). Then the *wise* will rise to be with the Lord, and they will receive the second portion of their allotted inheritance.

The second portion of their allotted inheritance is a glorious reward in the eternal life for being *wise* and for obeying the Lord's commands by evangelizing nonbelievers in their relational networks and bringing many to righteousness. The *wise* will understand Daniel's words and will walk out in their birthrights as believing believers, and then they will be rewarded with a glorious eternal inheritance for obeying the Lord and doing His kingdom exploits.

They are the *wise* ones who shine like the brightness of heaven just like the stars. The reason why they shine so brightly is because they are continually filled with the kingdom of heaven itself, as they are filled so much with the Holy Spirit that they are wearing the armor of light (see Rom. 13:12).[85]

Daniel shows that the Most High God wants believing believers to impact the people they are sent to with the kingdom of God. The Most High God wants to reward the believing believers with an allotted inheritance that will not be destroyed, stolen or attacked by moths or rust (see Matt. 6:19-20).

The believing believers will have their hearts set on obeying the Lord's commission and will preach the gospel of the kingdom in the entire world. That's where their treasure is, for they will have the Holy Spirit as their inheritance in this life (see Matt. 6:21). They will show that they belong to God and are obedient followers, and then they will be rewarded with a wonderful eternal inheritance.

The Bride of Christ is being awakened in this season and so they will become warriors who are clothed with the kingdom of God around them (see Luke 24:49). They will become the sons of God who will release the creation from its bondage and bring the good news of the kingdom into the lives of other people (see Rom. 8:19). They will shine with the brightness of the heavens, as they lead many to righteousness—for they will lead many to the Lord Jesus Christ, as He is the Only Righteous One (see Dan. 12:3; Ps. 119:137; Rom. 5:17, 19). Daniel's prophesy about the end of the end-times concerns the Bride of Christ who will shine like the stars in heaven, and she will bring many people to righteousness, which is leading them to Jesus Christ.

The Bride's Voice Must Speak Up, But Then it Will Never Speak Again!

There are some other Scriptures that refer to the Bride of Christ that are found in Revelation and they appear to resonate with what Daniel has shown us. One Scripture tells us,

> The light of a lamp will never shine in you again. The voice of the bridegroom and bride will never be heard in you again. *Your merchants were the world's great men*. By *your magic spell all the nations were led astray* (Rev. 18:23; emphasis added).

Implicitly, the light of the lamp was shining and the voice of the bride was speaking in all the nations. When the light of the lamp shines, it is because the Bride of Christ is clothed in the armor of light (see Rom. 13:12). When she is clothed in the armor of light, then she is then able to release the gifts of the Spirit into the world around her. And the Bride of Christ's voice will sound with the preaching of the gospel of the kingdom of God. In Chapter 2, we showed that one key aspect of the kingdom of God is being able to demonstrate it by releasing the gifts of the Spirit with healing, deliverance and prophecy (see Matt. 24:14).

The verse above speaks of the "*great men*" and how they cast their "*magic spell*" and *led astray the nations of the world*. In Revelation 12 it tells us that Satan is the one who leads the whole world *astray* (see Rev. 12:9). These great men appear to be in partnership with Satan, as they have both led the world astray.

The Illuminati elites are believed to be the authority over Freemasonry. One of the gods that Masons worship is Lucifer—the devil![86] *It appears as if the Illuminati elite have been used by Satan to cast their magic spells on the world.* Many of the Illuminati elite are reported to be involved in occult worship.[87] Saint Antony wrote about the evil spirits' plans stating "*if it were within their power, they would not let one of us Christians live, for the service of God is an abomination to the sinner.*"[88] In *Wake Up!* I wrote that the Illuminati's plan, right from the start, was to eliminate Christianity from the earth.[89] Clearly, they are in league with Satan, as they want to destroy Christianity completely from the face of the earth.

The Illuminati elite families have kept their plans secret from the general public for over three centuries, so they could implement their financial control and their manipulation over the world's cultures, politics, judicial systems, and resources. They are trying to eliminate Christianity completely from the earth. They appear to be the *"great men"* from Revelation 12, as they have high levels of intelligence in some areas. That's how they have seized the power and the financial control of most of the world's wealth. Some prophets have had revelation from God that Satan had appeared to one of the leaders of the Illuminati families, perhaps to Rothschild, and he was offered the kingdoms of the world if he would worship Satan. He apparently took him up on that offer, as Rothschild has become the richest family in the world, although that is not public information; consequently, Bill Gates is promoted to be the richest man in the world, but Gates is not the richest (see Matt. 4:8). However, both Rothschild and Gates push the evil plans of the Illuminati and they push for the depopulation of the world.[90]

The Illuminati elite families in addition to their money to control the world, they also use occult magic. They have their demonic plans to depopulate the world, destroy Christianity, and control the entire world and its resources. Believing believers who will become the Bride of Christ is the Godly solution to the Illuminati and their plans that have been inspired by Satan himself. The believing believers who will become the Bride of Christ are the *ONLY ONES* who can battle against these demonic forces that work through the Illuminati. True followers of Jesus Christ must arise today!

Therefore, the gospel of the kingdom of God will be preached to all nations at the end of the end-times by believing believers who will become the Bride of Christ. The Lord will finally get the gospel of the kingdom preached in power at the end of the end-times by the believing believers who will go out into the entire world. That's when "the earth will be filled with the knowledge of the glory of the Lord" (Hab. 2:14).

The voice of the bridegroom will have spoken through His end-times warriors, the Bride of Christ, when they preached the gospel of the kingdom, and they will spread the knowledge of the glory of the Lord throughout the earth. But finally its voice will cease to be heard. Neither the voice of the Bride of Christ, nor the Bridegroom's voice will ever be heard of again in the nations of the world (see Rev. 18:23).

The Bride of Christ Prepares For the Wedding with Righteous Acts

This next Scripture is important, as it gives us an understanding about the role of the Bride of Christ at the end of the end-times. It is found in Revelation 19 and says,

> Let us rejoice and be glad and give him glory! For the wedding of the Lamb has come, and His bride has made herself ready. Fine linen, bright and clean, was given her to wear. (Fine linen stands for the righteous acts of the saints) (Rev. 19:7-8).

The Bride of Christ has made herself ready! How does she make herself ready? She is clothed in "Fine Linen, bright and clean" (Rev. 19:8). This may sound like clothing, but could it also mean spiritual clothing? Could the bright linen actually be the armor of light? (see Rom. 13:12).

It may mean that, because the Greek word for "bright" is "*lampas.*" "*Lampas*" means "a light, lamp or a torch."[91] The Bride of Christ made herself ready by putting on the fine linen that is bright, which implies she put on the "armor of light" (Rom. 13:12).

Do you remember that when Jesus was transfigured, they described his clothes as being "white as the light" (Matt. 17:2). Jesus' clothing is the same clothing that the Bride of Christ will wear (see Rev. 19:14). It is *The Designer's Clothes*. Believing believers are to be clothed in Jesus Christ Himself (see Rom. 13:14).[92] When the Bride of Christ makes herself ready she will be clothed in the armor of light, and clothed in Jesus Christ Himself. That's why her clothes are bright and clean (see Rom. 13:12-14).

When the Bride of Christ is clothed in Jesus Christ then she is able to easily demonstrate who Jesus is to the world around her. Jesus did say we would be fruitful when He was in us and we were in Him (see John 15:5). But we can do nothing, if we are not in Him and He is not in us.

The Bride of Christ represents those believers who live at the end of the end-times, who are continually filled by the Spirit and have righteous acts, which are represented by the linen they have clothed themselves in (see Rev. 19:8). They are clothed by the righteous acts of sharing their faith. You can easily share your faith when you shine like the heavens, and you are clothed in the armor of light (see Rom. 13:12). Being clothed allows the *wise* to shine like the brightness of the heavens, and then they will lead many to righteousness by releasing the gifts of the Spirit in their relational networks.

Revelation also speaks about the washing of our robes,

> Blessed are those who wash their robes, that they may have the right to the tree of life and may go through the gates into the city (Rev 22:14).

When you have practiced the righteous acts of bringing people to be saved by Jesus Christ your linen garment will become bright and clean (see Rev. 19:8). That's what the Bride of Christ will do.

The Holy Spirit and the Bride of Christ Will Partner Together to Evangelize

The Bride of Christ is partnered by the Holy Spirit to evangelize, as that is implied by this Scripture,

> The Spirit and the bride say, 'Come!' And let him who hears say, 'Come.' Whoever is thirsty, let him come; and whoever wishes, let him take the free gift of the water of life (Rev 22:17).

The implication is that whoever is thirsty may come to the living water of life (see Isa. 55:1; John 7:38; Rev. 22:17). The Bride of Christ is partnered by the Holy Spirit and they both will call to nonbelievers who are thirsty to come to the living water (see Rev. 22:17; John 15:26-27).

But you cannot receive the free gift of the water of life, until you first ask Jesus to forgive you for your sins, and ask Him to become your Lord and Savior (see John 3:3-5; 3:16; 14:16-18). But when you have asked Jesus to be your Lord and Savior, then you can receive the free gift of the water of life, which is receiving the Holy Spirit. That's what makes you into a child of God, and it also makes you into the Warrior Bride who will glorify the Lord Jesus Christ when you live your life on the earth (see Song of Songs 6:10; Rev. 22:17).

The righteous acts of the Bride of Christ means that she will preach the gospel of the kingdom in power, because she is partnered by the Holy Spirit. The Bride of Christ will preach the gospel of the kingdom into the whole world (see Matt. 24:14; Rev 22:17).

The *wise* virgins have oil and Jesus taught that parable as one of the end of the end-times parables (See Matt. 25:1-13). The *wise* virgins are the only ones who make it into the wedding banquet. They are the Bride of Christ who will live at the end of the end-times, as they are obedient, as they choose to repeatedly ask and then wait, so they are continually filled by the Spirit until they will become clothed in Jesus Christ.

Perhaps Isaiah 60 is declaring to the Bride of Christ "Arise, shine, for your light has come, and the glory of the Lord rises upon you" (Is. 60:1-2). The sons of God who will to appear at the end of the end-times will also be clothed in Jesus Christ, and they will shine as well, as they also represent the Bride of Christ who will live at the end of the age (see Rom. 8:19; 13:14).

Jesus says He is Coming Like a Thief—So Better be Ready!

Jesus tells us, "Behold I come like a thief! Blessed is he who stays awake and keeps his clothes with him, so that he may not go naked and be shamefully exposed" (Rev. 16:15). Jesus wants believing believers to be awakened and to get dressed. Having oil represents having spiritual clothes that allows you to release the gifts of the Spirit and produce the righteous acts of bringing people to Jesus Christ to be saved.

Shining like the stars equates to the same thing—as the believing believers are to be continually filled by the Holy Spirit until they shine like stars; then they learn to release the gifts of the Spirit, and then they bring glory to the Lord Jesus Christ. That's how the Bride of Christ will preach the gospel of the kingdom and then the end will come (see Matt. 24:14). You will be *wise* if you take this revelation into your heart and act on it.

What is the Lord Looking for Today?

Jesus wondered "However, when the Son of Man comes, will He find faith on the earth?" (Luke 18:8b). So what is the Lord looking for today? The Lord Jesus Christ is looking for believing believers today who will be continually filled by the Spirit, will be clothed in Jesus Christ, and will be full of faith, so they can release the gifts of the Spirit into the world around them. The Lord wants the Bride of Christ to make herself ready by clothing herself in righteous acts of bringing people to Jesus Christ to be saved. The Great End-Times Harvest is going to sweep a great many people into a relationship with Jesus Christ and His church.

Will you be willing to dedicate yourself to God's purposes in this hour and begin to walk out your birthright because you are walking in Jesus Christ's Spirit? The world is groaning and waiting for the people of God to really become God's people. I hope you will learn to be continually filled by the Spirit, be clothed in Jesus Christ, and be full of faith. Then you can practice releasing the gifts of the Spirit until you can do it regularly, and then you will go out and bring in the harvest.

I bless you and hope you will enjoy walking out in your birthright at this time, and you will learn to get yourself ready, so you will become the Bride of Christ. It will be a wonderful time for the body of Christ, when the body wakes up, and realizes that you are called to become the Bride of Christ; then you will bring in the harvest.[93]

So I encourage you to wake up, get clothed in Jesus Christ, and learn to release the gifts of the Spirit in this season, so you will bring glory to the Lord by bringing in the harvest. You will become part of the Bride of Christ, and then you will be able to enter the wedding banquet at the end of the age (see Matt. 25:10-13). This will be an amazing time for the believing believers to really walk out their birthrights in Christ. I bless you and pray that you will capture all the heavenly blessings you are entitled to receive in Jesus Christ (see Eph. 1:3).

Chapter 8: Discussion Questions

1. Do you believe that you are called to become the Bride of Christ?
    a. What do you have to do to walk out as the Bride of Christ?

2. Do you believe that you need to be awakened to the things that the Lord wants you to do today?
    a. What things you are asleep to?
    b. What can you do to wake up?

3. Do you believe you need to get dressed in the armor of light to have your clothes with you?
    a. Do you think it is *wise* to avoid this prophetic warning about getting dressed in this hour?
    b. What do you need to do to get dressed?

4. Do you see how the Bride of Christ is to do the righteous acts at the end of the end-times?
    a. Are you prepared to sacrifice your life and do the righteous acts of bringing other people to the knowledge of Jesus Christ?
    b. What do you need to do to begin to start sharing your faith in Jesus Christ?

5. Do you see that the Scripture depicts it being *wise* to evangelize people at the end of the age?
    a. What barriers do you have to being *wise* and evangelizing other people?
    b. What do you need to do to begin to start evangelizing other people?

6. Are you willing to dedicate yourself to God's purposes in this hour?
    a. Do you want to walk out your birthright in this hour?
    b. What are the barriers to being continually filled by the Holy Spirit so you can release the gifts of the Spirit?
    c. What do you need to do to overcome these barriers?

7. Will you steel yourself in this hour and become all that the Lord has planned for you to become or will you remain asleep and fail to walk out in your birthright?

BIBLIOGRAPHY

[1] Gilligan, Neil, *Transformed by the Power of God: Learning to be Clothed in Jesus Christ,* Shippensburg: Destiny Image, 2010, 114.

[2] Orr, J Edwin, and Oxion, D Phil, *The Outpouring of the Spirit in Revival and Awakening and its Issues in Church Growth,* London, England: British Church Growth Association, 2000.

[3] Joyner, Rick, *The Vision: The Final Quest and The Call,* Nashville, TN: Thomas Nelson Publishers, 2000, 12-13.

[4] Weinlick, John R and Albert H. Frank, *The Moravian Church through the Ages: The Story of a Worldwide, Pre-Reformation Protestant Church,* Bethlehem, PA: The Department of Publications and Communications, Moravian Church, Northern Province, 1989.

Greenfield, John, *When the Spirit Came: The amazing story of the Moravian Revival of 1927,* Minneapolis: Bethany Fellowship, 1967, 13.

"A truly converted Catholic or Protestant, Calvinist, or Lutheran, Moravian or Armenian, Baptist or Quaker, when he is baptized with the Holy Ghost…," 57.

[5] Strong, James, *The Exhaustive Concordance of the Bible,* Nashville: Abingdon, 1890. (H2166; H2165).

[6] Gilligan, Neil, *Wake Up! Preparing for the End-Times Outpouring,* Nashville: Westbow Press, 2012, 111-113.

[7] Gilligan, Neil, *Surprisingly Supernatural: A Practical Guide to Releasing the Gifts of the Spirit.* Nashville: Westbow Press, 2012.

Wake Up! Encourages the Reader to Act like the First Christians Behaved

As I mentioned in the preface of this book that the Lord showed Himself in the clouds in my vision and that foreshadowed Him returning in the clouds in glory and power (see Mark 13:26). When the Lord spoke with His disciples about Him coming back He asked "when the Son of Man comes, will He find faith on the earth?" (Luke 18:8b). The key is if the Lord Jesus will find any believers who really believe when He comes back. The Christians who are alive today need to determine whether or not you want to live a life that pleases the Lord by having an increased level of faith and an increased level of His Spirit, because you are living at the end of the end-times.

Faith, belief and believing are essential for an active spiritual life. When we look in the New Testament we can easily see themes the Lord implies that we should know about faith:

- The first theme is having belief or faith in the Lord (see John 14:1; John 17:21; Acts 16:31; Romans 10:9).
- Another theme is to believe that the Lord has authority and power to do whatever He wants to do, which includes healing, driving out demons, multiplying food and changing the weather patterns (see Matt. 8:10; Matt. 15:28; Mark 9:23; Mark 11:24; Mark 11:22; Luke 7:9; Luke 8:25).
- Another theme is that with only a little faith we can move mountains (see Matt. 17:20; Matt. 21:21; 1 Cor. 13:2).
- Another theme is that the Lord wants believers to have faith to drive out demons (see Matt. 17:17).
- Another theme is that the Lord wants you to have faith that the Father will clothe you in power (see Luke 12:28; 24:49).
- Another theme shows we are called to have faith as our faith can pull on the Lord's healing power, so people will get healed (see Matt. 9:22 ; 14:31; Mark 5:34; Mark 10:52; Mark 16:17; Luke 8:48; Luke 18:42; James 5:15).
- Another theme is the believer is to have faith in order to operate in the gift of prophecy (see Rom. 12:6).

Faith is your life and you are to: stand in faith, walk by faith, be justified by faith, be saved through faith, live by faith, and by faith you will subdue kingdoms, bring forth righteousness, obtain promises with faith, and stop up lions' mouths in faith. And your faith is tested, so you will develop perseverance and overcome the world by believing that Jesus Christ is the Son of God (see John 1:12; 2 Cor. 1:24; 2 Co 5:7; Gal. 2:16; Eph. 2:8; Gal. 2:20; Gal. 3:11; Heb. 11:33; James 1:3; 1 John 5:5).

If you studied the Bible you would know that God is really pleased when we exhibit our faith. Hebrews 11 tells us that "without faith it is impossible to please God" (see Heb. 11:6). And Jesus wonders "when the Son of Man comes, will He find faith on the earth?" (Luke 18:8b). Jesus is still wondering if the Christians who profess to have faith in Him will be able to really believe all that the Scripture has for believers. Especially because you are living at the end of the end-times and you are called to have great faith. Jesus wants His followers to have great faith at the very end of the end-times just before He comes back for us. That's what I want to encourage you to grab hold of. I want you to see that the Lord really wants you to have more faith in what He can do through you, if you can only believe that He wants to work through you. That's why I am calling the believers who are full of faith believing believers. I hope that you will become a believing believer from reading this book, and practicing what it teaches.

[8] Smith, Oswald, J., *The Enduement of Power*, Edinburgh: Marshall, Morgan & Scott, 1965, 88.

[9] To find the Word of the Lord go to Christian International: http://www.christianinternational.org/ Then click on Articles→ then Click on→ Word of the Lord.

[10] Hamon, Bill, *The Day of the Saints: Equipping Believers for their Revolutionary Role in Ministry.* Shippensburg: Destiny Image, 2002.

[11] In this book I will alternate the usage of pronouns. This will help to cut the words down. I am aware that "*The Chicago Manual of Style* dictates that a singular antecedent use the construction *him or her, etc."* However, the Scripture states that believers have the right to "become children of

God" (John 1:12). We also are called "sons of God" when we have the Spirit of God testifying to that fact (see Romans 8:16). We are also called to be "The Bride of Christ" (see Rev. 19:7; 21:2). This is the paradox of our faith is that males are given feminine descriptions, i.e. Bride of Christ, and female believers are given male descriptions, i.e. sons of God. That's why Paul tells the believers that we are neither male nor females for we "are all one in Christ" but the issue is that we must be in Christ, which I implore in this book that we must be continually filled in Jesus Christ's Spirit until we are clothed *in Christ* (see Gal. 3:28; Rom. 13:14). When we are clothed *in Christ* we are all one in Him. Therefore, the gender pronouns really do not have any relevant meaning for true believers who are clothed *in Jesus Christ*. Because of this, I will use "she" sometimes and "he" other times to help reduce the word count and it also to helps us adjust to the reality that *we are one in Christ*, and it helps the reader wrestle with the paradox of being in God's kingdom.

[12] Paul C. Jong is an Asian author who wrote that people should not ask, as they might get the wrong spirit. However, with all the Scriptures that the Lord spoke about asking, I think Jong is off base. I do not recommend his book, but I refer to it here for reference purposes only (see Matt. 7:7; 7:11; 18:19; 21:22; Luke 11:9-13; John 11:22; 14:13-14; 15:7; 15:16; 16:19; 16:23-26). Jong, Paul C. *A Fail-Safe Way for You to Receive the Holy Spirit, Seoul: Hephzibal Publishing House, 2001.*

[13] Gilligan, Neil, *Transformed by the Power of God, 121-189.*

[14] To "be filled" from Ephesians 5:18 is found in the Strong's Concordance. The Greek word is: G4137, πληρόω, pleērooō, play-ro'-o and it means: "From G4134; *to make replete,* that is, (literally) *to cram* (a net), level up (a hollow), or (figuratively) to furnish (or imbue, diffuse, influence), satisfy, execute (an office), finish (a period or task), verify (or coincide with a prediction), etc.: - accomplish, X after, (be) complete, end, expire, *fill (up),* fulfil, (be, *make) full* (come), fully preach, *perfect,* supply."

"To make replete" means to be full, complete, or chock-full. *"Cram"* is to stuff, or *Fill up,* and also *"fill (up), "(make) full"* or *"perfect"* All of these imply what Paul said in the theme of Ephesians was for you to *be completely filled by the Holy Spirit so you obtain the fullness of God!*

[15] Gilligan, Neil, *Wake Up!, 74-116*; 9-10, 24, 54, 62-63, 67, 71, 114-115, 120, 134, 136, 141-142, 153-155, 166, 170, 172-173, 179, 185.

[16] Ibid, 119-122, 136-143.

[17] Bruce, F. F., *The Epistle to the Hebrews,* Revised Edition, Grand Rapids: Wm. B Eerdmans Publishing Co, 1990, 141.

[18] Otis, George Jr., *The Twilight Labyrinth: Why Does Spiritual Darkness Linger Where it Does?* Grand Rapids: Chosen Books, 1997, 72.

[19] Gilligan, Neil, *Transformed by the Power of God*, 63-66.

[20] Strong's (H1966, and H1984).

[21] From Dictionary.com (http://dictionary.reference.com/browse/Satan) the Cultural Dictionary has Satan's definition as "The devil. In the Bible, Satan is identified with the tempter who encourages the fall of Adam and Eve; *he is the accuser* who torments Job in the hope that he will curse God; the one who offers Jesus all the kingdoms of the world if Jesus will worship him (*see* Get thee behind me, Satan); and the evil one who puts betrayal in the heart of Judas. Satan will one day be confined in hell, but until then he is free to roam the Earth." Erhman, Bart D., *God's Problem: How the Bible Fails to Answer Our Most Important Questions—Why We Suffer,* (New York: HaperCollins, 2008) says, "The term Satan here is in Job does not appear to be a name so much as a description of his office. It literally means "The Adversary (or The Accuser)".

[22] The Toronto Airport Christian Fellowship has now changed its name to *"Catch the Fire."* However, the references made in this book were about the church when it was called the Toronto Airport Christian Fellowship; *therefore,* I do not mention the new name of the church in this book.

[23] See the website for "Transformed by the Power of God" book. Go to: www.transformedbythepowerofgod.com and then view the video and you will see several people describe that they feel "heat" or "fire" in front of me. That heat or fire is the cloaking that the Holy Spirit has made around me.

[24] I note this book here by Paul C. Jong as he teaches on receiving the Holy Spirit. In it he teaches that we cannot ask for the Holy Spirit, but that circumvents the Scriptures. I think he may be used by the enemy to keep people from being filled. I do not recommend this book:

Jong, Paul C. *A Fail-Safe Way for You to Receive the Holy Spirit,* Seoul: Hephzibal Publishing House, 2001.

[25] When I wrote "The prophetic word is always conditional" pertains to prophetic words that are given to people to receive and to walk them out. But prophetic words that God is responsible for, for example: Isaiah 7 says, "Therefore the Lord Himself will give you a sign: The virgin will be with child and will give birth to a son, and will call him Immanuel" (Isa. 7:14) are not conditional. God himself will give the prophetic sign and He will make it happen. But all words that people receive require them to have faith that God spoke the word, and they need to do actions in faith that will lead them into the reality of prophetic word coming to pass.

[26] Gove, Philip Babcock, Ph.D, *Webster's Third World International Dictionary,* Chicago: Merriam-Webster, 2002, 757.

[27] Strong's, (G191).

[28] Wimber, John, with Springer, Kevin, *Power Evangelism,* San Francisco, Harper & Row, Publishers, 1986, 12.

[29] Hamon, Bill, *Prophets and the Prophetic Movement,* Point Washington, FL: Christian International, 1990, 56. Note: the Orthodox Church has continued to have the prophetic gift operating for 2000 years.

[30] Dr. Paul Cox heads Aslan's Place website: www.aslansplace.com

[31] Sandford, John Loren, *Why Good People Mess Up,* Lake Mary, FL: Charisma House. 2007, 36, 35-53.

[32] Strong's, (G5590) ψυχή psuchē psoo-khay'

"From G5594; *breath*, that is, (by implication) *spirit*, abstractly or concretely (the *animal* sentient principle only; thus distinguished on the one hand from G4151, which is the rational and immortal *soul*; and on the other from G2222, which is mere *vitality*, even of plants: these terms thus exactly correspond respectively to the Hebrew [H5315], [H7307] and [H2416]: - heart (+ -ily), life, mind, soul, + us, + you."

[33] Lackie, Bill, Prophetic Activation...Preparing the Gift: Prophetic Activations Dictionary, Foundation and Basic Levels, Santa Rosa: Frontline Ministries, 2006. Contact Bill Lackie at Frontline International, 110 Prophets Parkway, Santa Rosa Beach, Florida 32459. 850-231-9101

[34] Virkler, Mark & Patti, *Communion with God*: Study Guide, Shippensburg: Destiny Image, 1995, 7-56.

[35] Lackie, 30.

[36] Lackie, 42.

[37] Wimber, John, and Springer, Kevin, *Power Healing*, London: British Library Cataloguing in Publication Data, 1986, 192.

[38] Brian Thomson *WLI course: School of Signs and Wonders*. RR4, Site 4, Box 50, Red Deer, AB, Canada: Wagner Leadership, 2007. E-mailed to author June 14: by Connie Thomson - WLI to me "Hi Neil, Brian gives you permission to reference his teaching in your book. Connie"

[39] The year before I had taken this ministry trip, I had begun to have "the sweats" and when I went to a doctor my blood pressure was elevated, but my blood test showed no problems with cholesterol levels so the doctor was a bit puzzled, as to why I appeared to have contracted heart disease. I explained that I had a tooth infection in my mouth for almost 2 years that was not treated. A doctor had prescribed antibiotics for me to take for over of 20 month period, but the antibiotics prescribed did not kill the bacteria! My new doctor concluded that the tooth infection had gone into my heart giving me heart disease.

I received healing prayers and the Lord Jesus Christ healed me! However, this evil spirit had attacked me with the dart when I was on that ministry trip, and was trying to bring back the heart disease symptoms and cause me to doubt and worry if the Lord had healed me. So I began to question: *Had I really been healed or not?* I began to buy into the demon's lie. But thankfully, the Lord intervened by drawing my attention to the devils' works by giving me that dream and reminding me of Acts 10:38, and then He healed me. God is so good!

[40] Campbell, T. Colin, and Campbell, Thomas M., *The China Study: The Most Comprehensive Study of Nutrition Ever Conducted and The Startling Implications for Diet, Weight Loss and Long-Term Health,* Dallas: BenBella Books, 2005, 2.

[41] Gilligan, *Wake Up!* 90-116.

[42] Ibid, 43-45.

[43] Brian Thomson *WLI course: School of Signs and Wonders.*

[44] Gilligan, *Wake Up!,* 151-153.

Steve and Christine Stewart's ministry website is: www.impactnations.com.

[45] The video on the website under Chapter 5 is called: "*Demonstration of Five Healing Miracles by Jesus Christ.*" The last miracle was a lady who had a detached retina, which resulted in her sight being completely darkened out. But she was miraculously healed and began to see light out of the formerly darkened eye, but she only had a smirk on her face. There was no jubilation or excitement from her receiving her miracle. Perhaps she was in shock.

[46] Also look at the video in Chapter 4 called: "*Jesus Heals a Deaf Woman working through a Believing Believer!*" This woman was deaf since 9 years of age. She gets up after being healed in both ears and puts on her coat and walks out. It was a miracle! No doctors could heal her for over twenty

years, but Jesus did in a few minutes. However, her response to being miraculously healed was muted. She was not excited either.

[47] Gilligan, *Wake Up! 18-71, 146-177.*

[48] Gilligan, *Transformed by the Power of God,* 119.

[49] MacNutt, Francis, *The Power to Heal,* Notre Dame, Indiana, Ave Maria Press, *1977.*

[50] Wright, Henry W., *A More Excellent Way: Be In Health,* Thomaston, Georgia, Pleasant Valley Publications, Seventh Edition, 2005.

[51] Discern and Discernment definitions derived from The Cambridge Advanced Learner's Dictionary - http://dictionary.cambridge.org/define.asp?key=22096&dict=CALD&topic=using-the-eyes; and The Compact Oxford dictionary http://www.askoxford.com/concise_oed/discern?view=uk

[52] Distinguish definition derived from The Cambridge Advanced Learner's Dictionary - http://dictionary.cambridge.org/define.asp?key=22689&dict=CALD.

[53] Strong's, (G1253).

[54] Strong's, (H995; G1262).

[55] Prophet Bob Jones spoke about God releasing the senses beginning in 2002 and 2003 to discern. On the blog post called "Bathed in Butter" Jones writes about this. URL: http://www.bobjones.org/Docs/Prophetic%20Archives/2003_11_ButterBath.htm

[56] On the "Stir the water" blog the author writes about how he had his five physical senses and his emotions opened up to receive revelation. To access it go to: http://www.stirthewater.com/blog/?p=1577&utm_source=MailingList&utm_medium=email&utm_campaign=mar_2010_enewsletter (Accessed March 21, 2010).

[57] Strong's, (G169).

[58] Gilligan, *Wake Up!*, 43-45.

[59] Strong's, (H259).

[60] Binding evil spirits on earth may affect the ruling spirits that operate from the second heaven, where the throne of Satan is. These ruling spirits may have been impeded from communicating with the evil spirits that were here on the earth, because I had exercised my authority to bind the evil spirits.

The context for the second heaven reference is found in 2 Corinthians 12 where Paul refers to his third heaven experience where he was caught up to paradise and found himself before the throne of God (see 2 Corinthians 12:2-4). The third heaven implies that the second heaven is a location between the first heaven, which is around our planet earth, and the third heaven where God's throne is. The second heaven is the domain of Satan, where the rulers, the authorities, the powers, the principalities, and the spiritual forces of evil in the heavenly realms operate from, which Paul wrote about it in Ephesians 6:12. Those rulers, and authorities, and powers control Satan's kingdoms on the earth, by controlling the evil spirits who are on the earth. And they ensure Satan's rule is carried out through the lesser evil spirits.

The Greek word for "heavenly realms" is: *epouranious* and it means "above the sky." The sky is the earth's sky and it can also be called our heavens, which is considered to be the first heavens. The heavenly realms (*epouranious*) are above our sky, which is beyond our heavens or stratosphere. The "heavenly realms" (*epouranious*) is where the spiritual forces dwell that Paul wrote about in Ephesians 6,

> ... *the spiritual forces of evil in the heavenly realms* (Ephesians 6:13).

Paul also writes in Ephesians 1 that,

> *Praise be to the God, and Father of our Lord Jesus Christ, who has blessed us in the heavenly realms with every spiritual blessings in Christ* (Ephesians 6:13).

Both of these verses quoted above have heavenly realms as the English translation for the Greek word *epouranious*. Therefore, we see in this context there can be a heavenly realm of evil, which is in the second heaven, and a heavenly realm of blessing from the Father in heaven, which is in the third heaven. The heavenly realms are also above our earthly sky, but we need to distinguish the second heavens where Satan's throne is, from the third heavens where God's throne is.

[61] Meyer, Robert T., trans. *Athanasius Life of St Antony,* New York: Newman Press, 1978, 31, 39, 40-41, 46.

[62] Ibid, 40-41.

[63] Ibid, 46.

[64] The Video is called: "Church Does Gay Exorcism on Teen" is on the book's website: under Chapter 6.

[65] Gilligan, *Wake Up!* 38-55.

[66] Newbigin, Lesslie, *Truth to Tell: The Gospel as Public Truth,* London: Wm. B. Eerdmans Publishing Co., 1991, 35-36, 56-57.

[67] Sexton, Colleen A., *Biography: J.K. Rowlings,* Minneapolis: Twenty-First Century Books, 2006, 85.

[68] Meyer, Robert T., 39, 40-41.

[69] This prophetic word was e-mailed to the author on April 28, 2011 and it addressed the same idea I have that believing believers need to awaken to the authority and power and gifts that the Lord has given us and clean up our spiritual environment.

SMALL STRAWS IN A SOFT WIND by Marsha Burns—4/28/11:

"When you came into and became a part of the Kingdom of God, you were given spiritual territory to maintain and rule over. You were given authority over the devil and the power to overcome temptation and to rule over your own flesh. *You have been appointed as watchmen to stay alert and be aware of any intrusion into your environment.* Now you must re-establish yourself in your authority by way of faith, and evaluate the condition of your spiritual atmosphere, and *then go to work to make it a clean habitation for My presence, says the Lord."*

Ephesians 2:19-22 "Now, therefore, you are no longer strangers and foreigners, but fellow citizens with the saints and members of the household of God, having been built on the foundation of the apostles and prophets, Jesus Christ Himself being the chief cornerstone, in whom the whole building, being joined together, grows into a holy temple in the Lord, in whom you also are being built together for a dwelling place of God in the Spirit." (e-mailed to the author Apr 28, 2011).

[70] Otis, George Jr., 70.

[71] I have posted a video called: *Incapacitating Demons with Swords* on the book's website: www.suprisinglysupernatural.com under Chapter 6. On this video I demonstrate that we not only can command evil spirits to leave, but we can ask for spiritual swords and attack the demons. I have seen this happen hundreds of times where the evil spirit falls to the ground after they want to steal, kill and destroy. It is our responsibility to try to destroy these evil spirits the best we can. Go to the book's website and watch the video. Then ask the Heavenly Father for a spiritual sword and confront the evil spirits whenever you can. That way they won't come back!

[72] Meyer, Robert T., 46.

[73] Gilligan, *Wake Up!* 43-45.

[74] Joyner, *12-13.*

[75] Gilligan, *Wake Up!,* 151-153.

[76] Newton, Phil A. *My Journey Through the Church Growth Movement,* Edited by Thomas A. Ascol, *The Founders Journal: Committed to Historic Baptist Principle,* Issue 30, Fall 1997. Newton cites in this journal that

there were differences in conversion with the vast majority being a gradual process and a smaller percentage being *sudden crisis-conversion experiences.* Releasing the gifts of the Spirit often times results in these *sudden crisis-conversion experiences* that Newton writes about.

Phil A. Newton is Lead Pastor at South Woods Baptist Church, 3175 Germantown Rd. S. Memphis, TN 38119. Newton is also an author and has looked at church growth topics with an evangelist perspective.

[77] C. Peter Wagner, editor, with Win Arn and Elmer Towns, *Church Growth: State of the Art,* Wheaton: Tyndale House Publishers, 1988, 296-297.

[78] Every Muslim that comes to Christ needs to have the *spirit of false religion* cast out of them. I learned this from an Iranian Christian Evangelist. I found that when ex-Muslims confess worshiping a false god, I then use the power of the Holy Spirit to drive it out of them and they almost always feel the *spirit of false religion* come up and out on their breath as they breathe out (evil spirits are spirit, so they are like the breath, and they can flow in and out of people on their breath).

[79] Go to the book's website: www.suprisinglysupernatural.com, and then look for the video titled: "Demonstration of Five Healing Miracles by Jesus Christ" under Chapter 5. On this video you will see several people who cry after Jesus healed them. They have tears of joy because what their doctors could not do; Jesus does; He heals all diseases. That's part of the good news of the gospel of the kingdom.

[80] The video on the book's website: is a video called "Muslim Demographics" under Chapter 6. And it shows that Muslims are apparently obeying the commands from Genesis which says, 'Be fruitful and increase in number; fill the earth and subdue it" (Gen. 1:28). Due to their large families they are going to take over the west if believing believers do not start releasing the gifts of the Sprit to show the Muslims that Jesus Christ is truly the Son of God and is the Savior of the world. This video "Muslim Demographics" tells us that in France, Muslims have a birth ratio 8:1; Europeans have 1:3; consequently, France will be under Islamic Law (Sharia Law) in about 39 years.

[81] Gilligan, Neil, *Wake Up!*, 90, 96, 111-113, 180-184.

[82] Gilligan, Neil, *Wake Up!*, 90, 96, 111-113, 180-184.

[83] Gilligan, Neil, *Transformed by the Power of God: Learning to be Clothed in Jesus Christ,* Shippensburg: Destiny Image, 2010.

Gilligan, Neil, *Wake Up! Preparing for the End-Times Outpouring,* Nashville: Westbow Press, 2012.

Gilligan, Neil, *Surprisingly Supernatural: A Practical Guide to Releasing the Gifts of the Spirit,* Nashville: Westbow Press, 2012.

[84] In 2006, I attended a *Global Awakening Healing School* taught by Randy Clark and when I was laying on the floor soaking in the Spirit, a seer prophet looked at me and testified to my friend Dee McKinney that "I looked at your friend and my spiritual eyes were opened and he was all on fire." Jamie Galloway another seer prophet looked at me in 2007 and said "you have a good fire in your spirit." In 2012, Kay a seer prophet prayed for me and said, "You have a very bright light in your spirit." Because I am clothed in Jesus Christ, I am clothed in the armor of light, which is stoked with the fire of God (see Rom. 13:12-14). This is the wardrobe for the wise virgins who make it into the wedding banquet at the end of the age (Matt. 25:1-13). I want to encourage all the believers who can read my writings to put on your spiritual clothes as well, for we are now in the end of the end-times.

[85] Stevens, Selwyn, *Unmasking Freemasonry: Removing the Hoodwink,* Wellington, NZ: Jubilee Resources International Inc., 2005, 32.

[86] The Illuminati Elites are reported to be conducting a child sacrifice on June 21, 2012 at The Kimball Castle aka The Cherokee Castle near Castle Rock Colorado Date: June 21, 2012; Time: 9pm to 6 am. URL: http://www.project.nsearch.com/profiles/blogs/insider-report-the-bushes-are-satanists-and-will-sacrifice-a-baby?xg_source=activity. Also Illuminati elites are known to participate in occult activities at the Bohemian Grove, in Northern California. Also see the blog post *Who are the Illuminati*: URL: http://www.jesus-is-savior.com/False%20Religions/Illuminati/who

are they.htm. Two more YouTube videos reveal the occult practices of the elite called: *The Bohemian Grove Exposed* ; and *ILLUMINATI RITUAL BOHEMIAN GROVE;* URL: http://www.youtube.com/watch?v=F2E HP97Rzc, One YouTube video linking Rothschild to HAARP is called: *A Rothschild Speaks - Listen Closely on the end talks about weather predictions (Haarp)* URL: http://www.youtube.com/watch?v=S0wve8O24Zw&feature=related

Evelyn de Rothschild Speaks - Geoengineering/HAARP Association?; URL: http://www.youtube.com/watch?v=sO_8dzG6aOw&feature=related

[87] Meyer, 40-41, 46.

[88] Gilligan, *Wake Up!* 90, 96.

[89] YouTube video called: *Bill Gates' Global Depopulation Agenda Phase 1*; URL: http://www.youtube.com/watch?v=fJZVAZh-TR8; there are many more videos showing Gates depopulation plans. Rothschild is behind the HAARP research that causes weather changes and earthquakes, which end up killing people.

[90] Strong's Concordance, G2985 λαμπάς *lampas lam-pas'* From G2989; a "lamp" or *flambeau:* - lamp, light, torch. Also related is G2984 Λάμεχ *Lamech lam'-ekh* Of Hebrew origin [H3929]; *Lamech* (that is, *Lemek*), a patriarch: - Lamech.

[91] Gilligan, Neil, *Transformed by the Power of God, 183-188.*

[92] Ann L. Ott is a prophet and she operates a ministry called *In His Presence Ministries* in Houston Texas. In her ministry Ann teaches the believers to prophesy and heal the sick and she takes the believers out on outreaches to bring in the harvest and glorify the Lord. Ann emailed the author the following:

> "Here is the prophetic word God gave me last Saturday night. This is about the calling and purpose of IHP! 08/27/2011 Word to Ann from the Lord concerning IHP. The reason IHP exists is because of these ministries who refused to let their people be trained or step out and do the

things God told them to do. They're sitting there in agony because they know they're called. No option for them. He is saying we exist because of that. We're going to open the flood gate. This is why we're going to grow so unbelievably. *I saw God crying because His churches have done this and haven't allowed the people to be trained or have not encouraged them to step out in their gifting. God is upset."* God Bless! Rev. Ann L. Ott (In His Presence Ministries 713-392-5940 www.annott.org).

ABOUT THE AUTHOR

Neil Gilligan, MCS, MPM, DPM, currently lives in Bellevue, Washington, and operates in the spiritual gifts of healings, miracles, prophecy, discernment, deliverance, evangelism, and teaching. He is called to empower the *Body of Christ* to learn to release the gifts of the Spirit and bring in the end-times harvest. Neil is a Licensed Minister in good standing with *International Fellowship of Ministries* (IFM) from Bothell, Washington. Neil's ministry is called: *Clothed in Jesus Christ Ministries* and you may e-mail Neil to arrange a *Surprisingly Supernatural Training School,* or to check his available schedule at: <u>surprisinglysupernatural@gmail.com</u>.

CPSIA information can be obtained at www.ICGtesting.com
Printed in the USA
BVOW011837081212

307602BV00001B/6/P